MW01283631
PARKS
The Bread Baker's Apprentice
VANCED BREAD AND PASTRY
A PROFESSIONAL APPROACH

Benjamin Delwiche

DESSERT COURSE

Benjamin Delwiche

DESSERT COURSE

Lessons in the *Whys* and *Hows* of Baking

Publisher Mike Sanders
Art & Design Director William Thomas
Editorial Director Ann Barton
Senior Editor Molly Ahuja
Designer Studio Noel
Illustrator Enya Todd
Photographer Haley Hunt Davis
Photo assistant David K Peng
Food Stylist Ryan Norton
Food Styling Assistants Jen Bolbat and Courtney Weis
Copyeditor Claire Safran
Proofreader Mira Park
Indexer Beverlee Day

First American Edition, 2024
Published in the United States by DK Publishing
1745 Broadway, 20th Floor, New York, NY 10019

The authorized representative in the EEA is Dorling Kindersley Verlag GmbH. Arnulfstr. 124, 80636 Munich, Germany

24 25 26 27 28 10 9 8 7 6 5 4 3 2 1
001-340246-APR/2025

A catalog record for this book is available from the Library of Congress.
ISBN 9780744095647

Printed and bound in China

www.dk.com

This book was made with Forest Stewardship Council™ certified paper – one small step in DK's commitment to a sustainable future.
Learn more at
www.dk.com/uk/information/sustainability

for Steph and Graham

TABLE OF CONTENTS

WELCOME

I grew up outside of Baltimore, a city known for its fudgy Berger cookies and even fudgier Smith Island cakes. Still, when I was growing up, it was on a rare occasion that my eight siblings and I would get dessert. If we wanted a sweet treat, we'd usually have to get creative and take matters into our own hands.

One of my very first bakes was a boxed cake made in the waffle maker. My brothers and I devised this plan when our parents were out of the house. The problem was simple: we wanted cake. But since we weren't allowed to use the oven and feared our parents would return at any moment, we needed a different heat source—and one that would work fast. Our solution was impulsive and messy. While I *can't* say that our smashed up waffle-cake hybrid was anything other than a baking disaster, I *can* say that the kitchen has been a place of ingenuity and playfulness for me for as long as I can remember.

When I was fifteen, I got my first job at a local bakery in Baltimore. I started sweeping the floors and, if I was lucky, cracking the hundreds of eggs necessary for mixing cookie dough. I watched the bakers closely, and I asked questions as often as I could. I wanted to learn it all so that *I* could be the one making the cookies, cakes, breads, and desserts in the shop. Slowly, I was given more responsibility and worked my way into each department in the shop: stacking and decorating layer cakes during the day and loading and unloading bread dough into the deck ovens at night.

After graduating from high school, my plan had always been to start college and pursue degrees in both math and education. Of course, I would continue to bake any chance I could, but teaching had long been my career aspiration. Luckily for me, it took no more than one week on campus to find a small, family-run bakery just a mile away that agreed to hire me. Just like before, I was assigned prep work while the owners of the bakery taught me everything they knew. When I wasn't in class or studying, I was at the bakery. And when I had breaks from school, I worked at the bakery back home.

For the past ten years, I have been a full-time math teacher and a part-time baker, working at bakeries on the weekends and school breaks and playing around in my kitchen many other nights of the week. Whether I end up with a key lime pie or a solution to a difficult problem, both baking and math fascinate me with their elegance, order, and complexity. As a teacher, I've learned how to share complex information in a relatable way to my students.

Many of us learned math by just memorizing formulas or repeating problem after problem, but I hope to show my students the beauty of the *whys* and the *hows* behind the procedures. As you will see in this book, the same holds true for my philosophy around baking. Following instructions is one thing. But confidently knowing the concepts that underlie the procedures is quite another.

In this book, I break down the mathematical and scientific elements of a recipe in a way that is approachable and understandable for even the most beginner of bakers. Like in math, the precision and structure of baking sometimes scares people away. The goal of this book is to empower bakers of all levels to broaden their skill sets by trying new recipes and learning the science behind fundamental principles. I hope to equip you with the knowledge of when precision is necessary and when you have the freedom to make decisions that stray from the recipe. When you learn the science behind a recipe, you are no longer tethered to it completely, and you can customize certain aspects to make the type of dessert you most want to eat.

I'm so thrilled that you've picked up this book and aspire to elevate your baking. Though I am now many years older and much more experienced, I am still, at heart, eleven years old and conspiring with my siblings to create a dessert in secret. I've never lost sight of the joy or the creativity in the technicalities of baking. I'm honored to share that joy with you.

Benjamin Delwiche
(benjaminthebaker)

BUTTER CAKES
WHITE CAKE
CHOCOLATE CAKE

HOW TO USE THIS BOOK

Above all else, this book is a celebration of the art and science of baking: the ingredients, the recipes, and the concepts that make a baked good both technically successful and undeniably delicious. Baking is notorious for being precise and unforgiving, and I hope to demystify the techniques and procedures that can intimidate home bakers and professional pastry chefs alike.

As bakers, we are tasked with both mastering difficult methods and also infusing them with our own creativity. After all, there are so many ways to create a chocolate chip cookie. Ask any group of people what kind of cookie they prefer, and you are likely to hear a laundry list of differing preferences: thin and crispy, thick and gooey, chewy, chocolatey, malty, salty, and so much more. For that reason, this book is not just a compilation of recipes. Instead, each recipe in this book is accompanied by a lesson that is meant to be instructive and eye-opening. Ultimately, by learning the fundamentals of baking, you will be able to tailor any recipe to fit your specific tastes.

In pursuit of this goal, this book is divided into three distinct sections:

- Section 1: "Breaking Down a Recipe"
  There is no process more fundamental to baking than measurement. Before anything goes in the oven or any mixing procedure begins, each ingredient must be accounted for and accurately measured. To demonstrate the importance of measurement, I will focus on the simplest cookies I know: shortbread. With just four primary ingredients (sugar, flour, butter, and salt), there is little margin for error when looking for succesful results.
- Section 2: "Mixing Methods"
  In this section we introduce ten different mixing methods that will be used in the recipes that follow. While all of these options might seem overwhelming, I encourage you to think of these methods as blueprints for future recipes where the pattern of mixing the ingredients impacts the overall outcome. Chocolate chip cookies and yellow cake might seem like totally different desserts on the surface, but both of them follow the same mixing method. Even though the ingredients, the time, and the temperature for baking differs, the way of constructing the dough or batter is the same.
- Section 3: "The Recipes"
  Each recipe section begins with a flow chart that shows the relationship between different variations of baked goods. These variations are based on the decisions that you (the baker) will make with ingredients and techniques. For instance, in the section on chocolate chip cookies, you will learn about the different types of cookies that result from a recipe that incorporates baking soda versus one that uses baking powder. When you explore these flow charts, pay close attention to what ingredients are changeable. Those adjustments will tell the story of the final baked good.

Whenever you are hoping to play around in the kitchen, I hope you will use this book in one of two ways. If you have a craving for a particular dessert or want to challenge yourself to learn a new approach, you can open up to any page you like. On the other hand, this book is also meant to be a course in baking, and the techniques and recipes are presented in a sequential and intentional order. A technique introduced at the beginning of the book will appear again and again throughout. In this way, you can see how your knowledge of fundamental techniques will build on itself and grow in complexity and creativity. My hope is that this book inspires you to both practice and play.

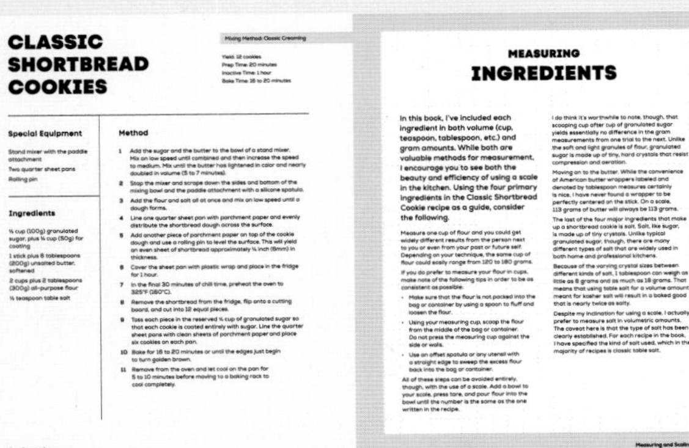

CLASSIC SHORTBREAD COOKIES

MEASURING INGREDIENTS

Measuring and Scaling

We will start with a number of recipes that function as case studies for the math that underlies so much of baking. Through these recipes, I will introduce you to the importance of measurements, ingredient ratios, and baker's percentages. The knowledge in this section can be used universally, whether you're baking a recipe from this book or not.

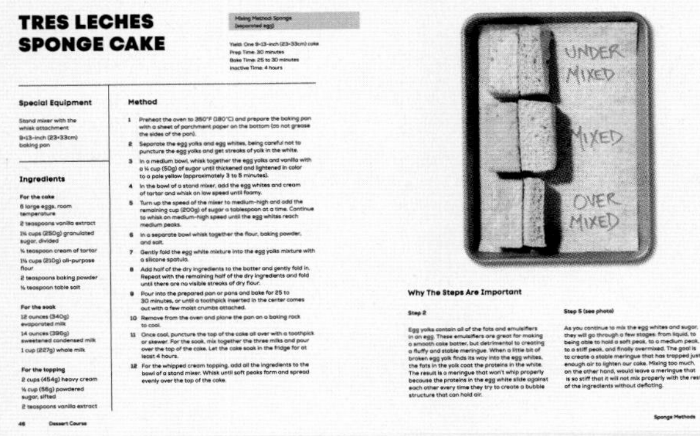

TRES LECHES SPONGE CAKE

Why The Steps Are Important

Mixing Methods and Why the Steps are Important

I will zoom in to a few steps of these recipes and include pictures illustrating different outcomes. Sometimes, I will explain common mistakes associated with each method, and other times I will show you how you can adjust these methods based on your preferences.

You'll want to refer back to these methods as you continue baking through The Recipes section and beyond.

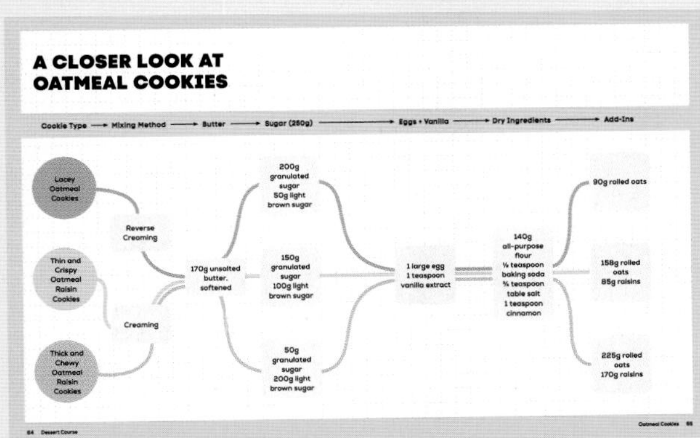

A CLOSER LOOK AT OATMEAL COOKIES

The Recipes

Each recipe section begins with a flow chart that shows the relationship between different variations of baked goods. When you explore these flow charts, pay close attention to what ingredients are changed. Those adjustments will tell the story of the final baked good.

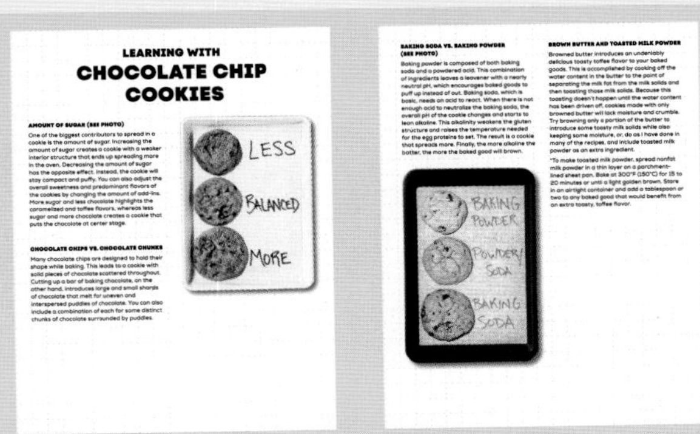

LEARNING WITH CHOCOLATE CHIP COOKIES

Learning With

To conclude each recipe grouping, there will be a set of lessons that are meant to explain the variations between recipes in that section. To offer explanations that go beyond just words, many of these lessons include a photo of the actual results when following a recipe three different ways.

TOOLS USED

Hand Tools

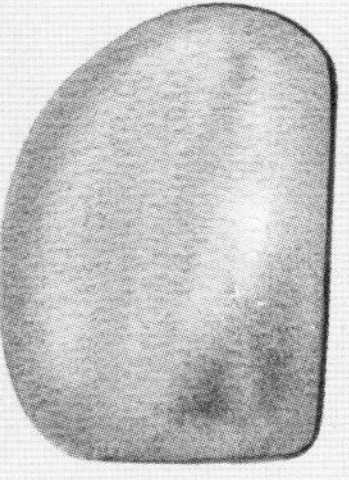

Plastic dough scraper

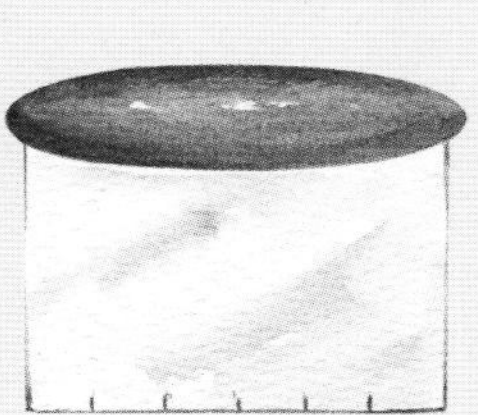

Metal bench scraper

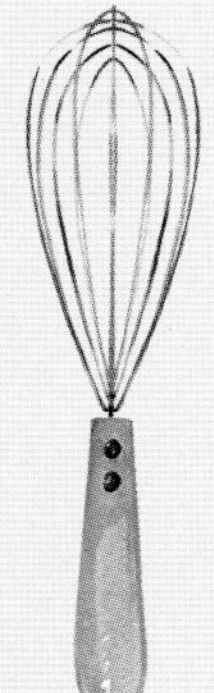

Balloon whisk

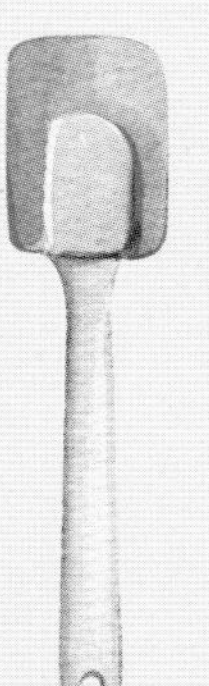

Silicone spatula

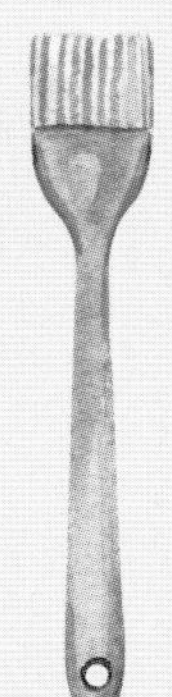

Pastry brush

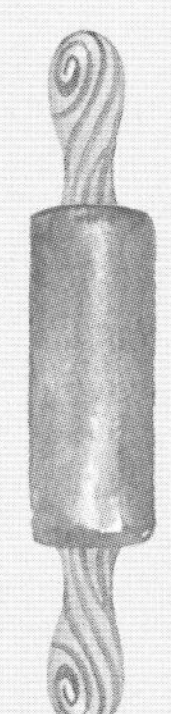

Rolling pin

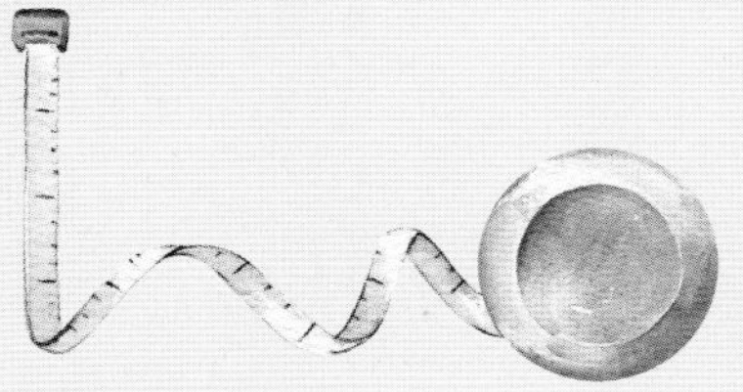

Ruler or tape measure

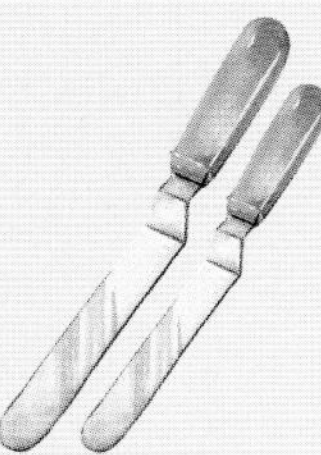

Offset spatulas (large and small)

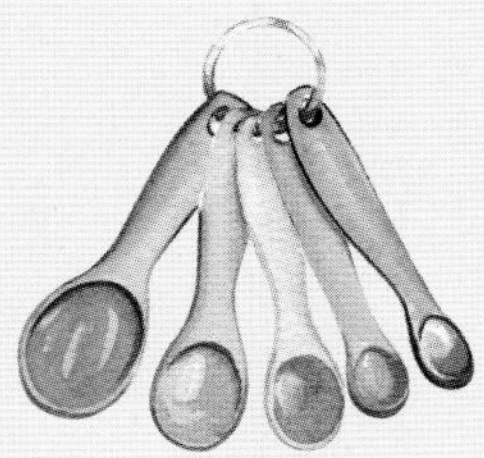

Measuring spoons

Cookie cutters (in various shapes and sizes)

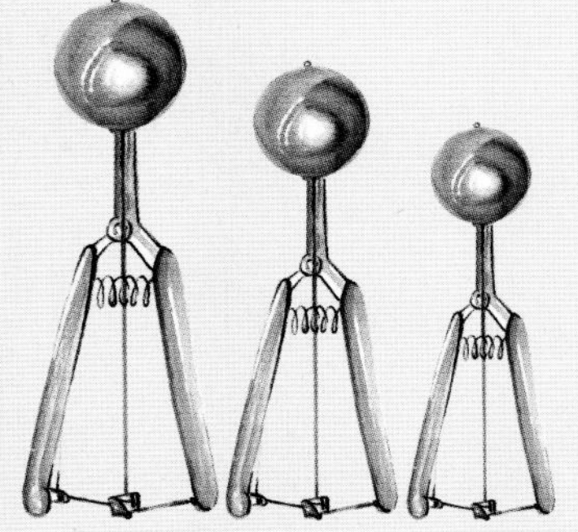

Cookie scoops (in various sizes)

Sieve

Small Appliances

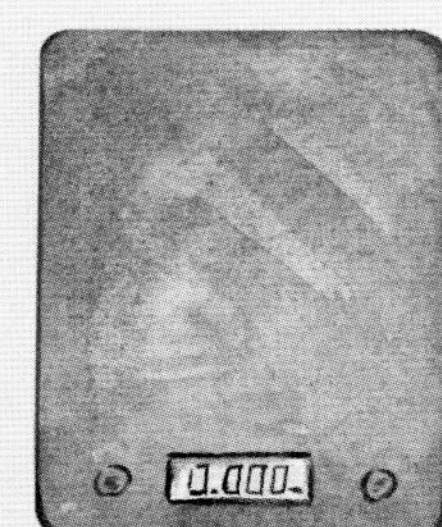

Digital scale

Instant-read thermometer

Cookware

Saucepan

Large Appliances

Stand mixer with the whisk, paddle, and hook attachments

Blender

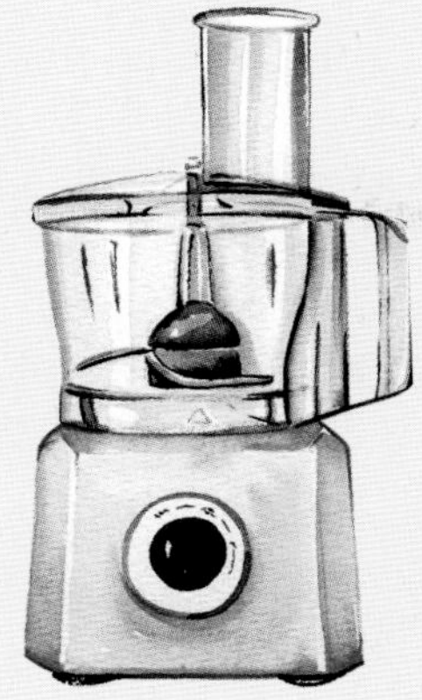

Food processor

Bakeware

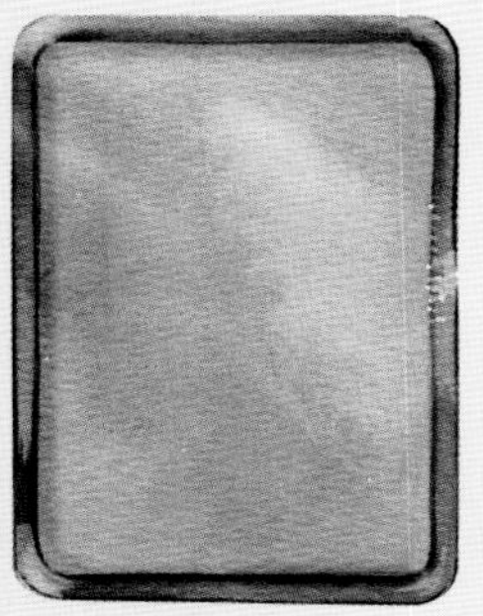

Quarter sheet pan

9×5-inch (23×13 cm)

Half sheet pan

9×13-inch (23×33 cm) baking pan

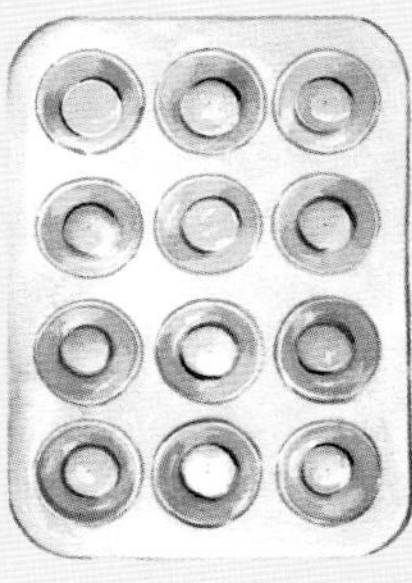

12-cup muffin tin

9×9-inch (23×23 cm) square baking pan

loaf pan

9-inch (23cm) pie pan (at least 2 inches (5cm) deep)

8×3-inch (20×8 cm) round cake pan

9×2-inch (23×5 cm) round cake pan

parchment paper and plastic wrap

GRADE AA
BUTTER
FIRST QUALITY
TAYLOR
CAPACITY

MEASURING AND SCALING

CLASSIC SHORTBREAD COOKIES

Mixing Method: Classic Creaming

Yield: 12 cookies
Prep Time: 20 minutes
Inactive Time: 1 hour
Bake Time: 16 to 20 minutes

Special Equipment

Stand mixer with the paddle attachment

Two quarter sheet pans

Rolling pin

Ingredients

½ cup (100g) granulated sugar, plus ¼ cup (50g) for coating

1 stick plus 6 tablespoons (200g) unsalted butter, softened

2 cups plus 2 tablespoons (300g) all-purpose flour

½ teaspoon table salt

Method

1. Add the sugar and the butter to the bowl of a stand mixer. Mix on low speed until combined and then increase the speed to medium. Mix until the butter has lightened in color and nearly doubled in volume (5 to 7 minutes).
2. Stop the mixer and scrape down the sides and bottom of the mixing bowl and the paddle attachment with a silicone spatula.
3. Add the flour and salt all at once and mix on low speed until a dough forms.
4. Line one quarter sheet pan with parchment paper and evenly distribute the shortbread dough across the surface.
5. Add another piece of parchment paper on top of the cookie dough and use a rolling pin to level the surface. This will yield an even sheet of shortbread approximately ¼ inch (6mm) in thickness.
6. Cover the sheet pan with plastic wrap and place in the fridge for 1 hour.
7. In the final 30 minutes of chill time, preheat the oven to 325°F (160°C).
8. Remove the shortbread from the fridge, flip onto a cutting board, and cut into 12 equal pieces.
9. Toss each piece in the reserved ¼ cup of granulated sugar so that each cookie is coated entirely with sugar. Line the quarter sheet pans with clean sheets of parchment paper and place six cookies on each pan.
10. Bake for 16 to 20 minutes or until the edges just begin to turn golden brown.
11. Remove from the oven and let cool on the pan for 5 to 10 minutes before moving to a baking rack to cool completely.

MEASURING INGREDIENTS

In this book, I've included each ingredient in both volume (cup, teaspoon, tablespoon, etc.) and gram amounts. While both are valuable methods for measurement, I encourage you to see both the beauty and efficiency of using a scale in the kitchen. Using the four primary ingredients in the Classic Shortbread Cookie recipe as a guide, consider the following.

Measure one cup of flour and you could get widely different results from the person next to you or even from your past or future self. Depending on your technique, the same cup of flour could easily range from 120 to 180 grams.

If you do prefer to measure your flour in cups, make note of the following tips in order to be as consistent as possible:

- Make sure that the flour is not packed into the bag or container by using a spoon to fluff and loosen the flour.
- Using your measuring cup, scoop the flour from the middle of the bag or container. Do not press the measuring cup against the side or walls.
- Use an offset spatula or any utensil with a straight edge to sweep the excess flour back into the bag or container.

All of these steps can be avoided entirely, though, with the use of a scale. Add a bowl to your scale, press tare, and pour flour into the bowl until the number is the same as the one written in the recipe.

I do think it's worthwhile to note, though, that scooping cup after cup of granulated sugar yields essentially no difference in the gram measurements from one trial to the next. Unlike the soft and light granules of flour, granulated sugar is made up of tiny, hard crystals that resist compression and aeration.

Moving on to the butter. While the convenience of American butter wrappers labeled and denoted by tablespoon measures certainly is nice, I have never found a wrapper to be perfectly centered on the stick. On a scale, 113 grams of butter will always be 113 grams.

The last of the four major ingredients that make up a shortbread cookie is salt. Salt, like sugar, is made up of tiny crystals. Unlike typical granulated sugar, though, there are many different types of salt that are widely used in both home and professional kitchens.

Because of the varying crystal sizes between different kinds of salt, 1 tablespoon can weigh as little as 8 grams and as much as 18 grams. That means that using table salt for a volume amount meant for kosher salt will result in a baked good that is nearly twice as salty.

Despite my inclination for using a scale, I actually prefer to measure salt in volumetric amounts. The caveat here is that the type of salt has been clearly established. For each recipe in the book, I have specified the kind of salt used, which in the majority of recipes is classic table salt.

CRISPY SHORTBREAD COOKIES

Mixing Method: Classic Creaming

Yield: 12 cookies
Prep Time: 20 minutes
Inactive Time: 1 hour
Bake Time: 16 to 20 minutes

Special Equipment

Stand mixer with the paddle attachment

Two quarter sheet pans

Rolling pin

Ingredients

½ cup (100g) granulated sugar, plus ¼ cup (50g) for coating

1 stick plus 6 tablespoons (200g) unsalted butter, softened

1¼ cups plus 2 tablespoons (200g) all-purpose flour

¾ cup (100g) white rice flour

½ teaspoon table salt

Method

1 Follow the method outlined in the Classic Shortbread Cookies on page 16, adding the white rice flour along with the all-purpose flour and salt in step 3.

INTRODUCTING

RECIPE RATIOS

Aside from the ability to achieve consistent results (which I consider to be the most valuable benefit), the second biggest benefit of using a scale is in being able to quickly and easily adjust your recipe to achieve different yields. Baking recipes are often called formulas for this very reason. They are, at their core, a list of ingredient ratios paired with a technique. While it is relatively quick to scale a recipe by doubling or halving, it is often more helpful to be able to scale a recipe based on a given amount of one ingredient or on a specific yield.

Take a close look at the Crispy Shortbread Cookies recipe and you will quickly notice the beauty of the relationship between the gram amounts of each ingredient. Many ingredient amounts are the same and others are either double or half depending on the direction of the comparison. To express this recipe or any recipe in ratios, start by making sure that all ingredient amounts are expressed in grams. From there, pick the ingredient with the smallest amount and label it as 1 part. To determine the corresponding number of parts for any ingredient, divide its weight by the weight of the ingredient with the smallest amount.

To break it down: in any scaling of the Crispy Shortbread Cookies, the gram amounts of butter and all-purpose flour are twice the amount of sugar, and the amount of rice flour is the same as the amount of sugar.

CRISPY SHORTBREAD COOKIE RATIOS

INGREDIENT	AMOUNT	RATIOS
granulated sugar	100g	1
unsalted butter, softened	200g	200/100 = 2
all-purpose flour	200g	200/100 = 2
white rice flour	100g	1

TENDER SHORTBREAD COOKIES

Mixing Method: Classic Creaming

Yield: 12 cookies
Prep Time: 20 minutes
Inactive Time: 1 hour
Bake Time: 16 to 20 minutes

Special Equipment

Stand mixer with the paddle attachment

Two quarter sheet pans

Rolling pin

Ingredients

1 cup (114g) powdered sugar, sifted

2 sticks (228g) unsalted butter, softened

2 cups (285g) all-purpose flour

½ teaspoon table salt

¼ cup (50g) granulated sugar, for coating

Method

1 Follow the method outlined in the Classic Shortbread cookies on page 16, using powdered sugar in place of the granulated sugar in the first step.

USING RATIOS TO

SCALE A RECIPE

Scenario 1: You look in your fridge and find that you have only 228 grams of unsalted butter. As you take the butter out of the fridge to let it soften, you run the following calculations:

In the Tender Shortbread Cookies recipe, the relative amount of butter is 4 parts. If 4 parts is equal to 228 grams, then 1 part is 228 / 4 = 57g. To determine the amounts of the other ingredients, multiply the ingredient ratio by 57.

Scenario 2: You know you need to make exactly 33 cookies and you want each raw cookie to weigh 24g. This means the total dough should weigh 33 × 24 = 792g. To determine the exact amount for each ingredient, follow the slight variation from the procedure described in scenario 1:

The total number of parts in the Tender Shortbread Cookies recipe is 2 + 4 + 5 = 11. With these eleven parts representing the whole batch, one part would be 792 / 11 = 72. This time, to determine the amounts of each ingredient, multiply the ingredient ratio by 72.

TENDER SHORTBREAD COOKIES RATIOS

INGREDIENT	RATIO	Scenario 1 Amounts	Scenario 2 Amounts
powdered sugar, sifted	2	2 × 57 = 114g	2 × 72 = 144g
unsalted butter, softened	4	228g	4 × 72 = 288g
all-purpose flour	5	5 × 57 = 285g	5 × 72 = 360g
Total	11	11 × 57 = 627g	792g

CHOCOLATE SHORTBREAD COOKIES

Mixing Method: Classic Creaming

Yield: 12 cookies
Prep Time: 20 minutes
Inactive Time: 1 hour
Bake Time: 16 to 20 minutes

Special Equipment

Stand mixer with the paddle attachment

Two quarter sheet pans

Rolling pin

Ingredients

½ cup (100g) granulated sugar, plus ¼ cup (50g) for coating

1 stick plus 6 tablespoons (200g) unsalted butter, softened

1¾ cups plus 1 tablespoon (255g) all-purpose flour

½ cup (45g) Dutch-process cocoa powder

½ teaspoon table salt

Method

1 Follow the method outlined in the Classic Shortbread Cookies on page 16, adding the cocoa powder along with the all-purpose flour and salt in step 3.

INTRODUCING

BAKER'S PERCENTAGES

Recipe ratios are nice and extremely helpful, but they have their limitations. To truly represent the Classic Shortbread Cookies recipe (which includes salt), in ratios, we would have to say 100:200:300:3. Not entirely unmanageable, but certainly not as nice as 1:2:3. As the number of ingredients grows, it becomes more difficult to remember a long string of numbers and the ingredients they represent.

Enter the last stop in this opening section on how to decipher a recipe: baker's percentages.

Instead of stopping at ratios to represent the relationship between ingredients in a recipe, many bakers will write their recipes based on percentages. Just as with ratios, it is important that each ingredient start in the same unit of measurement before calculating the percentages. We will continue to express ingredient amounts in grams.

In order to calculate baker's percentages, each ingredient amount is expressed as a percent of the amount of flour in the recipe.

$$\frac{\text{Grams of ingredient}}{\text{Grams of flour}} \times 100 = \textbf{baker's percentage}$$

CHOCOLATE SHORTBREAD COOKIE BAKER'S PERCENTAGES

INGREDIENT	AMOUNT	BAKER'S PERCENTAGES
granulated sugar	100g	100/255 × 100 = 39%
unsalted butter, softened	200g	200/255 × 100 = 78%
all-purpose flour	255g	255/255 × 100 = 100%
Dutch-process cocoa powder	45g	45/255 × 100 = 18%
table salt	3g	3/255 × 100 = 1.2%

ALMOND SHORTBREAD COOKIES

Mixing Method: Classic Creaming

Yield: 12 cookies
Prep Time: 20 minutes
Inactive Time: 1 hour
Bake Time: 16 to 20 minutes

Special Equipment

Stand mixer with the paddle attachment

Two quarter sheet pans

Rolling pin

Ingredients

½ cup (100g) granulated sugar, plus ¼ cup (50g) for coating

1 stick plus 6 tablespoons (200g) unsalted butter, softened

1¾ cups plus 1 tablespoon (255g) all-purpose flour

1 cup (90g) almond flour

½ teaspoon table salt

Method

1 Follow the method outlined in the Classic Shortbread cookies on page 16, adding the almond flour along with the all-purpose flour and salt in step 3.

USING BAKER'S PERCENTAGES TO SCALE RECIPES

Scenario 3: You are low on sugar and want to make Almond Shortbread Cookies. Aside from the amount for coating the cookies, you have just 78g of sugar left. To determine your new recipe, follow the procedure below:

Start by figuring out the 100% amount by dividing the amount of sugar you have by its percent. This will determine the amount of flour in the recipe. Here, that means 78 / 39% = 200. This means that the amount represented by 100% is 200g. To find the amount of any other ingredient, multiply its percentage by 200.

Scenario 4: Just as in Scenario 2, you want to make 33 cookies that each weigh 24g or an entire batch that weighs 792g. This time, though, your formula is expressed in baker's percentages. Determine how much of each ingredient you need to make the perfect amount of Almond Shortbread Cookies.

In the Almond Shortbread Cookies recipe, the sum of all the percentages is 253.2%. This means that the amount of flour, which is measured at 100%, is a relative fraction of 100/253.2 of the entire batch, or 100 / 253.2 × 792 = 313g. From here, we can use this flour amount and the baker's percentages to determine the exact amount, in grams, for each ingredient.

ALMOND SHORTBREAD COOKIE SCENARIOS

Ingredient	BAKER'S %	SCENARIO 3 AMOUNTS	SCENARIO 4 AMOUNTS
granulated sugar	39%	78g	39% × 313 = 122g
unsalted butter, softened	78%	78% × 200 = 156g	78% × 313 = 244g
all-purpose flour	100%	200g	313g
almond flour	35%	35% × 200 = 70g	35% × 313 = 109g
table salt	1.2%	1.2% × 200 = 2g	1.2% × 313 = 4g
Total	253.2%	253.2% × 200 = 506g	792g

USING BAKER'S PERCENTAGES TO

COMPARE RECIPES

Finally, let me demonstrate the value of baker's percentages when comparing recipes.

Take the following example. I have found two chocolate chip cookie recipes and want to know about the relative butteriness of each cookie. Not only does this have an impact on taste, but also on the spread and texture of the final cookie. To start, let's ignore all the other ingredients and only look at the amount of butter in each cookie.

INGREDIENT	COOKIE X (AMOUNT)	COOKIE Y (AMOUNT)
unsalted butter, softened	227g	283g

Purely by looking at the amount of butter contained in each cookie, we might come to the conclusion that Cookie Y is more buttery. What this picture is lacking, however, is a view of the entire batch of cookies. Let's zoom out a little and consider the yield of the entire batch of cookies.

INGREDIENT	COOKIE X (AMOUNT)	COOKIE Y (AMOUNT)	COOKIE Y (% OF WHOLE)	COOKIE Y (% OF WHOLE)
unsalted butter, softened	227g	16%	283g	15%
TOTAL	1410g		1928g	

We can now see that Cookie Y has a much larger yield, so it makes sense that we would use more butter. If we make a comparison to the entire batch, we find that the relative amounts of butter are almost identical. This might suggest that the cookies will have the same amount of relative butteriness. Still, though, we don't have a complete picture of what's going on. Let's zoom out one more time and consider the impact of the other ingredients in each recipe.

With a broader view (see table on the top of page 27), we can now see that, when looking relative to the other ingredients in the recipe, Cookie X has much more butter than Cookie Y. The amount of chocolate chips and nuts in Cookie X disproportionately threw off our calculations when comparing our butter amount to the whole batch. (It is true that the amount of add-ins has an effect on the spread and structure of a cookie, but this role is significantly less than the amount of fat in the cookie base). Because flour provides the majority of the structure in a cookie (and most traditional baked goods for that matter), it follows that we should focus our comparisons around its weight. When doing exactly that, we can see that the push/pull of structure and spread between flour and fat leans toward spread for Cookie X and structure for Cookie Y.

INGREDIENT	COOKIE X (AMOUNT)	COOKIE X (BAKER'S %)	COOKIE Y (AMOUNT)	COOKIE Y (BAKER'S %)
unsalted butter, softened	227g	72%	283g	59%
all-purpose flour	315g	100%	477g	100%
chocolate chips	340g	108	567g	119%
walnuts	113g	36%	0g	0%

Finally, when Cookie Z enters the picture, baker's percentages allow us to immediately see that it is merely a scaling of Cookie X where the recipe developer has opted for no walnuts and slightly more chocolate chips.

INGREDIENT	COOKIE X (AMOUNT)	COOKIE X (BAKER'S %)	COOKIE Y (AMOUNT)	COOKIE Y (BAKER'S %)	COOKIE Z (AMOUNT)	COOKIE Z (BAKER'S %)
unsalted butter, softened	227g	72%	283g	59%	283g	72%
granulated sugar	150g	48%	225g	47%	188g	48%
light brown sugar	150g	48%	250g	52%	188g	48%
eggs	100g	32%	100g	21%	125g	32%
vanilla	5g	2%	10g	2%	8g	2%
all-purpose flour	315g	100%	477g	100%	394g	100%
baking soda	4g	1.3%	5g	1%	5g	1.3%
baking powder	0g	0%	6g	1.3%	0g	0%
table salt	6g	2%	5g	1%	8g	2%
chocolate chips	340g	108%	567g	119%	454g	115%
walnuts	113g	36%	0g	0%	0g	0%
TOTAL	1410g		1928g		1653g	

Classic
Classic

MIXING METHODS

THE

ALL IN ONE

METHOD IN BRIEF

The first mixing method we will cover is the one with the fewest steps. While there are not many baking recipes that follow such a quick procedure, the following popovers are a perfect example of one that does. Add everything to the mixing bowl—or in this case, blender—and mix until combined.

1 Add all the ingredients to a mixing bowl, blender, food processor, or bowl of a stand mixer. Mix gently at first to combine all the ingredients and then continue mixing until smooth. There should not be visible streaks of any one ingredient after mixing.

THE

WET AND DRY

METHOD IN BRIEF

The perfect example for the Wet and Dry Method is a classic muffin. For this reason, the method is also commonly referred to as the muffin method. I prefer the name Wet and Dry Method so as not to limit its power to create a coarse and fluffy texture to muffins alone. This method especially shines when using liquid sweeteners like honey and/or melted fats or oils.

1. Whisk all the dry ingredients together in one bowl.
2. In a separate bowl, whisk together all the wet ingredients, including the sugar.
3. Add the dry ingredients to the wet ingredients and mix with a silicone spatula just until there are no more streaks of dry flour. There may be some lumps left in the batter, but that's okay!

POPOVERS

Mixing Method: All In One

Yield: 12 popovers
Prep Time: 10 minutes
Inactive Time: 1 hour
Bake Time: 25 to 30 minutes

Special Equipment

Blender

12-cup muffin pan

Ingredients

1¼ cups (284g) whole milk

2 tablespoons (28g) water

5 large eggs

1 teaspoon granulated sugar

½ teaspoon table salt

1½ cups (210g) all-purpose flour

Method

1. Add all the ingredients to a blender and blend on low speed until combined. Increase the speed to medium-low and blend until smooth (1 to 2 minutes). There should not be any visible streaks of dry flour or eggs.
2. Pour the popover batter into a measuring cup, cover with plastic wrap, and let sit at room temperature for 1 hour or in the refrigerator for up to 24 hours.
3. In the final 30 minutes of resting time, preheat the oven to 450°F (230°C).
4. Lightly grease each of the 12 muffin cups with nonstick baking spray. Divide the popover batter evenly between the 12 cups (approximately ¼ cup or 60g per cup).
5. Bake for 25 to 30 minutes or until golden brown and crisp on the outside.
6. Remove from the oven and let cool in the pan for 5 to 10 minutes before moving to a baking rack to cool completely.

Why The Steps Are Important

Step 1

Popovers get their name for the incredible pop they experience when they go into a hot oven. This rise is due to the high amount of liquid in the batter turning into steam. The starch in the flour and the protein in both the flour and eggs are then responsible for the popovers setting and maintaining their shape once the baking is complete. If some of the flour is tied up in small clumps and the eggs are in streaks instead of being evenly distributed, the popovers will struggle to maintain their shape. Even worse, the texture will be speckled with hard clumps of dry or rubbery flour and ribbons of scrambled eggs.

Step 2 (see photo)

Allowing the batter to rest accomplishes two key things. The first is that it allows the flour in the batter to fully hydrate. This leads to a popover that rises higher and better holds its shape. The second is that resting allows the formation of a more complex flavor. There are enzymes in flour that, when activated by water, break down the starches and proteins in the batter, resulting in a popover with a deeper, more complex flavor.

BLUEBERRY MUFFINS

Mixing Method: Wet and Dry

Yield: 12 muffins
Prep Time: 20 minutes
Inactive Time: 30 minutes
Bake Time: 17 to 22 minutes

Special Equipment

12-cup muffin pan

#16 scoop

Ingredients

2 cups (280g) all-purpose flour

1½ teaspoons baking powder

¼ teaspoon baking soda

½ teaspoon table salt

¾ cup (150g) granulated sugar

¼ cup (84g) honey

¾ cup (170g) buttermilk

½ cup (100g) vegetable oil

2 large eggs

1 teaspoon vanilla extract

1 cup (170g) wild blueberries, fresh or frozen

¼ cup (50g) turbinado sugar, for sprinkling on top

Method

1. Preheat the oven to 400°F (200°C) and line each of the muffin cups with a paper muffin liner.
2. In a small bowl, whisk together the flour, baking powder, baking soda, and salt until evenly distributed.
3. In a medium bowl, whisk together the sugar, honey, buttermilk, oil, eggs, and vanilla.
4. Add the dry ingredients to the wet ingredients and, using a silicone spatula, mix together just until you can't see any streaks of dry flour. There will still be some lumps in the batter, but that's okay!
5. Using a silicone spatula, gently fold the blueberries into the muffin batter.
6. Divide the muffin batter evenly between the muffin cups (roughly one #16 scoop) and sprinkle the top of each muffin with approximately 1 teaspoon of turbinado sugar.
7. Bake for 17 to 22 minutes or until a toothpick inserted in the center comes out with a few moist crumbs attached.
8. Remove from the oven and let cool in the pan for 5 to 10 minutes before moving to a baking rack to cool completely.

Why The Steps Are Important

Step 1 (see photo)

When the wet and dry ingredients meet, you will want to combine them in as few stirs of the spatula as possible. Stirring just a few times is great for preventing gluten development but not great in making sure that your leaveners (baking soda or baking powder) are evenly distributed. When these leaveners don't mix evenly into the batter, the resulting muffin can rise unevenly or not at all. Because gluten won't form until the liquid meets the flour, take the time early on to evenly distribute the leaveners with the other dry ingredients.

Step 3 (see photo)

It is satisfying to mix the batter until it's smooth and to see every lump disappear, but with all the extra mixing, something else has formed: gluten, and too much of it. If you cut open your muffins and find long vertical holes called tunnels inside, you may be guilty of overmixing. These tunnels are often an indication of too much gluten development and will lead to a tough muffin.

(Note: You may be wondering why I am being particular about mixing the ingredients together here, but told you to just add all the popover ingredients to a blender and let it spin. The big difference is the hydration of the batter. Because the popover batter is so thin, the odds of developing too much gluten are very slim.)

THE

CLASSIC CREAMING

METHOD IN BRIEF

Traditional pound cake gets its name from the amounts of each ingredient it contains: one pound each of sugar, butter, eggs, and flour. The only leavening agent in this original cake is the air mixed into the batter when creaming the butter and sugar. While many modern pound cakes, including my own, adjust these ratios slightly and include baking powder as an additional leavener, the success of the cake still relies on the air incorporated during the creaming step of the mixing process.

1. Add the sugar and softened fat to the bowl of a stand mixer fitted with the paddle attachment. Mix on low speed until combined and then increase the speed to medium. Mix until the fat has lightened in color and nearly doubled in volume (5 to 7 minutes).
2. Reduce the speed of the mixer to medium and add the eggs one at a time. Wait until each egg is fully incorporated before adding the next.
3. Stop the mixer and, using a silicone spatula, scrape down the sides and bottom of the mixing bowl and the paddle attachment. Return the bowl to the mixer and mix on medium speed for another 30 seconds.
4. Depending on whether you are making a cake or a cookie, follow the procedure below:

- For a cake, separately mix the dry and wet ingredients. Alternate adding the dry and wet ingredients to the mixing bowl, with three additions of the dry and two of the wet. Stop mixing as soon as you can't see any streaks of dry flour.
- For a cookie, mix the dry ingredients together in a separate bowl. Add all at once to the mixing bowl. Mix on low speed until there are no visible streaks of dry flour. Finish by mixing in any add-ins.

Notes on the fat in the recipe:

In order to effectively incorporate air into the batter when mixing the sugar and fat, the fat must be soft enough to be flexible and pliable but not so soft that it melts or can't hold onto any of the air from mixing. For butter, this means a temperature of 60 to 65°F (16 to 18°C).

There are, however, benefits to using melted fats and/or oils in certain cases. The final mix will not have the same amount of air trapped inside, but that could be exactly what we want (see the Chocolate Chip Blondies on page 94). When using melted butter and/or oils, shorten the first step to 1 to 2 minutes, mixing just until the butter and fat have combined.

THE REVERSE CREAMING METHOD IN BRIEF

My ideal coffee cake is soft, delicate, but just sturdy enough to support the weight of the cinnamon crumb that rests on top. Mixing the flour with the fat in the first step of the Reverse Creaming Method helps limit gluten development and creates a cake that bakes up with a velvety texture inside and a level top.

1 Add the dry ingredients, including the sugar, to the bowl of a stand mixer fitted with the paddle attachment. Mix briefly to evenly distribute the ingredients.

2 Add the fat and mix on low speed until the mixture resembles coarse crumbs.

3 Depending on whether you are making a cake or a cookie, follow the procedure below:

4 For a cake, add ½ to ¾ of the liquid (excluding the eggs) to the mixing bowl in order to fully moisten the dry ingredients. Mix on low until combined and then on medium speed for a full minute and a half. Stop the mixer and scrape the bottom and sides of the mixing bowl and the paddle attachment.

5 Whisk the remaining liquid with the eggs and add to the mixing bowl in two additions, mixing for 20 seconds in between each addition.

6 For a cookie, whisk the eggs together with any extracts and then add into the mixer. Mix until incorporated and the cookie dough is smooth. Finish by mixing in any add-ins.

VANILLA-ALMOND POUND CAKE

Mixing Method: Classic Creaming

Yield: One 9×5-inch (23×13cm) loaf
Prep Time: 20 minutes
Bake Time: 55 to 65 minutes

Special Equipment

Stand mixer with the paddle attachment

9×5-inch (23×13cm) loaf pan

Ingredients

For the cake

2 sticks (227g) unsalted butter, softened

1¼ cups (250g) granulated sugar

3 large eggs

1¾ cups plus 2 tablespoons (240g) cake flour, sifted

1 teaspoon baking powder

½ teaspoon table salt

½ cup (113g) whole milk

2 teaspoons vanilla extract

1 teaspoon almond extract

For the glaze

1 cup (113g) powdered sugar, sifted

¼ cup (57g) whole milk

1 teaspoon vanilla extract

Method

1. Preheat the oven to 350°F (180°C). Prepare the loaf pan with nonstick baking spray and a parchment paper sling across the width of the pan (see illustration below).
2. Add the butter and sugar to the bowl of a stand mixer. Mix on low speed until combined and then increase the speed to medium. Mix until the butter has lightened in color and nearly doubled in volume (5 to 7 minutes).
3. Reduce the speed of the mixer to medium and add the eggs one at a time. Wait until each egg is fully incorporated before adding the next.
4. Stop the mixer and scrape down the sides and bottom of the mixing bowl and the paddle attachment with a silicone spatula. Return the bowl to the mixer and mix on medium speed for another 30 seconds.
5. In a medium bowl, mix together the flour, baking powder, and salt. In a measuring cup, combine the milk and vanilla and almond extracts.
6. Start by adding one third of the dry mixture to the stand mixer bowl and mix on low speed until combined. With the mixer still running, stream in half of the milk mixture, again mixing just until combined. Continue alternating the dry and wet ingredients until all the dry has been added. Stop mixing as soon as there are no more visible streaks of dry flour.
7. Pour the pound cake batter into the prepared pan and bake for 55 to 65 minutes or until a toothpick inserted in the center comes out with moist crumbs attached.
8. Remove the cake from the oven and let cool for 5 minutes while making the glaze.
9. For the glaze, mix the powdered sugar, milk, and vanilla extract together until smooth.
10. Lift the cake from the pan using the parchment paper and place on a wire rack. Immediately brush all over with the glaze and let cool completely.

Why The Steps Are Important

Step 2 (see photo)

The Creaming Method is named for this very step. As the butter and sugar mix, the coarse crystals of sugar tear into the softened butter and create tiny pockets of air in the batter. As you continue to mix, the volume of the batter increases and the color lightens, both visible signs of the amount of air added. When the batter hits the oven, both the heat and any added leaveners (baking powder or baking soda) cause the already created air bubbles to expand and create a taller, lighter, and less dense final product. Technically, it is possible to over-cream the butter and sugar, but it takes an excessive amount of over mixing for this to happen.

Step 3

Eggs are made up of approximately 75% water. Just like with the classic elementary school experiment of mixing water and oil, the fat from the butter and water in the eggs don't necessarily want to mix. That is, unless there is an emulsifier present. Luckily, egg yolks have the exact emulsifier, lecithin, that we need. The lecithin can only do its job, when given time to slowly encourage the water and fat to mix. If you add the eggs all at once, the mixture will split and the water and fat will never mix. This leads to a cake that bakes unevenly and has a splotchy appearance and inconsistent interior texture.

Step 6 (see photo)

The goal with pound cake is a dense but tender cake. The quickest way to lose that tenderness is by developing too much gluten. Staggering the additions of the wet and dry ingredients expedites the process of everything coming together into a smooth batter with as little mixing as possible. Overmixing, on the other hand, leads to a gummy and tough interior.

CINNAMON COFFEE CAKE

Mixing Method: Reverse Creaming

Yield: One 9×9-inch (23×23cm) cake
Prep Time: 30 minutes
Bake Time: 40 to 45 minutes

Special Equipment

Stand mixer with the paddle attachment

9×9-inch (23×23cm) square baking pan

Ingredients

For the cake

1¾ cups (228g) cake flour, sifted

2 teaspoons baking powder

½ teaspoon table salt

1¼ cups (250g) granulated sugar

1 stick (113g) unsalted butter, softened

½ cup (113g) buttermilk

3 large eggs

2 teaspoons vanilla extract

For the crumb

½ cup (100g) light brown sugar

1¾ cups (228g) cake flour, sifted

2 teaspoons cinnamon

¼ teaspoon table salt

2 teaspoons vanilla extract

1 stick (113g) unsalted butter, softened

Method

For the cake

1 Preheat the oven to 350°F (180°C) and prepare the baking pan with nonstick baking spray and a parchment paper sling across the width of the pan (see page 38).

2 Add the flour, baking powder, salt, and sugar to the bowl of a stand mixer. Mix on low speed to evenly distribute the ingredients.

3 Add the butter to the mixing bowl and mix on low speed until the dry ingredients are completely coated with the butter and the mixture resembles coarse crumbs.

4 Add ¾ of the buttermilk and turn the mixer speed up to medium. Mix for a full minute and a half until smooth and slightly aerated. Stop the mixer and scrape the bottom and sides of the mixing bowl and the paddle attachment.

5 Whisk the remaining buttermilk together with the eggs and vanilla. Add the liquid into the batter in two additions, letting the mixer run on medium-low for 20 seconds between each addition.

6 Pour the cake batter into the prepared pan and smooth the top.

For the crumb

7 In the same mixing bowl that you made the cake in, mix together all the dry ingredients.

8 Add the butter and mix on medium-low speed until coarse crumbs form.

For assembly

9 Sprinkle the crumbs on top of the cake batter and bake for 40 to 45 minutes or until golden brown and a toothpick inserted in the center comes out with just a few moist crumbs attached.

10 Remove from the oven and let cool in the pan for 5 to 10 minutes before lifting from the pan using the parchment paper and moving to a baking rack to cool completely.

Why The Steps Are Important

Step 3

The beauty of the Reverse Creaming Method is the fine and velvety texture it helps create. The way that it is able to accomplish this plush interior is by minimizing gluten formation. As we saw in the Wet and Dry Method (page 31), one way to reduce gluten development is by minimizing mixing. The other way is to coat the flour in fat and discourage the proteins from linking and creating a stretchy web.

Step 4 (see photo)

For the most part, this mixing method calls for moderate mixing speeds and minimal mixing times. Still, though, the cake needs some physical aeration to work in conjunction with the leavening to create a nice rise in the oven (unlike the Creaming Method, the rise will be modest, but that again is part of the allure of the Reverse Creaming Method: a nice, level top).

THE

SPONGE (WHOLE EGG)

METHOD IN BRIEF

No baked good showcases the extraordinary power of eggs to provide structure in baked goods more than a sponge cake. Mixing whole eggs and egg yolks with sugar forms the foundation of this whole recipe. The air trapped in the mix during this step lightens the cake and the high percentage of eggs allow for less flour to be used later on. The result is a delicate cake that is fluffy and light with a rich golden color.

1. Add the sugar and eggs to the bowl of a stand mixer fitted with the whisk attachment. Start by mixing on low speed until all the ingredients are combined, then turn the speed up to medium to medium-high and whisk until the mixture has thickened and nearly tripled in volume (7 to 10 minutes).
2. With the mixer running, slowly stream in any melted fat, oil, or liquid ingredients.
3. In a small bowl, sift together the flour and other dry ingredients. Remove the bowl from the mixer and, using a silicone spatula, gently fold in the dry ingredients until just combined.

SPONGE (SEPARATED EGG)

METHOD IN BRIEF

Sponge cakes, with their light and airy interior texture, are particularly well suited for soaking. Because of the lack of fat in the recipe, the cake on its own is inherently drier than many other types of cakes, such as the butter cakes that have become the standard for many American birthday cakes.

1. Separate the egg yolks from the egg whites and whisk the yolks together with a portion of the sugar until thickened, lightened in color, and approximately doubled in volume.
2. Mix any melted fat, oil, or other liquid ingredients in with the egg yolks and sugar.
3. Add the egg whites and cream of tartar to the bowl of a stand mixer fitted with the whisk attachment. Start mixing on low until the egg whites are foamy. Turn up the speed to medium-high and add the remaining sugar one tablespoon at a time. Continue whisking until the egg whites reach medium peaks.
4. Gently fold the egg yolk and egg white mixtures together.
5. Sift the dry ingredients together and fold into the egg mixture in two to three additions.

HOT MILK SPONGE CAKE*

Mixing Method: Sponge (whole egg)

Yield: Two 8-inch (20cm) cakes
Prep Time: 30 minutes
Bake Time: 25 to 30 minutes

Special Equipment

Stand mixer with the whisk attachment

Two 8×3-inch (20×8cm) round cake pans

Ingredients

1¼ cups (250g) granulated sugar

3 large eggs, room temperature

3 egg yolks, room temperature

½ cup (113g) whole milk

2 tablespoons (28g) unsalted butter

2 teaspoons vanilla extract

1½ cups (195g) cake flour, sifted

1½ teaspoons baking powder

½ teaspoon table salt

Method

1. Preheat the oven to 350°F (180°C) and prepare both cake pans with a circle of parchment paper on the bottom (do not grease the sides of the pan).
2. Add the granulated sugar, eggs, and egg yolks to the bowl of a stand mixer. Start by whisking on low speed until all the ingredients are combined, then turn the speed up to medium-high and whisk until the mixture has thickened and nearly tripled in volume (7 to 10 minutes).
3. While the eggs and sugar mix, add the milk and butter to a small pot set over medium heat. Heat until the mixture comes just below a boil, remove from heat, and set aside.
4. In a small bowl, sift together the flour, baking powder, and salt until evenly combined.
5. Add the vanilla to the warm milk mixture and, with the mixer running, slowly stream in the liquid.
6. Remove the bowl from the mixer and add half of the dry ingredients. Using a silicone spatula, fold the dry ingredients into the egg mixture. Once almost entirely combined, add the remaining dry ingredients and continue folding just until there are no more visible streaks of flour.
7. Divide the batter evenly between the prepared pans and bake for 25 to 30 minutes or until a toothpick inserted in the center comes out with a few moist crumbs attached.
8. Remove from the oven and cool upside down in the pan set on a baking rack.

*Make it a Boston cream pie by adding a layer of Banana Cream Pie filling (minus the bananas), (see page 146) on top of one of the cakes, then layering the other cake on top and finishing with dark chocolate ganache (see page 270).

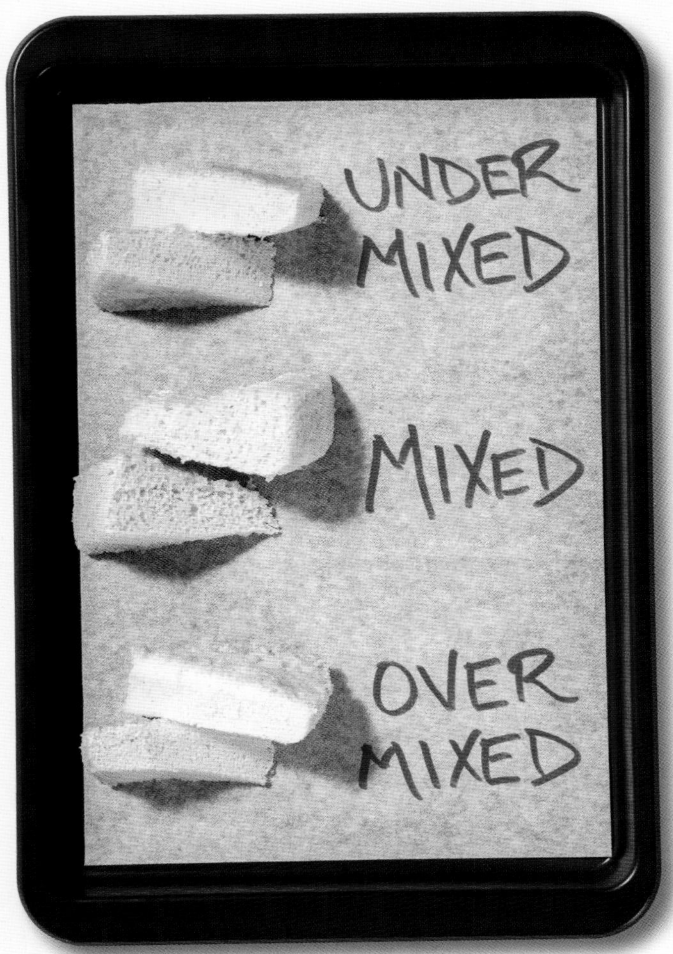

Why The Steps Are Important

Step 2 (see photo)

This recipe would not be possible if not for the eggs. They provide two primary functions: structure and aeration. In addition to the baking powder, this cake relies on the physical aeration of the eggs for leavening. Cutting this step short would result in an overly liquid batter that would bake into a dense and rubbery cake.

Step 6 (see photo)

If whipping is on one end of the spectrum of mixing intensity, folding is on the other. The entire purpose is to combine two sets of ingredients with as little mixing as possible and while being as gentle as possible. The first few steps of the Sponge Cake method are all designed with one goal in mind: aeration. The final baked good benefits from the drastic increase in volume that the eggs and sugar experience early on. As long as your eggs are whipped to the correct point, the final batter can withstand a fair amount of mixing without experiencing a considerable decrease in volume. A heavy hand and vigorous mixing, though, will leave you with a short and dense cake. For this reason, I prefer to take these final steps into my own hands and not rely on a potentially overly powerful mixer.

TRES LECHES SPONGE CAKE

Mixing Method: Sponge (separated egg)

Yield: One 9×13-inch (23×33cm) cake
Prep Time: 30 minutes
Bake Time: 25 to 30 minutes
Inactive Time: 4 hours

Special Equipment

Stand mixer with the whisk attachment

9×13-inch (23×33cm) baking pan

Ingredients

For the cake

6 large eggs, room temperature

2 teaspoons vanilla extract

1¼ cups (250g) granulated sugar, divided

¼ teaspoon cream of tartar

1½ cups (210g) all-purpose flour

2 teaspoons baking powder

½ teaspoon table salt

For the soak

12 ounces (340g) evaporated milk

14 ounces (396g) sweetened condensed milk

1 cup (227g) whole milk

For the topping

2 cups (454g) heavy cream

½ cup (56g) powdered sugar, sifted

2 teaspoons vanilla extract

Method

1. Preheat the oven to 350°F (180°C) and prepare the baking pan with a sheet of parchment paper on the bottom (do not grease the sides of the pan).
2. Separate the egg yolks and egg whites, being careful not to puncture the egg yolks and get streaks of yolk in the white.
3. In a medium bowl, whisk together the egg yolks and vanilla with a ¼ cup (50g) of sugar until thickened and lightened in color to a pale yellow (approximately 3 to 5 minutes).
4. In the bowl of a stand mixer, add the egg whites and cream of tartar and whisk on low speed until foamy.
5. Turn up the speed of the mixer to medium-high and add the remaining cup (200g) of sugar a tablespoon at a time. Continue to whisk on medium-high speed until the egg whites reach medium peaks.
6. In a separate bowl whisk together the flour, baking powder, and salt.
7. Gently fold the egg white mixture into the egg yolks mixture with a silicone spatula.
8. Add half of the dry ingredients to the batter and gently fold in. Repeat with the remaining half of the dry ingredients and fold until there are no visible streaks of dry flour.
9. Pour into the prepared pan or pans and bake for 25 to 30 minutes, or until a toothpick inserted in the center comes out with a few moist crumbs attached.
10. Remove from the oven and plane the pan on a baking rack to cool.
11. Once cool, puncture the top of the cake all over with a toothpick or skewer. For the soak, mix together the three milks and pour over the top of the cake. Let the cake soak in the fridge for at least 4 hours.
12. For the whipped cream topping, add all the ingredients to the bowl of a stand mixer. Whisk until soft peaks form and spread evenly over the top of the cake.

Why The Steps Are Important

Step 2

Egg yolks contain all of the fats and emulsifiers in an egg. These emulsifiers are great for making a smooth cake batter, but detrimental to creating a fluffy and stable meringue. When a little bit of broken egg yolk finds its way into the egg whites, the fats in the yolk coat the proteins in the white. The result is a meringue that won't whip properly because the proteins in the egg white slide against each other every time they try to create a bubble structure that can hold air.

Step 5 (see photo)

As you continue to mix the egg whites and sugar, they will go through a few stages: from liquid, to being able to hold a soft peak, to a medium peak, to a stiff peak, and finally overmixed. The goal is to create a stable meringue that has trapped just enough air to lighten our cake. Mixing too much, on the other hand, would leave a meringue that is so stiff that it will not mix properly with the rest of the ingredients without deflating.

THE

FULL KNEAD

METHOD IN BRIEF

In many areas of baking, the warnings of over mixing caution against excess gluten development. Traditionally, however, the script is completely reversed in the world of bread making. The formation of chewy gluten can make a cookie, cake, or muffin tough but provides exactly the structure and texture we want in bread. Add a few enrichments in the form of whole milk, egg, sugar, and butter and you get these soft and fluffy dinner rolls.

1. Add the water, milk, or other liquid to a mixing bowl along with the instant yeast. Stir briefly and leave for a minute to let the yeast dissolve.
2. Add the remaining ingredients and mix until the dough reaches full gluten development and passes the windowpane test (see page 50).
3. Add the dough to a lightly greased bowl and cover with plastic wrap. Let rise until approximately doubled in size.
4. Deflate the dough, divide, and shape.
5. Cover the dough and let rise until it's doubled to tripled in size and passes the poke test (see page 51)

THE LOW KNEAD METHOD IN BRIEF

Yes, gluten forms with mixing, but it also forms with time. Mix flour and water together and after an extended period of time, the dough that has formed will be as elastic as one that has been mixed in an industrial mixer. An extended resting period also allows for the formation of a more complex flavor as enzymes present in the flour and yeast break down the proteins and starches in the dough. Focaccia is the perfect example of this simple mixing method. Without time, all you taste is olive oil. With time, the flavor is so much more.

1. Add the water and yeast to a mixing bowl and stir briefly. Leave for a minute to allow the yeast time to dissolve.
2. Add the remaining ingredients and mix just until the dough comes together.
3. Cover the bowl with plastic wrap and let rest for 30 minutes.
4. After 30 minutes, wet your hands with water and fold the dough by grabbing a piece of dough on the edge, stretching it upward, and folding into the middle (see illustration below). Continue this process working your way around the perimeter of the bowl until the dough no longer stretches upward (approximately 10 to 12 times).
5. Flip the dough over in the bowl so that the smooth side is up and cover the bowl with plastic wrap. Set in the refrigerator overnight.
6. Remove the dough from the fridge and fold one more time. Let rest to allow the dough time to relax and make for easier shaping in the next step.
7. Shape the dough and let rise until it's doubled to tripled in size and passes the poke test (see page 51).

DINNER ROLLS

Mixing Method: Full Knead

Yield: 12 rolls
Prep Time: 20 minutes
Inactive Time: 2½ hours
Bake Time: 20 to 25 minutes

Special Equipment

Stand mixer with the hook attachment

9×13-inch (23×33cm) baking pan

Ingredients

¼ cup (57g) whole milk

½ cup (113g) water

1¼ teaspoons instant yeast

1 large egg

2½ cups (350g) all-purpose flour

2 tablespoons (25g) granulated sugar

2 tablespoons (28g) unsalted butter, softened, plus 2 tablespoons (28g), melted for brushing

1 teaspoon table salt

1 tablespoon flaky salt, for sprinkling on top

Method

1. Add the milk, water, and yeast to the bowl of a stand mixer. Let sit for one minute to allow the yeast time to dissolve.
2. Add the egg, flour, sugar, softened butter, and table salt to the mixing bowl.
3. Start mixing on low speed until the dough comes together. Turn up the speed to medium-low and mix until the dough reaches full gluten development and passes the windowpane test (see illustration below) (approximately 7 to 10 minutes).
4. Add the dough to a lightly greased bowl and cover with plastic wrap. Let rise at room temperature for an hour or until approximately doubled in size.
5. Remove the dough from the mixing bowl, deflate, and transfer it to a lightly floured work surface. Divide the dough into 12 equal pieces (approximately 53g each) and shape into rounds.
6. Prepare the baking pan with a sheet of parchment paper and evenly space the dough balls in the pan. Cover with a lid or a piece of lightly greased plastic wrap and let rise (proof) for an hour to an hour and a half or until it's nearly doubled to tripled in size and passes the poke test (see page 51).
7. In the final 30 minutes of proofing, preheat the oven to 375°F (190°C).
8. Bake the rolls for 20 to 25 minutes or until golden brown.
9. Remove from the oven, brush with the melted butter, sprinkle with flaky salt, and let cool in the pan for 5 to 10 minutes before moving to a baking rack to cool completely.

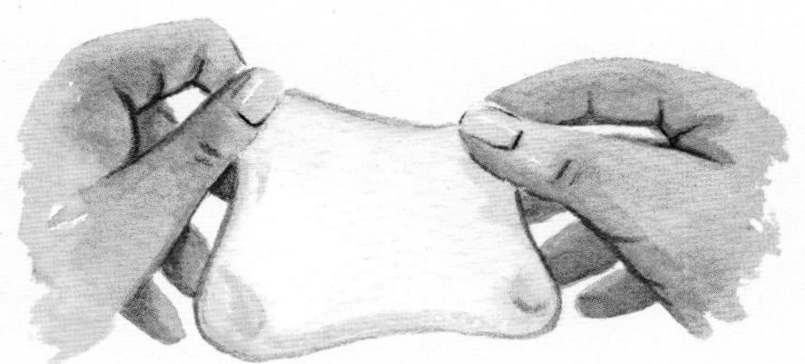

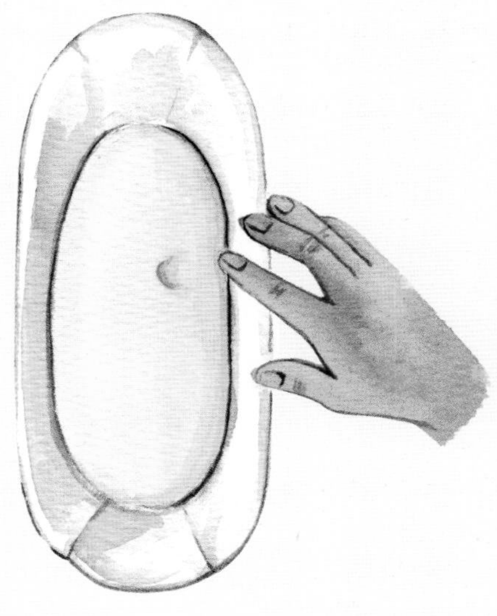

Why The Steps Are Important

Step 3

When wheat flour and water mix, two proteins in the flour (gliadin and glutenin) unwind and begin to form a flexible web that helps form the structure of bread dough. One way to develop gluten is to work the bread dough and force this elastic network to form. Stopping short of full gluten development (without the benefit of an extended rest time, as we will see in the next section) would lead to a short and dense final product instead of the tall and fluffy one we are after. Technically, it is possible to overmix and over develop gluten but I have only ever seen or heard of that happening in large industrial mixers that have power that goes far beyond mixing by hand or even that of a typical home stand mixer.

Step 6 (see photo)

Properly proofed dough will spring back slightly when gently pressed. If the dough springs back quickly and completely, there has not been enough time for the dough to rise. The result is a roll or loaf of bread that can burst as it bakes and has a dense interior texture. If the dough does not spring back at all, the roll is likely overproofed. By the time the dough hits the heat of the oven, it is prone to deflating and developing a coarse interior.

FOCACCIA

Mixing Method: Low Knead

Yield: One 9×13-inch (23×33cm) loaf
Prep Time: 15 minutes
Inactive Time: 14 hours
Bake Time: 40 to 45 minutes

Special Equipment

9×13-inch (23×33cm) baking pan

Ingredients

2 cups (454g) water

1¼ teaspoons instant yeast

3¾ cups (525g) bread flour

1½ tablespoons (19g) olive oil, plus 4 tablespoons (50g) for coating

1¾ teaspoons table salt

1 to 2 tablespoons flaky salt, for sprinkling on top

Method

1. Add the water and yeast to a medium bowl and let sit for one minute to allow the yeast time to dissolve.
2. Add the flour, oil, and table salt to the bowl and mix until a dough comes together. Cover the bowl with plastic wrap and let rest for 30 minutes.
3. After 30 minutes, wet your hands with water and fold the dough by grabbing a piece on the edge, stretching it upward, and folding into the middle. Continue this process working your way around the perimeter of the bowl until the dough no longer stretches upward (approximately 10 to 12 times) (see illustration on page 49).
4. Flip the dough over in the bowl so that the smooth side is up and cover the bowl with plastic wrap. Set in the refrigerator overnight or up to 18 hours.
5. Prepare the baking pan with a sheet of parchment paper and 2 tablespoons of the remaining olive oil spread evenly.
6. Dump the bread dough onto the baking pan so that the smooth side (the top) is in contact with the oil-coated parchment. Fold the dough by bringing the top to the middle, bottom to the middle, left to the middle, and right to the middle. Once folded, flip over one more time so that smooth side is up. Cover with a lid or lightly greased plastic wrap and let rest for 30 minutes.
7. Remove the plastic wrap (but do not get rid of it) and pour another tablespoon of the reserved olive oil on top of the dough. Gently push and stretch the dough to fit the pan. Do not tear the dough. It's okay if the corners are not completely filled in. Re-cover and let rise for an hour and half or until the dough ripples from side to side when you shake the pan.
8. In the final 30 minutes of proofing, preheat the oven to 450°F (230°C).
9. Pour the last tablespoon of olive oil on top of the dough, use your fingertips to dimple the dough all over, and sprinkle flaky salt evenly across the top.
10. Bake for 40 to 45 minutes or until golden brown.
11. Remove from the oven and let cool in the pan for 5 to 10 minutes before moving to a baking rack to cool completely.

Why The Steps Are Important

Step 4 (see photo)

I am classifying this dough as low knead instead of no knead because of these few folds I've included in the recipe. As covered in the next step, gluten will form with time, but these folds help strengthen the dough just enough to aid in a loaf that rises high and has an open interior structure. After just 30 minutes of sitting on the counter, the dough will already begin to develop some structure and strength. Try to perform these folds immediately after mixing and the dough will easily rip and tear.

Step 5

One way to develop gluten is through mixing, but it is not the only way. Gluten will also form as the dough rests and the flour hydrates. The benefit of leaving the bread dough overnight in the fridge is not even just about the formation of gluten. This extra time where the bread dough is left alone allows the enzymes present in the flour and the yeast to get to work, and more fermentation time leads to more flavor.

THE

ROUGH PUFF

METHOD IN BRIEF

Most baked goods aim to have an even distribution of each ingredient, including fat, at each step before continuing on. Not the case with pie dough. An uneven mixing of the butter into the dry ingredients leads to a pie dough that is both tender and flaky. Some of the butter ties up the protein in the flour granules to prevent gluten development and a tough dough. The rest creates thin sheets of butter in the dough for a satisfying, crispy texture.

1 Combine all the dry ingredients together in a mixing bowl.

2 Add cubes of cold butter and use a silicone spatula to mix briefly so that each cube of butter is covered in flour. Flatten each cube of butter between your fingertips. Again using your fingertips, work half of the flattened disks into the flour until they have almost been entirely incorporated.

3 Pour the cold liquid into the bowl and use the silicone spatula to mix until a dough starts to come together.

4 Wrap the dough in plastic wrap and refrigerate for 30 minutes.

5 Remove the dough from the plastic wrap and place on a very lightly floured work surface. Roll the dough out into a rough rectangle approximately ¼ inch (6mm) thick. Fold the dough in thirds like a letter.

6 Rotate the dough 90 degrees and repeat rolling and folding. Refrigerate the dough after every two folds.

7 Repeat the rolling and folding process as many times as indicated in the recipe.

THE

FULL PUFF

METHOD IN BRIEF

If there were a perfect example of exponential growth in the baking world, it would be puff pastry. Start with just one layer of butter between two layers of dough. A few rolls and folds later, all of a sudden those numbers are in the hundreds or even thousands. Temperature is key here to make sure that each layer stays separate, but, as long as they do, you will get a pastry that puffs far beyond what you thought it could.

1. Add all the ingredients, except for the lamination butter, to a mixing bowl and mix briefly to form a smooth dough (1 to 2 minutes).
2. Wrap the dough in plastic wrap and chill in the fridge for 1 hour.
3. Roll the lamination butter between two sheets of parchment until it is roughly ½ inch (1cm) thick. Wrap in plastic and place in the fridge.
4. Remove the lamination butter from the fridge 5 to 10 minutes before the dough. This will allow time for the butter to be pliable but still cold when locking in.
5. Roll the dough into a rectangle the same width and twice as long as the lamination butter block.
6. Add the butter block to the center of the dough and fold the two halves of dough over the butter to meet in the middle.
7. Roll the dough and butter into a rectangle roughly ¼ to ⅜ inch (6 to 10mm) thick. Fold the dough in thirds like a letter.
8. Rotate the dough 90 degrees and repeat rolling and folding. Refrigerate the dough after every 2 folds.
9. Repeat the rolling and folding process as many times as indicated in the recipe.

PIE DOUGH

Mixing Method: Rough Puff

Yield: Top and bottom of one 9-inch (23cm) pie

Prep Time: 40 minutes

Inactive Time: 1½ hours

Special Equipment

Rolling pin

Ingredients

2 cups plus 2 tablespoons (298g) all-purpose flour, plus more for dusting

1 tablespoon (13g) granulated sugar

1 teaspoon table salt

2 sticks (227g) unsalted butter, cold and cut into cubes

½ cup (113g) cold water

Method

1. In a medium bowl, mix together the flour, sugar, and salt using a silicone spatula.
2. Add the cubes of cold butter and use the silicone spatula to mix briefly so that each cube of butter is covered in flour. Flatten each cube of butter between your fingertips, working quickly so as to not heat up the butter. Again using your fingertips, work half of the flattened disks into the flour until they have almost been entirely incorporated (see illustration below).
3. Pour the cold water into the bowl and use the silicone spatula to mix until a dough starts to come together. At this point the dough will look dry, but resist the urge to add extra water.
4. Transfer the dough onto a sheet of plastic wrap and bring the corners of the plastic together to encase the dough inside. Squeeze together so that the dough comes together inside the stretched plastic.
5. Chill the dough in the refrigerator for 30 minutes.
6. Remove the dough from the plastic wrap and place on a very lightly floured work surface. Roll the dough out into a rough rectangle approximately ¼ inch (6mm) thick. Fold the dough in thirds like a letter.
7. Rotate the dough 90 degrees and repeat this rolling and folding process.
8. Cover the dough with plastic wrap and let chill in the refrigerator for at least an hour before using. If not using within two days, wrap in an extra layer of plastic wrap and place in the freezer for long-term storage.

Why The Steps Are Important

Step 2

As you continue to work the butter into flour, you are coating more of the flour granules with fat and helping prevent the formation of gluten later on. This leads to a tender dough that almost melts in your mouth. Leaving the butter in large chunks, on the other hand, allows for the formation of flaky layers later on during the process of rolling and folding. To maximize both tenderness and flakiness, I like to incorporate some of the butter all the way into the dough and leave some in large pieces for the lamination that happens later.

Step 3 (see photo)

Just as with the Low Knead Method, the dough will come together over time. Even though the dough looks dry and crumbly at this step, give it some time to rest in the fridge and allow the flour to fully hydrate for a dough that comes together and holds its shape. Adding too much water to the dough at this point will leave a pie dough that is stretchy and tough and will require an excessive amount of flour during the rolling and folding procedure later on.

PUFF PASTRY DOUGH

Mixing Method: Full Puff

Yield: One sheet of puff pastry

Prep Time: 1 hour

Inactive Time: 4 hours

Special Equipment

Stand mixer with the paddle attachment (optional)

Rolling pin

Ingredients

For the dough

2¼ cups (315g) all-purpose flour, plus more for dusting

1 teaspoon table salt

¾ cup (151g) cold water

3 tablespoons (42g) unsalted butter, melted and cooled

For the lamination

2 sticks (227g) unsalted European-style butter for locking in, cool but pliable

Method

1. To make the dough, mix together the flour, salt, water, and melted butter either by hand or in the bowl of a stand mixer. Mix until the ingredients are evenly distributed and the dough is smooth (1 to 2 minutes).
2. Transfer the dough to a very lightly floured work surface and roll into a rough rectangle (this will help later when locking in the butter). Wrap the dough in plastic wrap and chill in the fridge for 1 hour.
3. While the dough chills, place the laminating butter between two sheets of parchment. Roll the butter into a rectangle ½ inch (1cm) thick and place in the fridge.
4. Remove the butter from the fridge 5 to 10 minutes before the dough is ready. This will allow time for the butter to be pliable but still cold when locking in.
5. Roll the dough into a rectangle the same width and twice as long as the butter block.
6. Add the butter block to the center of the dough and fold the two halves over the butter to meet in the middle (see illustration below).
7. Roll the dough and butter into a rectangle roughly ¼ to ⅜ inch (6 to 10mm) thick. Fold the dough in thirds like a letter, rotate 90 degrees, and repeat the rolling and folding one more time.
8. Wrap the dough in plastic wrap and chill in the refrigerator for 30 minutes.
9. Repeat the process of rolling and folding 2 to 4 more times for a total of between 4 to 6 total folds. Only perform 2 folds at a time and chill for 30 minutes between each pair of folds. After the last fold, chill for at least 1 hour before using.

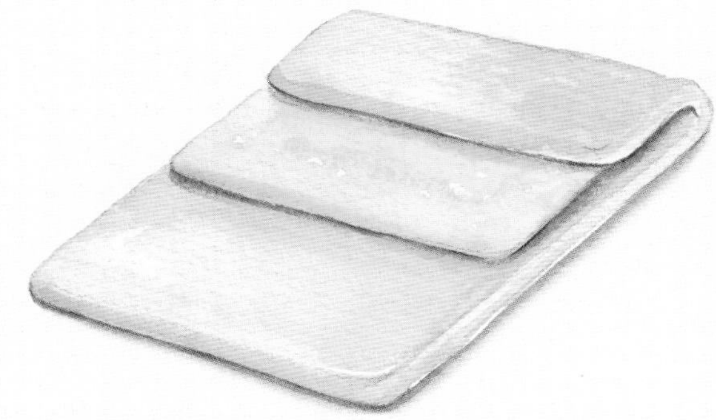

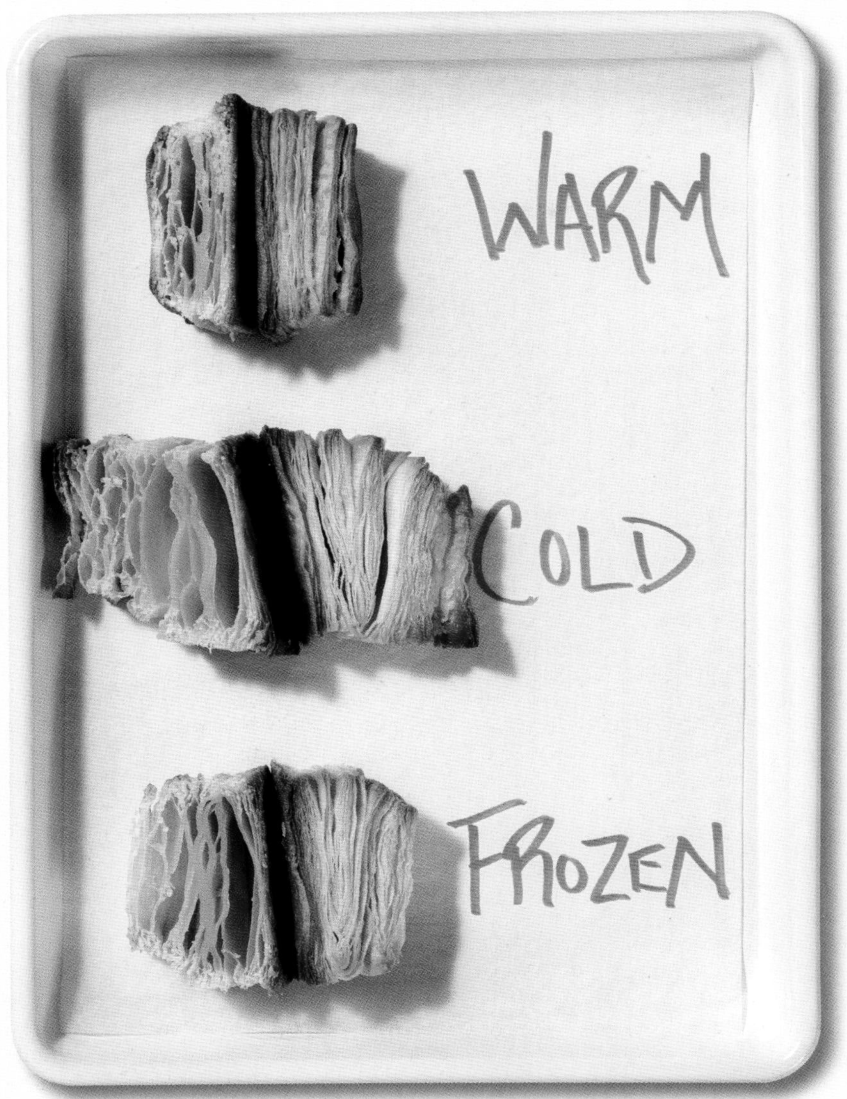

Why The Steps Are Important

Step 4 (see photo)

Both the butter and dough should be cold when you roll and fold them together. It is entirely possible, though, for the butter to be too cold. When this happens, the butter shatters inside the dough and instead of having a thin sheet of butter stretching across the entire surface, you end up with small disparate pieces scattered throughout. When you are ready to roll and fold, the butter should be just warm enough to be flexible, but no more.

Step 8 (see photo)

Keeping the layers separate means you have to keep the dough and butter cold. When everything warms up, the butter melts into the dough and you end up with a very tender, but not very flaky pastry dough. Especially when working by hand, speed is important and chilling time is crucial. This relaxing time also allows the gluten in the dough to relax so that the dough doesn't stretch and spring back on itself as you roll.

OIL/
BUTTER
OIL
NOT
DISSOLVED
DISSOLVED
BROWN
SUGAR
NONE
SOFTENED
CUBES
BLOCK
NONE
SHINY
DULL
DARK
NONE
1 tsp
1 tbsp
UNDER
MIXED
MIXED

THE RECIPES

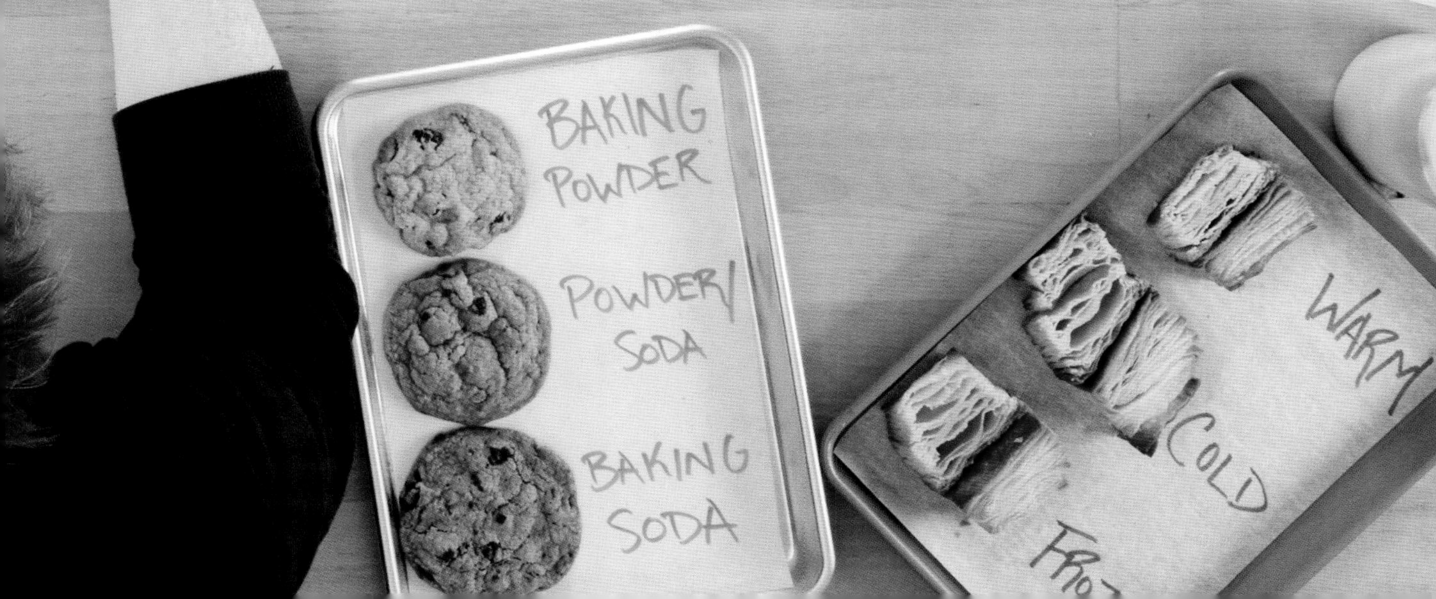

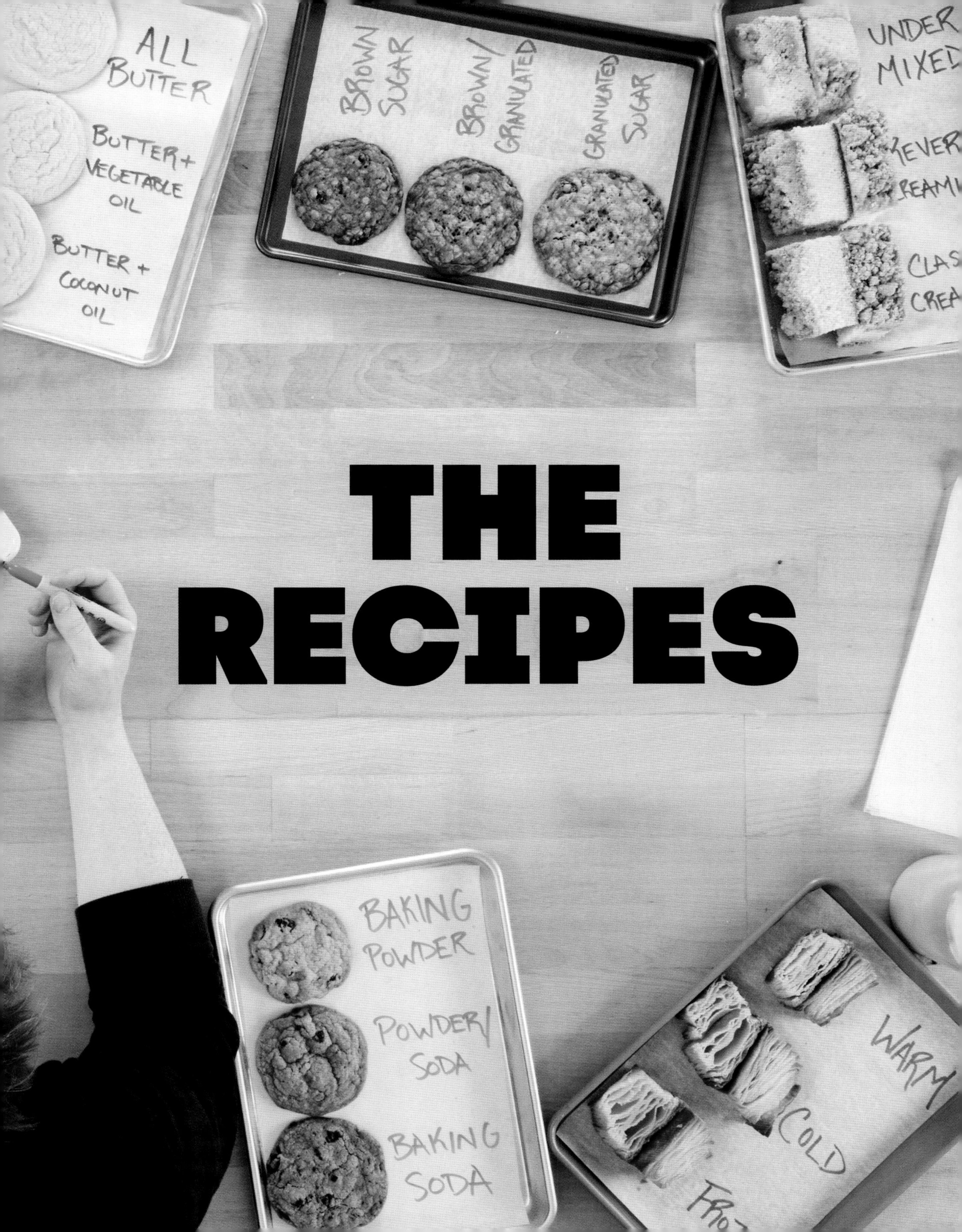
ALL BUTTER
BUTTER + VEGETABLE OIL
BUTTER + COCONUT OIL
BROWN SUGAR
BROWN/GRANULATED
GRANULATED SUGAR
UNDER
BAKING POWDER
POWDER/SODA
BAKING SODA
WARM
COLD

OATMEAL COOKIES

A CLOSER LOOK AT OATMEAL COOKIES

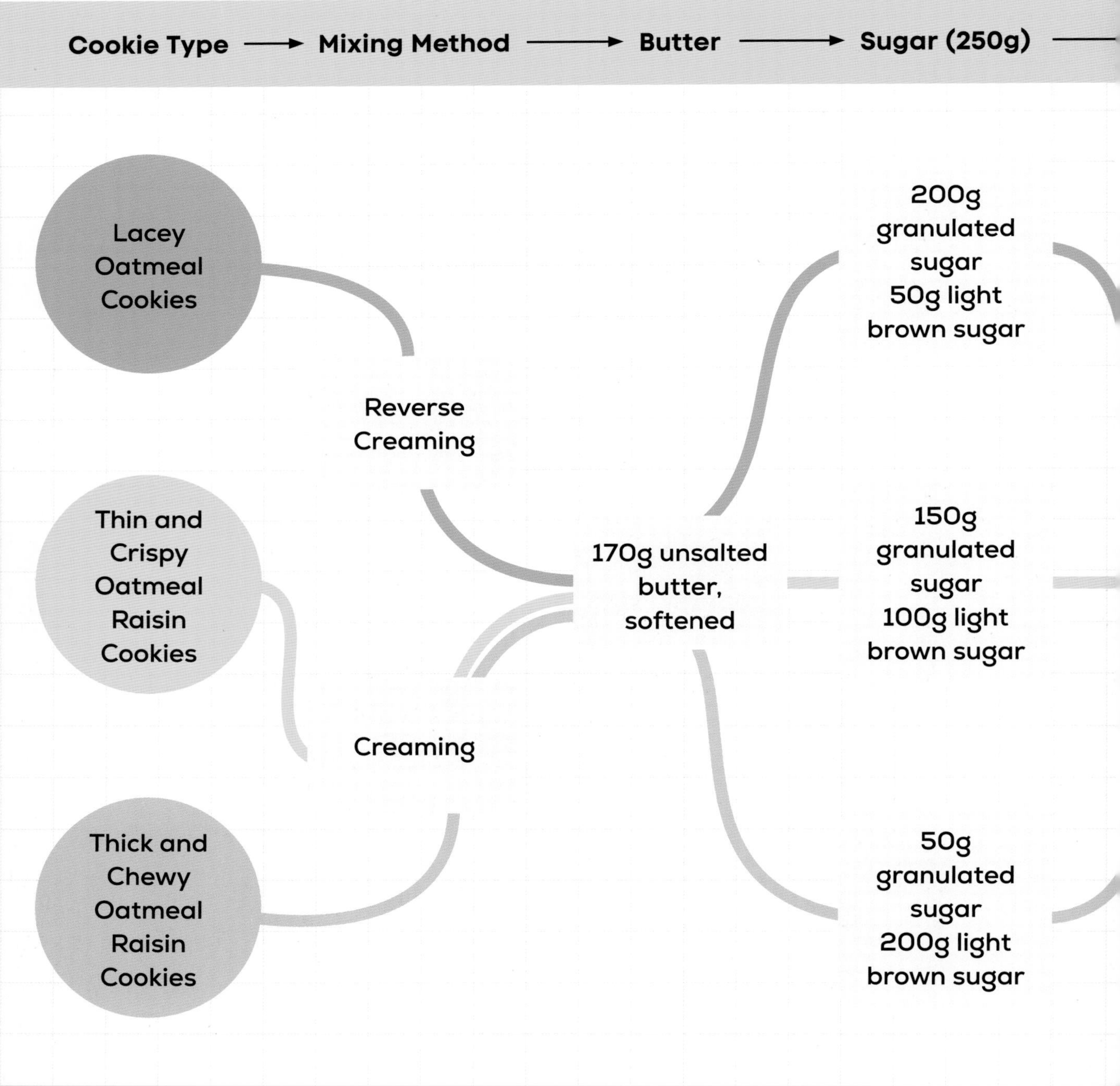

Cookie Type → Mixing Method → Butter → Sugar (250g) →

Lacey Oatmeal Cookies

Thin and Crispy Oatmeal Raisin Cookies

Thick and Chewy Oatmeal Raisin Cookies

Reverse Creaming

Creaming

170g unsalted butter, softened

200g granulated sugar
50g light brown sugar

150g granulated sugar
100g light brown sugar

50g granulated sugar
200g light brown sugar

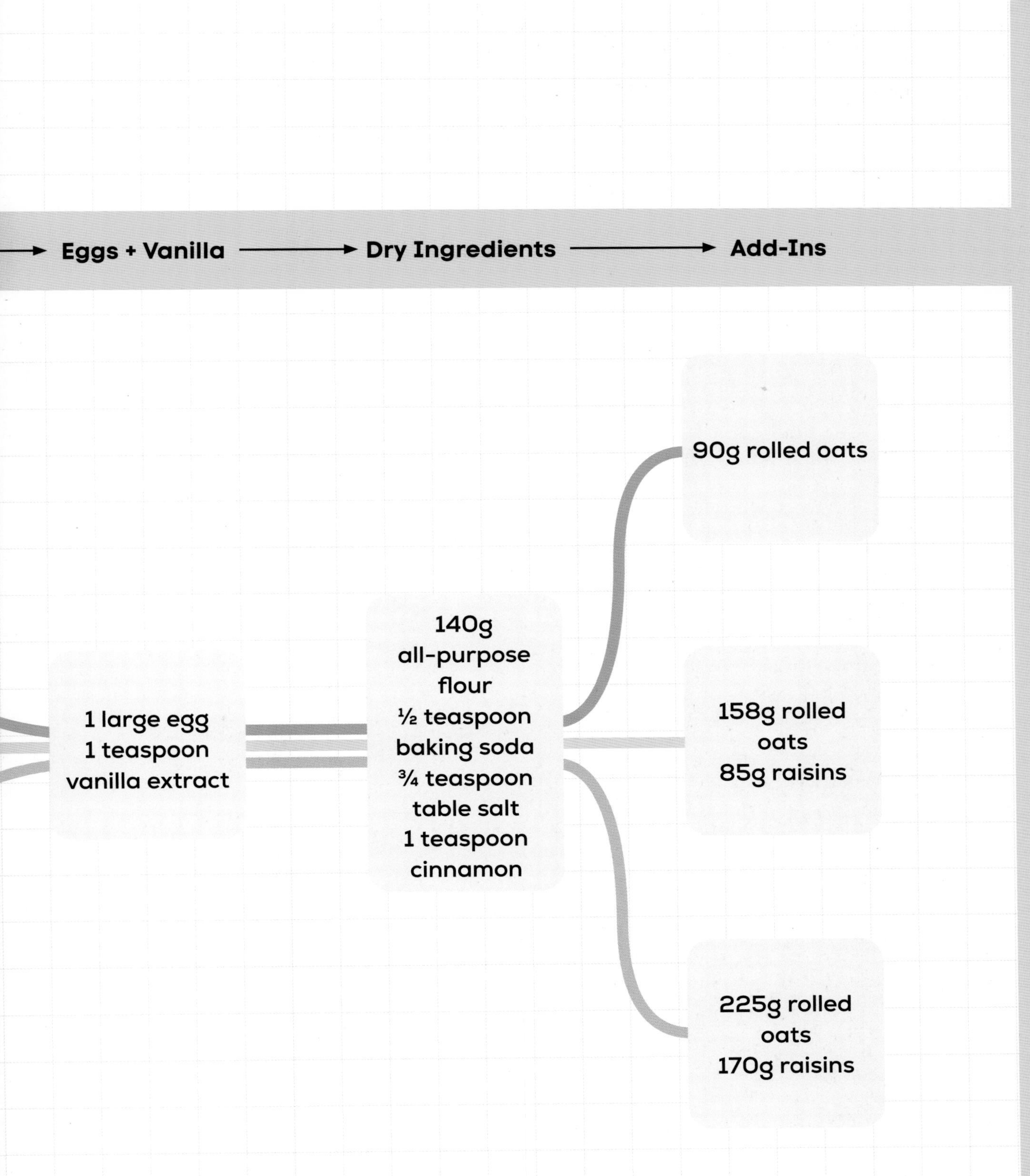

Eggs + Vanilla
Dry Ingredients
Add-Ins
1 large egg
1 teaspoon
vanilla extract
140g
all-purpose
flour
½ teaspoon
baking soda
¾ teaspoon
table salt
1 teaspoon
cinnamon
90g rolled oats
158g rolled
oats
85g raisins
225g rolled
oats
170g raisins

LACEY OATMEAL COOKIES

Mixing Method: Reverse Creaming

Yield: 22 to 24 cookies
Prep Time: 20 minutes
Inactive Time: 30 minutes
Bake Time: 18 to 20 minutes

Special Equipment

Stand mixer with the paddle attachment

#40 scoop

Half sheet pans

Ingredients

1 cup (140g) all-purpose flour

1 cup (200g) granulated sugar

¼ cup (50g) light brown sugar

1 teaspoon cinnamon

¾ teaspoon table salt

½ teaspoon baking soda

1½ sticks (170g) unsalted butter, softened

1 large egg

1 teaspoon vanilla extract

1 cup (90g) rolled oats

Method

1. Follow the Reverse Creaming Method outlined on page 37.
2. Cover the cookie dough and chill in the refrigerator for 30 minutes. In the meantime, preheat the oven to 325°F (160°C).
3. Divide the dough into cookies, each about the size of 1½ tablespoons or measuring 30g. For the quickest and easiest portioning, use a #40 size scoop.
4. Arrange 6 cookies on each half sheet pan lined with parchment paper.
5. Bake for 18 to 20 minutes or until golden brown and crisp.
6. Remove the sheet pan from the oven and let the cookies cool on the pan for 5 to 10 minutes before moving to a baking rack to cool completely.

THIN AND CRISPY OATMEAL RAISIN COOKIES

Mixing Method: Classic Creaming

Yield: 20 to 22 cookies
Prep Time: 20 minutes
Inactive Time: 30 minutes
Bake Time: 18 to 20 minutes

Special Equipment

Stand mixer with the paddle attachment

#30 scoop

Half sheet pans

Ingredients

1½ sticks (170g) unsalted butter, softened

¾ cup (150g) granulated sugar

½ cup (100g) light brown sugar

1 large egg

1 teaspoon vanilla extract

1 cup (140g) all-purpose flour

1 teaspoon cinnamon

¾ teaspoon table salt

½ teaspoon baking soda

1¾ cup (158g) rolled oats

½ cup (85g) raisins

Method

1. Follow the Classic Creaming Method outlined on page 36.
2. Cover the cookie dough and chill in the refrigerator for 30 minutes. In the meantime, preheat the oven to 350°F (180°C).
3. Divide the dough into cookies, each about the size of 2 tablespoons or measuring 40g. For the quickest and easiest portioning, use a #30 size scoop.
4. Arrange 6 cookies on each half sheet pan lined with parchment paper.
5. Bake for 18 to 20 minutes or until golden brown and crisp.
6. Remove from the oven and let cool on the pan for 5 to 10 minutes before moving to a baking rack to cool completely.

THICK AND CHEWY OATMEAL RAISIN COOKIES

Mixing Method: Classic Creaming

Yield: 16 to 18 cookies
Prep Time: 20 minutes
Inactive Time: 30 minutes
Bake Time: 16 to 18 minutes

Special Equipment

Stand mixer with the paddle attachment

#20 scoop

Half sheet pans

Ingredients

1½ sticks (170g) unsalted butter, softened

¼ cup (50g) granulated sugar

1 cup (200g) light brown sugar

1 large egg

1 teaspoon vanilla extract

1 cup (140g) all-purpose flour

1 teaspoon cinnamon

¾ teaspoon table salt

½ teaspoon baking soda

2½ cups (225g) rolled oats

1 cup (170g) raisins

Method

1 Follow the Classic Creaming Method outlined on page 36.

2 Cover the cookie dough and chill in the refrigerator for 30 minutes. In the meantime, preheat the oven to 375°F (190°C).

3 Divide the dough into cookies, each about the size of 3 tablespoons or measuring 60g. For the quickest and easiest portioning, use a #20 size scoop.

4 Arrange 8 cookies on each half sheet pan lined with parchment paper.

5 Bake for 16 to 18 minutes or until golden brown but the edge is still soft.

6 Remove from the oven and let cool on the pan for 5 to 10 minutes before moving to a baking rack to cool completely.

LEARNING WITH OATMEAL COOKIES

LETTING THE DOUGH CHILL IN THE FRIDGE (SEE PHOTO)

Letting the cookie dough chill in the refrigerator before baking allows time for the flour (and any other dry ingredients like oats) to fully hydrate and the fat to solidify. It also allows for the development of a more complex flavor. Enzymes present in the flour have time to break down some of the proteins and starches in the dough and set the stage for a deeper flavor. Cookies baked right away will still be delicious, but try a 30-minute rest as a good starting point. For a more pronounced effect, let the dough chill overnight.

GRANULATED SUGAR VS. BROWN SUGAR (SEE PHOTO)

When using the Creaming Method, the coarse crystals of granulated sugar will puncture the fat and create pockets of air that encourage the cookie to spread. Brown sugar, with its relatively softer granules, is not as well suited for this task, so the resulting cookie stays more compact. Additionally, the reaction between any alkaline baking soda and the slight acidity of brown sugar creates a cookie that puffs up. Lastly, brown sugar is more hygroscopic than white sugar. This water-loving property means that cookies made with brown sugar will hold onto moisture better.

CHOCOLATE CHIP COOKIES

A CLOSER LOOK AT CHOCOLATE CHIP COOKIES

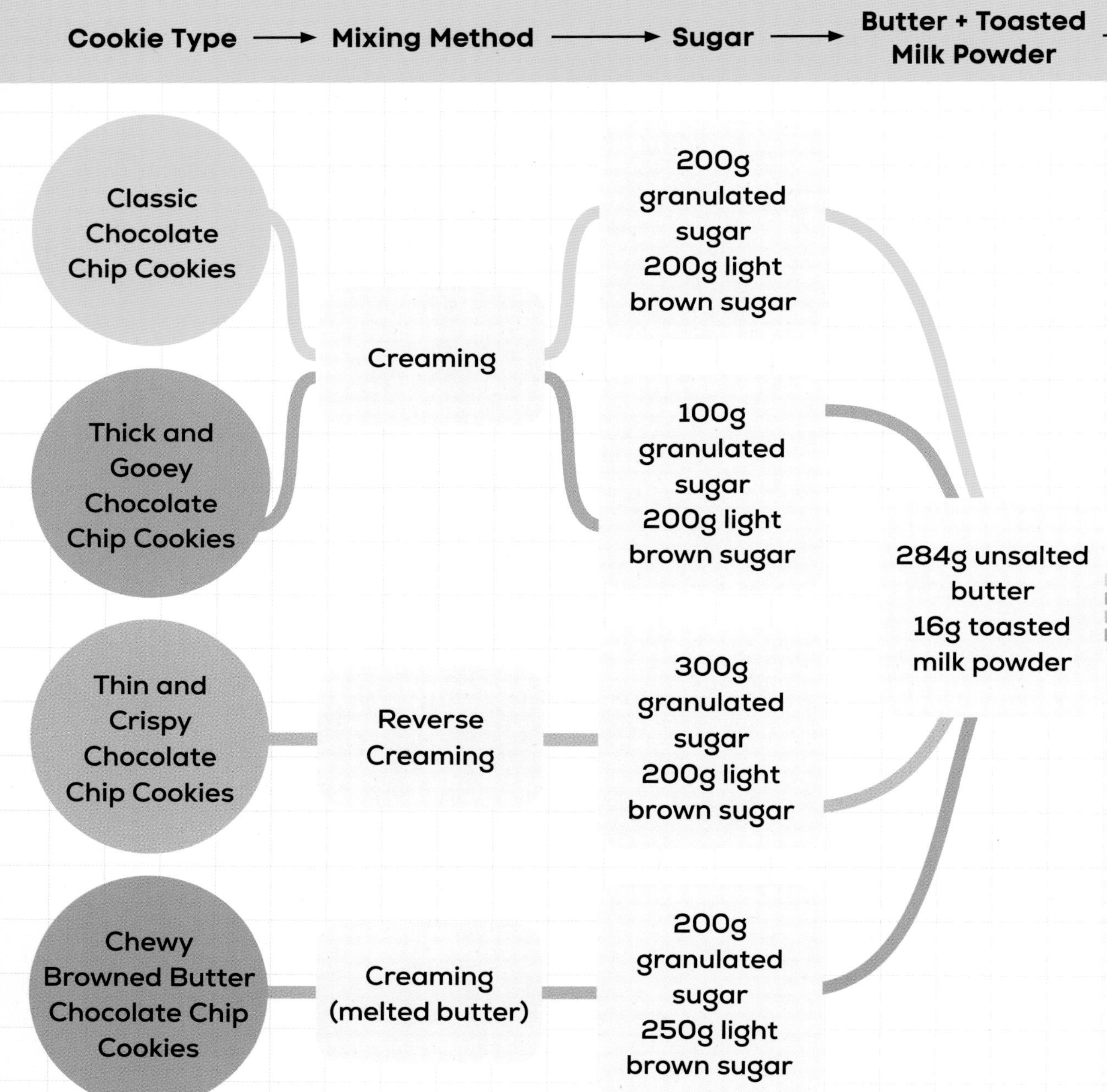

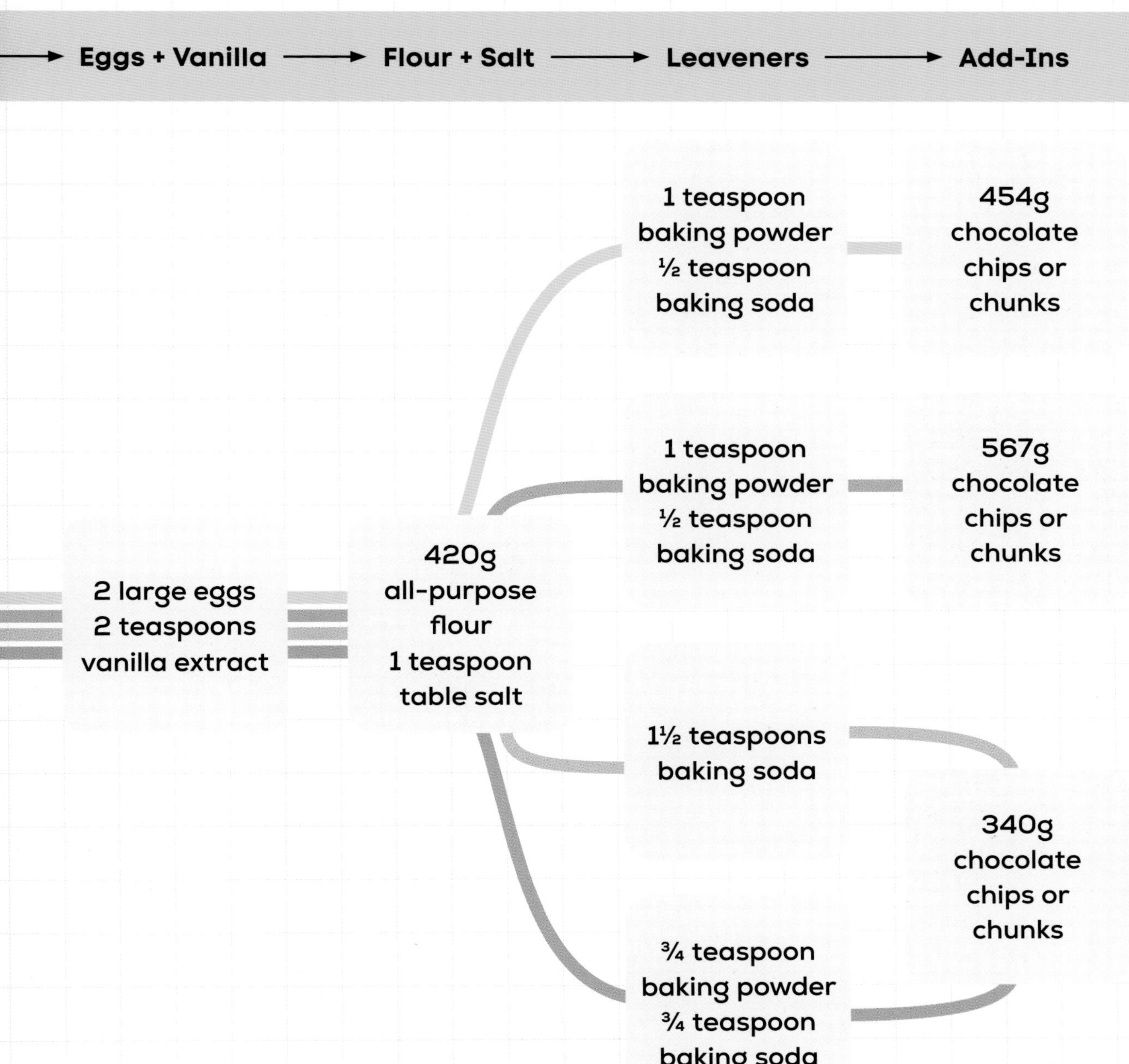

Eggs + Vanilla
Flour + Salt
Leaveners
Add-Ins
2 large eggs
2 teaspoons
vanilla extract
420g
all-purpose
flour
1 teaspoon
table salt
1 teaspoon
baking powder
½ teaspoon
baking soda
454g
chocolate
chips or
chunks
1 teaspoon
baking powder
½ teaspoon
baking soda
567g
chocolate
chips or
chunks
1½ teaspoons
baking soda
¾ teaspoon
baking powder
¾ teaspoon
baking soda
340g
chocolate
chips or
chunks

CLASSIC CHOCOLATE CHIP COOKIES

Mixing Method: Classic Creaming

Yield: 26 to 28 cookies
Prep Time: 20 minutes
Bake Time: 13 to 15 minutes

Special Equipment

Stand mixer with the paddle attachment

#20 scoop

Half sheet pans

Ingredients

1 cup (200g) granulated sugar

1 cup (200g) light brown sugar

2 tablespoons toasted milk powder (see page 79)

2½ sticks (284g) unsalted butter, softened

2 large eggs

2 teaspoons vanilla extract

3 cups (420g) all-purpose flour

1 teaspoon baking soda

½ teaspoon baking powder

1 teaspoon table salt

16 ounces (454g) chocolate chips or chunks

Method

1. Follow the Classic Creaming Method outlined on page 36, including the toasted milk powder with the sugar and butter in the first step.
2. Optionally, cover the cookie dough and chill in the refrigerator for 30 minutes or up to overnight. Preheat the oven to 375°F (190°C) 30 minutes before baking.
3. Divide the dough into cookies, each about the size of 3 tablespoons or weighing 60g. For the quickest and easiest portioning, use a #20 size scoop.
4. Arrange 8 cookies on each half sheet pan lined with parchment paper.
5. Bake for 13 to 15 minutes or until golden brown but the edge is still soft.
6. Remove from the oven and let cool on the pan for 5 to 10 minutes before moving to a baking rack to cool completely.

THICK AND GOOEY CHOCOLATE CHIP COOKIES

Mixing Method: Classic Creaming (melted butter)

Yield: 12 to 14 cookies
Prep Time: 20 minutes
Bake Time: 16 to 18 minutes

Special Equipment

Stand mixer with the paddle attachment

#10 scoop

Half sheet pans

Ingredients

½ cup (100g) granulated sugar

1 cup (200g) light brown sugar

2 tablespoons toasted milk powder (see page 79)

2½ sticks (284g) unsalted butter, melted and cooled

2 large eggs

2 teaspoons vanilla extract

3 cups (420g) all-purpose flour

1½ teaspoons baking powder

1 teaspoon table salt

20 ounces (567g) chocolate chips or chunks

Method

1. Follow the Classic Creaming Method outlined on page 36, including the toasted milk powder with the sugar and butter in the first step.
2. Optionally, cover the cookie dough and chill in the refrigerator for 30 minutes or up to overnight. Preheat the oven to 375°F (190°C) 30 minutes before baking.
3. Divide the dough into cookies, each about the size of ⅓ cup or weighing 120g. For the quickest and easiest portioning, use a #10 size scoop.
4. Arrange 6 cookies on each half sheet pan lined with parchment paper.
5. Bake for 16 to 18 minutes or until golden brown but the edge is still soft.
6. Remove from the oven and let cool on the pan for 5 to 10 minutes before moving to a baking rack to cool completely.

THIN AND CRISPY CHOCOLATE CHIP COOKIES

Mixing Method: Reverse Creaming

Yield: 40 to 42 cookies
Prep Time: 20 minutes
Bake Time: 18 to 20 minutes

Special Equipment

Stand mixer with the paddle attachment

#30 scoop

Half sheet pans

Ingredients

1½ cup (300g) granulated sugar

1 cup (200g) light brown sugar

2 tablespoons toasted milk powder (see page 79)

3 cups (420g) all-purpose flour

1½ teaspoons baking soda

1 teaspoon table salt

2½ sticks (284g) unsalted butter, softened

2 large eggs

2 teaspoons vanilla extract

12 ounces (340g) chocolate chips or chunks

Method

1 Follow the Reverse Creaming Method outlined on page 37.

2 Optionally, cover the cookie dough and chill in the refrigerator for 30 minutes or up to overnight. Preheat the oven to 325°F (160°C) 30 minutes before baking.

3 Divide the dough into cookies, each about the size of 2 tablespoons or weighing 40g. For the quickest and easiest portioning, use a #30 size scoop.

4 Arrange 6 cookies on each half sheet pan lined with parchment paper.

5 Bake for 18 to 20 minutes or until golden brown and crisp.

6 Remove from the oven and let cool on the pan for 5 to 10 minutes before moving to a baking rack to cool completely.

CHEWY BROWNED BUTTER CHOCOLATE CHIP COOKIES

Mixing Method: Classic Creaming (melted butter)

Yield: 26 to 28 cookies
Prep Time: 30 minutes
Bake Time: 13 to 15 minutes

Special Equipment

Stand mixer with the paddle attachment

#20 scoop

Half sheet pans

Ingredients

2½ sticks (284g) unsalted butter

1 cup (200g) granulated sugar

1¼ cups (250g) light brown sugar

2 tablespoons toasted milk powder (see page 79)

2 large eggs

2 teaspoons vanilla extract

3 cups (420g) all-purpose flour

¾ teaspoon baking soda

¾ teaspoon baking powder

1 teaspoon table salt

12 ounces (340g) chocolate chips or chunks

Method

1. Add 1½ sticks (170g) of the butter to a small saucepan set over medium heat. Stir continuously with a silicone spatula until the milk solids separate and turn light golden brown. Turn off the heat and immediately add the other remaining butter to the pot. Let the butter cool for 10 minutes before continuing on.
2. Follow the Classic Creaming Method outlined on page 36, including the toasted milk powder with the sugar and butter in the first step.
3. Optionally, cover the cookie dough and chill in the refrigerator for 30 minutes or up to overnight. Preheat the oven to 375°F (190°C) 30 minutes before baking.
4. Divide the dough into cookies, each about the size of 3 tablespoons or weighing 60g. For the quickest and easiest portioning, use a #20 size scoop.
5. Arrange 8 cookies on each half sheet pan lined with parchment paper.
6. Bake for 13 to 15 minutes or until golden brown but the edge is still soft.
7. Remove from the oven and let cool on the pan for 5 to 10 minutes before moving to a baking rack to cool completely.

LEARNING WITH

CHOCOLATE CHIP COOKIES

AMOUNT OF SUGAR (SEE PHOTO)

One of the biggest contributors to spread in a cookie is the amount of sugar. Increasing the amount of sugar creates a cookie with a weaker interior structure that ends up spreading more in the oven. Decreasing the amount of sugar has the opposite effect. Instead, the cookie will stay compact and puffy. You can also adjust the overall sweetness and predominant flavors of the cookies by changing the amount of add-ins. More sugar and less chocolate highlights the caramelized and toffee flavors, whereas less sugar and more chocolate creates a cookie that puts the chocolate at center stage.

CHOCOLATE CHIPS VS. CHOCOLATE CHUNKS

Many chocolate chips are designed to hold their shape while baking. This leads to a cookie with solid pieces of chocolate scattered throughout. Cutting up a bar of baking chocolate, on the other hand, introduces large and small shards of chocolate that melt for uneven and interspersed puddles of chocolate. You can also include a combination of each for some distinct chunks of chocolate surrounded by puddles.

BAKING SODA VS. BAKING POWDER (SEE PHOTO)

Baking powder is composed of both baking soda and a powdered acid. This combination of ingredients leaves a leavener with a nearly neutral pH, which encourages baked goods to puff up instead of out. Baking soda, which is basic, needs an acid to react. When there is not enough acid to neutralize the baking soda, the overall pH of the cookie changes and starts to lean alkaline. This alkalinity weakens the gluten structure and raises the temperature needed for the egg proteins to set. The result is a cookie that spreads more. Finally, the more alkaline the batter, the more the baked good will brown.

BROWN BUTTER AND TOASTED MILK POWDER

Browned butter introduces an undeniably delicious toasty toffee flavor to your baked goods. This is accomplished by cooking off the water content in the butter to the point of separating the milk fat from the milk solids and then toasting those milk solids. Because this toasting doesn't happen until the water content has been driven off, cookies made with only browned butter will lack moisture and crumble. Try browning only a portion of the butter to introduce some toasty milk solids while also keeping some moisture, or, do as I have done in many of the recipes, and include toasted milk powder as an extra ingredient.

*To make toasted milk powder, spread nonfat milk powder in a thin layer on a parchment-lined sheet pan. Bake at 300°F (150°C) for 15 to 20 minutes or until a light golden brown. Store in an airtight container and add a tablespoon or two to any baked good that would benefit from an extra toasty, toffee flavor.

PEANUT BUTTER COOKIES

A CLOSER LOOK AT PEANUT BUTTER COOKIES

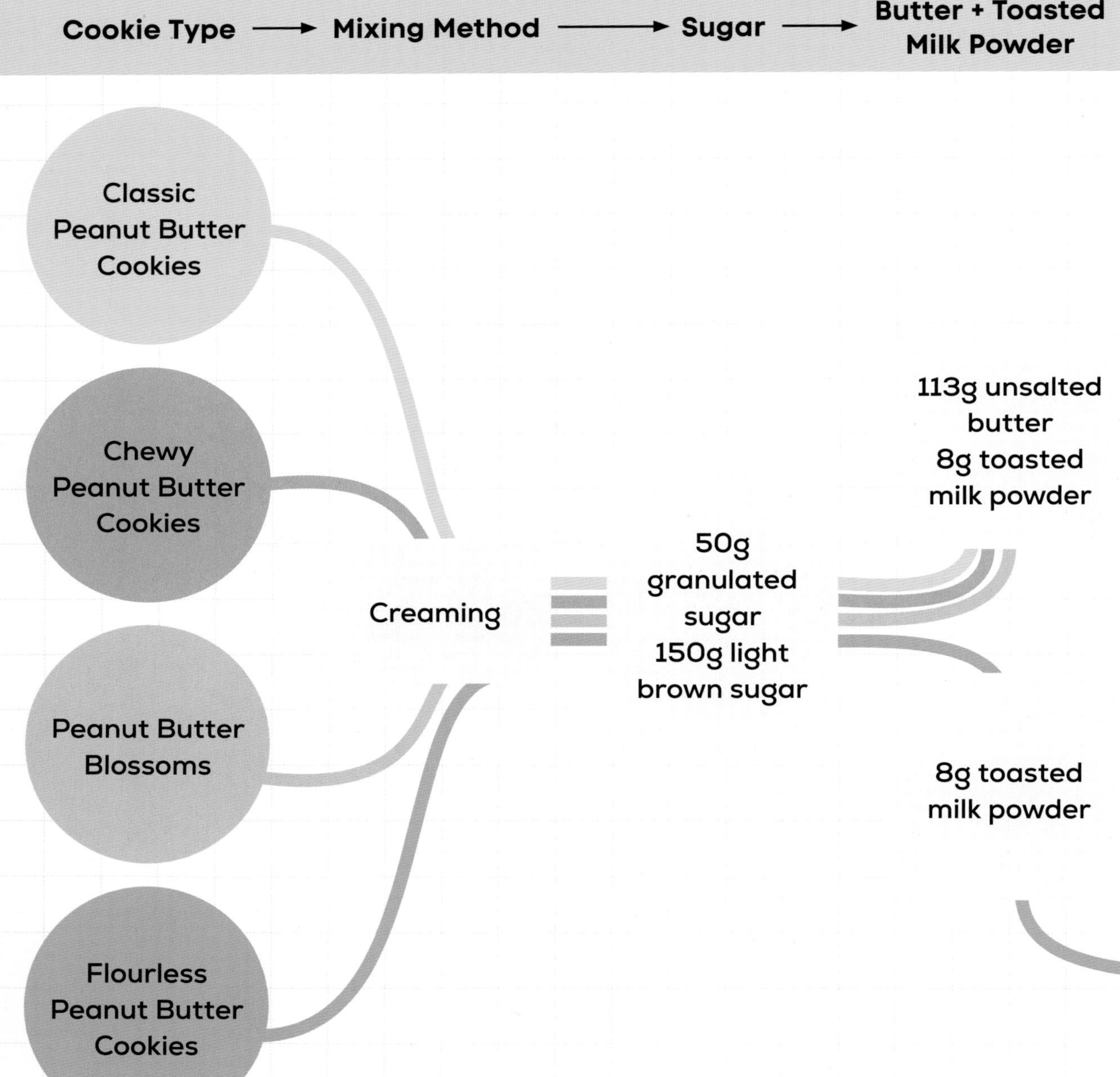

→ Peanut Butter → Eggs + Vanilla → Flour → Baking Soda + Salt

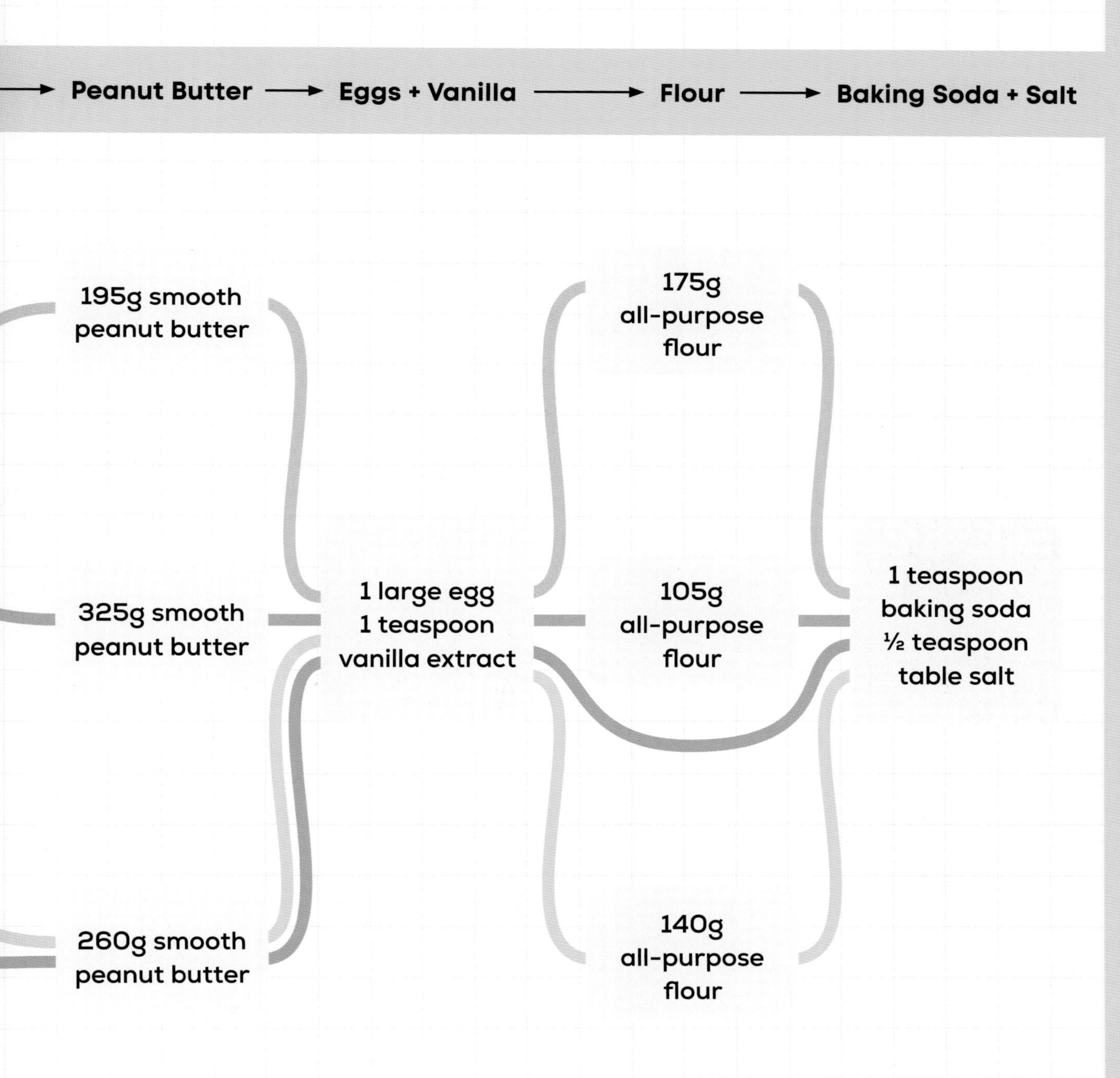

CLASSIC PEANUT BUTTER COOKIES

Mixing Method: Classic Creaming

Yield: 18 to 20 cookies
Prep Time: 20 minutes
Bake Time: 14 to 16 minutes

Special Equipment

Stand mixer with the paddle attachment

#30 scoop

Half sheet pans

Ingredients

¼ cup (50g) granulated sugar, plus ¼ cup (50g) for rolling

¾ cup (150g) light brown sugar

1 tablespoon toasted milk powder (see page 79)

1 cup (260g) smooth peanut butter

1 stick (113g) unsalted butter, softened

1 large egg

1 teaspoon vanilla extract

1 cup (140g) all-purpose flour

1 teaspoon baking soda

½ teaspoon table salt

Method

1. Preheat the oven to 350°F (180°C)
2. Follow the Classic Creaming Method outlined on page 36, including the peanut butter and toasted milk powder with the sugar and butter in the first step.
3. Divide the dough into cookies, each about the size of 2 tablespoons or weighing 40g. For the quickest and easiest portioning, use a #30 size scoop.
4. Roll each cookie dough ball in granulated sugar and arrange 8 cookies on each half sheet pan lined with parchment paper. Before placing in the oven, press the cookies down with the tines of a fork, first one way and then again perpendicular to the first press.
5. Bake for 14 to 16 minutes or until golden and the edge is just set.
6. Remove from the oven and let cool on the pan for 5 to 10 minutes before moving to a baking rack to cool completely.

CHEWY PEANUT BUTTER COOKIES

Mixing Method: Classic Creaming

Yield: 12 to 14 cookies
Prep Time: 20 minutes
Bake Time: 14 to 16 minutes

Special Equipment

Stand mixer with the paddle attachment

#20 scoop

Half sheet pans

Ingredients

¼ cup (50g) granulated sugar

¾ cup (150g) light brown sugar

1 tablespoon toasted milk powder (see page 79)

1¼ cups (325g) smooth peanut butter

1 stick (113g) unsalted butter, softened

1 large egg

1 teaspoon vanilla extract

¾ cup (105g) all-purpose flour

1 teaspoon baking soda

½ teaspoon table salt

Method

1. Preheat the oven to 375°F (190°C)
2. Follow the Classic Creaming Method outlined on page 36, including the peanut butter and toasted milk powder with the sugar and butter in the first step.
3. Divide the dough into cookies, each about the size of 3 tablespoons or weighing 60g. For the quickest and easiest portioning, use a #20 size scoop.
4. Arrange 6 cookies on each half sheet pan lined with parchment paper.
5. Bake for 14 to 16 minutes or until golden and the edge is still soft.
6. Remove from the oven and let cool on the pan for 5 to 10 minutes before moving to a baking rack to cool completely.

PEANUT BUTTER BLOSSOMS

Mixing Method: Classic Creaming

Yield: 24 to 26 cookies
Prep Time: 20 minutes
Bake Time: 14 to 16 minutes

Special Equipment

Stand mixer with the paddle attachment

#40 scoop

Half sheet pans

Ingredients

¼ cup (50g) granulated sugar, plus ¼ cup (50g) for rolling

¾ cup (150g) light brown sugar

1 tablespoon toasted milk powder (see page 79)

¾ cup (195g) smooth peanut butter

1 stick (113g) unsalted butter, softened

1 large egg

1 teaspoon vanilla extract

1¼ cups (175g) all-purpose flour

1 teaspoon baking soda

½ teaspoon table salt

24 to 26 pieces of milk chocolate

Method

1. Preheat the oven to 350°F (180°C)
2. Follow the Classic Creaming Method outlined on page 36, including the peanut butter and toasted milk powder with the sugar and butter in the first step.
3. Divide the dough into cookies, each about the size of 1½ tablespoons or measuring 30g. For the quickest and easiest portioning, use a #40 size scoop.
4. Roll each cookie dough ball in granulated sugar and arrange 12 cookies on each half sheet pan lined with parchment paper.
5. Bake for 14 to 16 minutes or until golden and the edge is just set.
6. Remove from the oven and immediately press a piece of milk chocolate into the top of each cookie. Let cool on the pan for 5 to 10 minutes before moving to a baking rack to cool completely.

FLOURLESS PEANUT BUTTER COOKIES

Mixing Method: Classic Creaming

Yield: 12 to 14 cookies
Prep Time: 20 minutes
Bake Time: 14 to 16 minutes

Special Equipment

Stand mixer with the paddle attachment

#30 scoop

Half sheet pans

Ingredients

¼ cup (50g) granulated sugar, plus ¼ cup (50g) for rolling

¾ cup (150g) light brown sugar

1 tablespoon toasted milk powder (see page 79)

1 cup (260g) smooth peanut butter

1 large egg

1 teaspoon vanilla extract

1 teaspoon baking soda

½ teaspoon table salt

Method

1 Preheat the oven to 350°F (180°C).

2 Follow the Classic Creaming Method outlined on page 36, including the peanut butter and toasted milk powder in the first step. (Because there is no butter, don't worry about mixing until the mixture has lightened in color and increased in volume. Instead, mix together for 1 to 2 minutes to create a smooth paste with the sugar, toasted milk powder, and peanut butter.)

3 Divide the dough into cookies, each about the size of 2 tablespoons or weighing 40g. For the quickest and easiest portioning, use a #30 size scoop.

4 Arrange 8 cookies on each half sheet pan lined with parchment paper.

5 Bake for 14 to 16 minutes or until golden and the edge is just set.

6 Remove from the oven and let cool on the pan for 5 to 10 minutes before moving to a baking rack to cool completely.

NONE
CUP
FORK

LEARNING WITH
PEANUT BUTTER COOKIES

AMOUNT OF FAT

As the amount of peanut butter changed between the different variations presented, so too did the amount of fat in the cookie. An increased amount of fat encourages spread and, because gluten can't form when the flour particles have been greased, the result is a cookie with a more tender texture.

AMOUNT OF FLOUR

Though perhaps obvious, it is still worth noting that the amount of flour in a recipe can impact the spread, texture, and flavor of a cookie. As discussed in the Notes on Baker's Percentages section (page 23), adjusting the amount of flour changes the relative percentage of each ingredient compared to this main structure builder. Adjusting this amount a little can prove beneficial in gently tweaking a recipe, but if you go too far, the resulting baked good will taste of flour and not much else.

SQUISHING THE DOUGH (SEE PHOTO, PAGE 88)

In addition to all the chemical changes you can make in your cookie batter, we cannot ignore the physical ones. For example, the crisscross pattern on a classic peanut butter cookie is more than just decoration. Squishing the dough encourages the spread of the cookie into its final shape. Adjust the shape of your cookie before it goes in the oven and that may be all you need to achieve your desired result.

OVEN TEMPERATURE

Many of the recipes in this book call for one of three temperatures: 325°F, 350°F, or 375°F (160°C, 180°C, or 190°C). The difference? At lower temperatures, the interior of the cookie, or other baked good, takes longer to set up. This allows more time for the cookie to spread and lose moisture. The result is a thinner and crispier final result. At higher temperatures, the edge of the cookie will set more quickly, which leads to a thicker cookie with a softer interior.

CHOCOLATE CHIP COOKIE BARS

A CLOSER LOOK AT CHOCOLATE CHIP COOKIE BARS

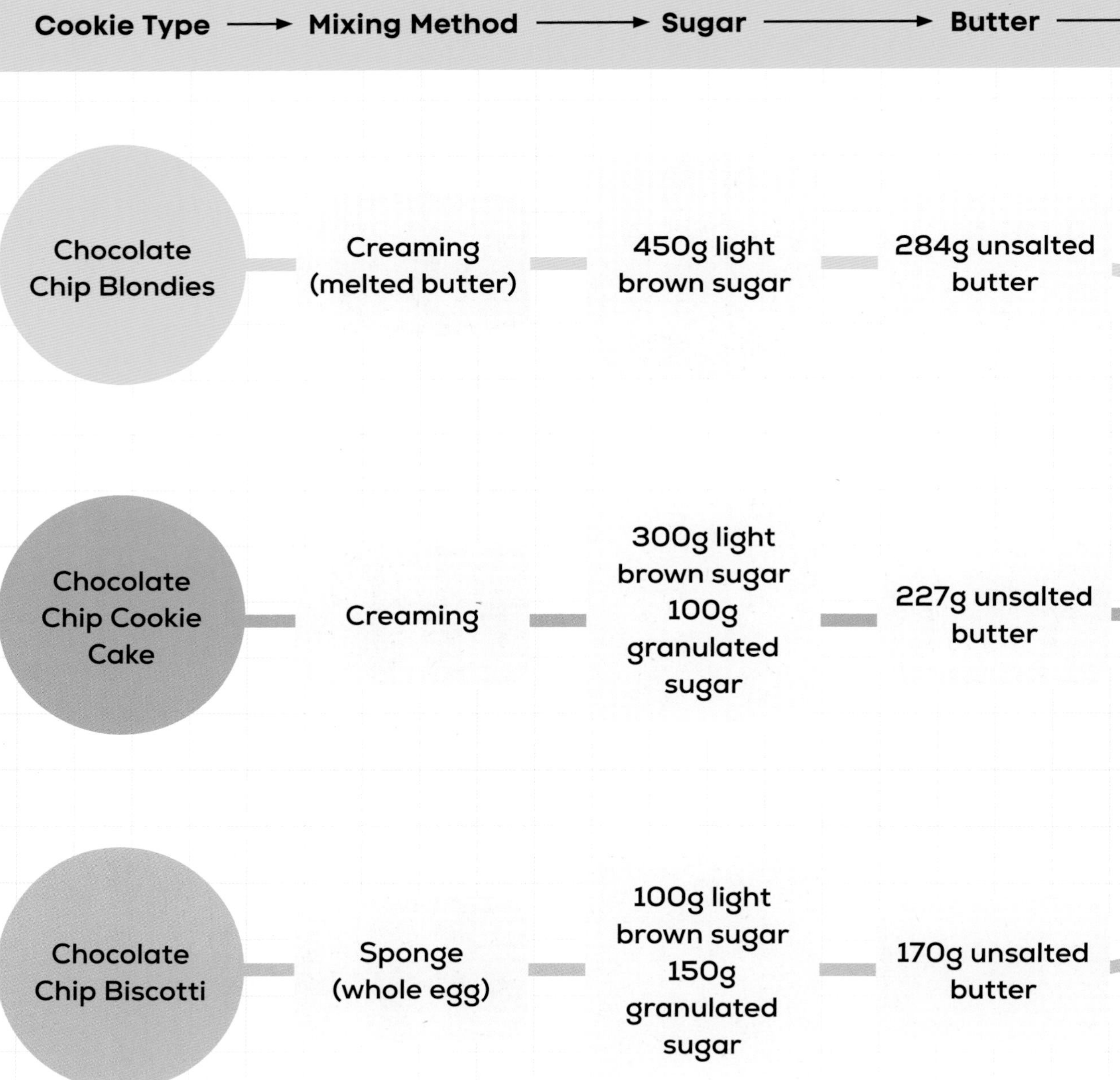

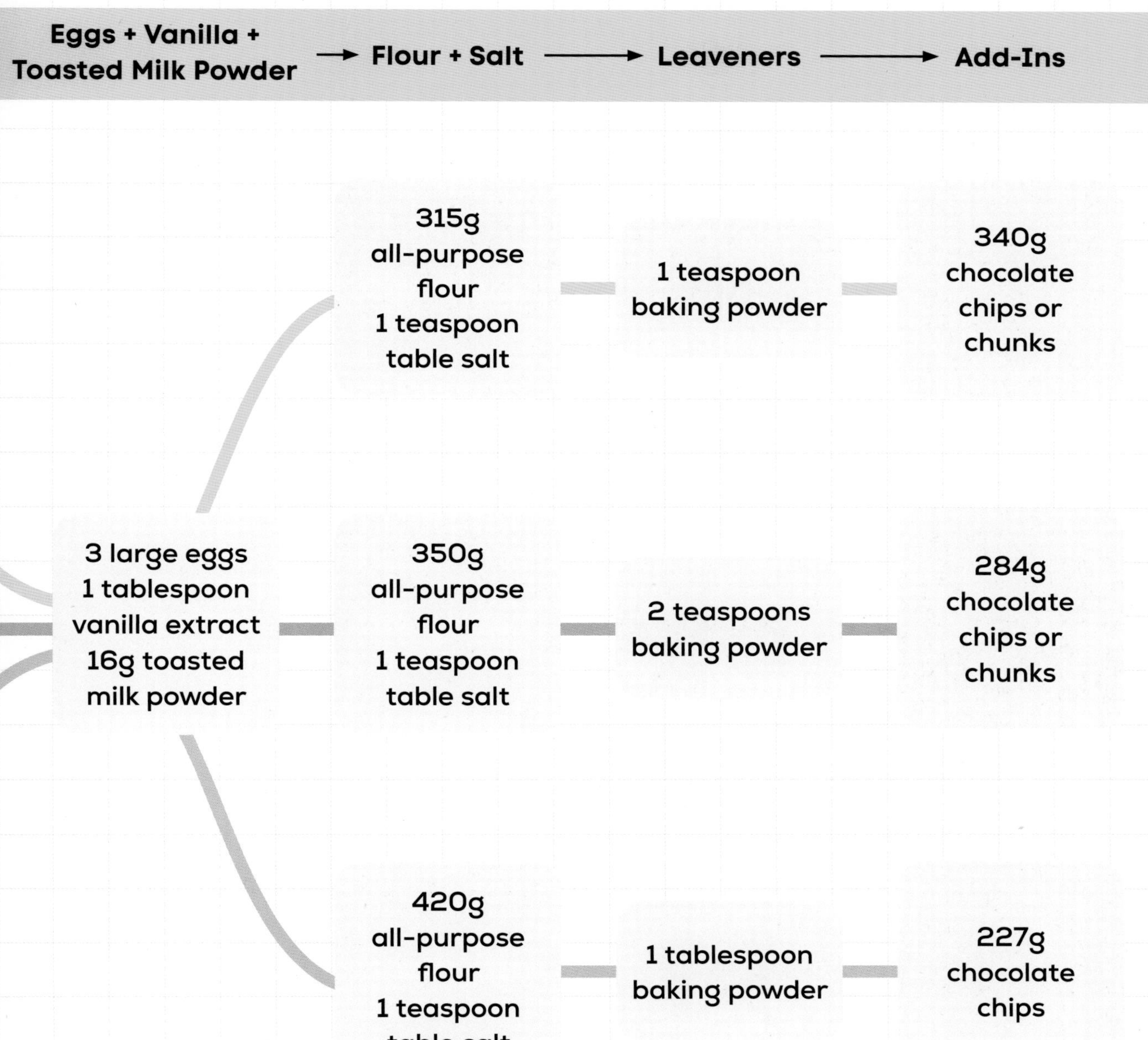
Eggs + Vanilla + Toasted Milk Powder
Flour + Salt
Leaveners
Add-Ins
315g all-purpose flour 1 teaspoon table salt
1 teaspoon baking powder
340g chocolate chips or chunks
3 large eggs 1 tablespoon vanilla extract 16g toasted milk powder
350g all-purpose flour 1 teaspoon table salt
2 teaspoons baking powder
284g chocolate chips or chunks
420g all-purpose flour 1 teaspoon table salt
1 tablespoon baking powder
227g chocolate chips

CHOCOLATE CHIP BLONDIES

Mixing Method: Classic Creaming (melted butter)

Yield: One 9×13-inch (23×33cm) pan, about 12 to 24 blondies depending on their size

Prep Time: 20 minutes

Bake Time: 35 to 40 minutes

Special Equipment

9×13-inch (23×33cm) baking pan

Stand mixer with the paddle attachment

Ingredients

2¼ cups (450g) light brown sugar

2½ sticks (284g) unsalted butter, melted and cooled

2 tablespoons toasted milk powder (see page 79)

3 large eggs

1 tablespoon vanilla extract

2¼ cups (315g) all-purpose flour

1 teaspoon baking powder

1 teaspoon table salt

12 ounces (340g) chocolate chips or chunks

Method

1. Preheat the oven to 350°F (180°C) and prepare the pan with nonstick baking spray and a parchment paper sling across the width of the pan (see page 38).
2. Follow the Classic Creaming Method outlined on page 36, including the toasted milk powder with the sugar and butter in the first step.
3. Spread the blondie batter evenly in the prepared pan and bake for 35 to 40 minutes or until a light golden brown.
4. Remove from the oven and set the pan on a baking rack to cool completely.
5. Once cool, lift out using the parchment paper sling and cut into squares.

CHOCOLATE CHIP COOKIE CAKE

Mixing Method: Classic Creaming

Yield: Two 8×3-inch (20×8cm) round cakes

Prep Time: 20 minutes

Bake Time: 30 to 35 minutes

Special Equipment

Stand mixer with the paddle attachment

Two 8×3-inch (20×8cm) round cake pans

Ingredients

1½ cups (300g) light brown sugar

½ cup (100g) granulated sugar

2 sticks (227g) unsalted butter, softened

2 tablespoons toasted milk powder (see page 79)

3 large eggs

1 tablespoon vanilla extract

2½ cups (350g) all-purpose flour

2 teaspoons baking powder

1 teaspoon table salt

10 ounces (284g) chocolate chips or chunks

Method

1 Preheat the oven to 350°F (180°C) and prepare the cake pans with nonstick baking spray and a circle of parchment paper on the bottom.

2 Follow the Classic Creaming Method outlined on page 36, including the toasted milk powder with the sugar and butter in the first step.

3 Divide the cookie dough evenly between the two cake pans and smooth the tops.

4 Bake for 30 to 35 minutes or until a light golden brown.

5 Remove from the oven and let cool for 5 to 10 minutes before flipping the cookie cake rounds onto a baking rack to cool completely.

CHOCOLATE CHIP BISCOTTI

Mixing Method: Sponge (whole egg)

Yield: 32 to 36 biscotti
Prep Time: 30 minutes
First Bake Time: 25 to 30 minutes
Inactive Time: 30 minutes
Second Bake Time: 15 to 20 minutes

Special Equipment

Stand mixer with the whisk attachment

Half sheet pans

Ingredients

½ cup (100g) light brown sugar

¾ cup (150g) granulated sugar

3 large eggs, room temperature

1½ sticks (170g) unsalted butter, melted and cooled

2 tablespoons toasted milk powder (see page 79)

1 tablespoon vanilla extract

3 cups (420g) all-purpose flour

1 tablespoon baking powder

1 teaspoon table salt

8 ounces (227g) chocolate chips or chunks

Method

1. Preheat the oven to 350°F (180°C).
2. Follow the Sponge (Whole Egg) Method outlined on page 42, adding the toasted milk powder and vanilla with the melted butter. Finish by gently mixing in the chocolate once all the dry ingredients have been incorporated.
3. Divide the biscotti dough in two and with each half, form a 12×3-inch (30×8cm) rectangle. Place each rectangle on its own half sheet pan lined with parchment paper.
4. Bake for 25 to 30 minutes or until puffed and a light golden brown.
5. Let cool on the pan for 30 minutes. In the meantime, turn the oven down to 325°F (160°C).
6. Slice each biscotti log on an angle to create individual biscotti roughly ½ inch (1cm) wide.
7. Arrange the biscotti on the half sheet pan so that they are standing up and spaced at least a half inch away from each other.
8. Return the biscotti to the oven for 15 to 20 minutes or until dry to the touch.
9. Remove from the oven and let cool completely on the pan.

LEARNING WITH

CHOCOLATE CHIP COOKIE BARS

MELTED BUTTER VS. SOFTENED BUTTER

When using the Creaming Method, the butter must be just the right temperature (around 60 to 65°F or 16 to 18°C) in order for air to be incorporated into the batter or dough. If the butter is too cold or too hot, it won't be able to hold on to any of that air from mixing. This denser result, though, may not be a bad thing. A cookie or bar made with melted butter will be denser and chewier than its softened butter counterpart.

MIXING METHOD

Altering the method used to mix your cookies or bars will change both the amount of air whipped into your baked good and the amount of dissolved sugar. Mixing the sugar and eggs in the first steps allows for some of the sugar to dissolve in the water of the eggs. In addition to increased aeration, the final product will have a smoother surface. In the case of brownies, as we will see next, dissolved sugar is the key to that thin, shiny layer that sits on top.

AMOUNT OF BAKING POWDER (SEE PHOTO)

Increasing the amount of baking powder in a recipe results in a baked good that both rises higher and has a more open and airy texture. There is, however, a tipping point. Go too far and all of a sudden that cookie or cake that once looked puffed up in the oven will have collapsed the next time you take a peek.

BROWNIES

A CLOSER LOOK AT BROWNIES

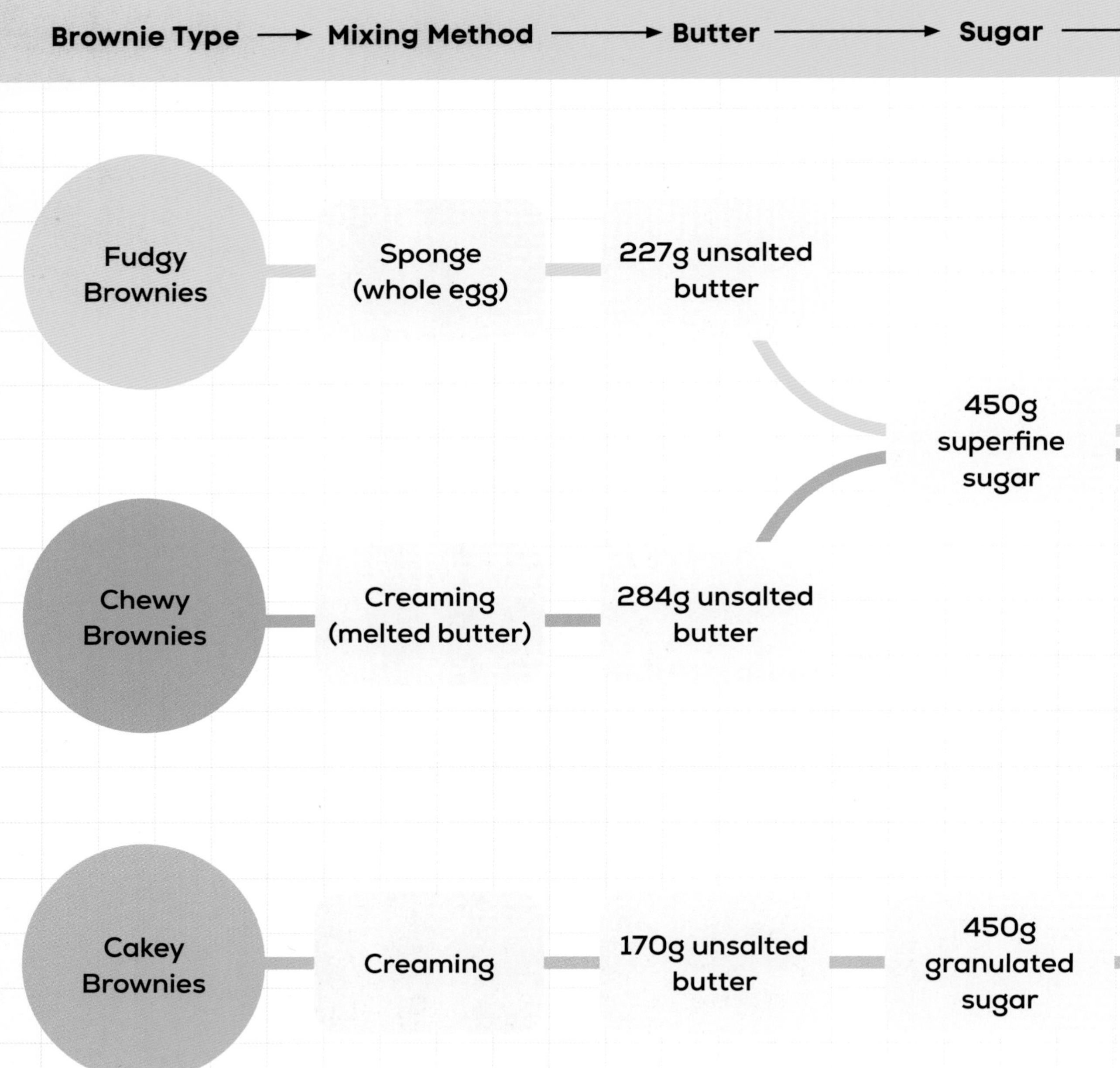

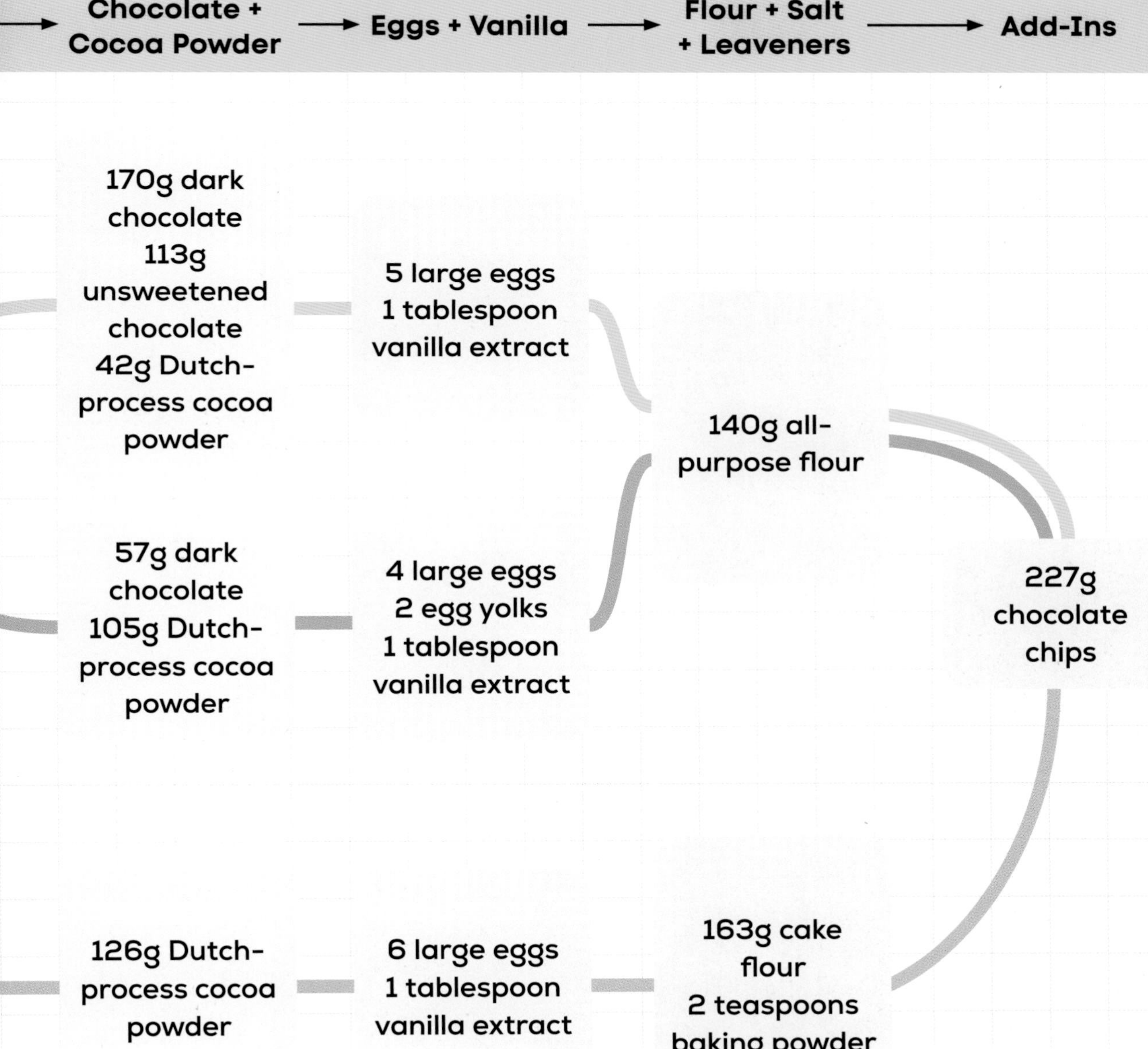
Chocolate + Cocoa Powder
Eggs + Vanilla
Flour + Salt + Leaveners
Add-Ins
170g dark chocolate
113g unsweetened chocolate
42g Dutch-process cocoa powder
5 large eggs
1 tablespoon vanilla extract
140g all-purpose flour
227g chocolate chips
57g dark chocolate
105g Dutch-process cocoa powder
4 large eggs
2 egg yolks
1 tablespoon vanilla extract
126g Dutch-process cocoa powder
6 large eggs
1 tablespoon vanilla extract
163g cake flour
2 teaspoons baking powder

FUDGY BROWNIES

Mixing Method: Sponge (Whole Egg)

Yield: One 9×13-inch (23×33cm) pan, about 12 to 24 brownies depending on their size

Prep Time: 30 minutes

Bake Time: 25 to 30 minutes

Special Equipment

Stand mixer with the whisk attachment

9×13-inch (23×33cm) baking pan

Ingredients

2 sticks (227g) unsalted butter

2 ounces (57g) dark chocolate (around 70%), finely chopped

4 ounces (113g) unsweetened chocolate, finely chopped

½ cup (42g) Dutch-process cocoa powder

2¼ cups (450g) superfine sugar

5 large eggs, room temperature

1 tablespoon vanilla extract

1 cup (140g) all-purpose flour

1 teaspoon table salt

8 ounces (227g) chocolate chips

Method

1. Preheat the oven to 350°F (180°C) and prepare the pan with nonstick baking spray and a parchment paper sling across the width of the pan (see page 38).
2. Add the butter and both chocolates to a medium bowl set over a pan of simmering water. Stir together with a silicone spatula until the butter and chocolate have melted. Once melted, remove from the heat and immediately mix in the cocoa powder.
3. Follow the Sponge (Whole Egg) method outlined on page 42, adding the chocolate mixture from the previous step after whisking the eggs and sugar together. Finish by mixing in the chocolate chips.
4. Smooth out in the prepared pan and bake for 25 to 30 minutes or until a toothpick inserted in the center comes out with streaks of thick batter (the toothpick should not come out clean nor should it come out entirely coated with shiny, wet batter).
5. Remove from the oven and set the pan on a baking rack to cool completely.
6. Once cool, lift out using the parchment paper sling and cut into squares.

CHEWY BROWNIES

Mixing Method: Classic Creaming (melted butter)

Yield: One 9×13-inch (23×33cm) pan, about 12 to 24 brownies depending on their size

Prep Time: 30 minutes

Bake Time: 25 to 30 minutes

Special Equipment

9×13-inch (23×33cm) baking pan

Ingredients

2¼ cups (450g) superfine sugar

2½ sticks (284g) unsalted butter

1¼ cups (105g) Dutch-process cocoa powder

2 ounces (57g) dark chocolate (around 70%), finely chopped

4 large eggs

2 egg yolks

1 tablespoon vanilla extract

1 cup (140g) all-purpose flour

1 teaspoon table salt

8 ounces (227g) chocolate chips

Method

1. Preheat the oven to 350°F (180°C) and prepare the pan with nonstick baking spray and a parchment paper sling across the width of the pan (see page 38).
2. Add the sugar to a medium size bowl and add the butter to a small pot set over medium heat.
3. When the butter comes to a boil, remove from the heat and immediately pour over the sugar. Stir with a silicone spatula to evenly distribute the melted butter over the sugar and to allow the sugar to dissolve.
4. Immediately add the cocoa powder and finely chopped chocolate to the bowl and mix until the chocolate is melted and a smooth paste forms.
5. Continue by following the Classic Creaming Method outlined on page 36, picking up with step 2 where the eggs are added.
6. Smooth out in the prepared pan and bake for 25 to 30 minutes or until a toothpick inserted in the center comes out with streaks of thick batter (the toothpick should not come out clean nor should it come out entirely coated with shiny, wet batter).
7. Remove from the oven and set the pan on a baking rack to cool completely.
8. Once cool, lift out using the parchment paper sling and cut into squares.

CAKEY BROWNIES

Mixing Method: Classic Creaming

Yield: One 9×13-inch (23×33cm) pan, about 12 to 24 brownies depending on their size

Prep Time: 30 minutes

Bake Time: 25 to 30 minutes

Special Equipment

Stand mixer with the paddle attachment

9×13-inch (23×33cm) baking pan

Ingredients

1½ sticks (170g) unsalted butter, softened

1¼ cups (250g) granulated sugar

1 cup (200g) light brown sugar

6 large eggs

1 tablespoon vanilla extract

1¼ cups (163g) cake flour, sifted

1½ cups (126g) Dutch-process cocoa powder

1 teaspoon table salt

2 teaspoons baking powder

8 ounces (227g) chocolate chips

Method

1. Preheat the oven to 350°F (180°C) and prepare the pan with nonstick baking spray and a parchment paper sling across the width of the pan (see page 38).
2. Follow the Creaming Method outlined on page 36.
3. Smooth out in the prepared pan and bake for 25 to 30 minutes or until a toothpick inserted in the center comes out with a few moist crumbs attached.
4. Remove from the oven and set the pan on a baking rack to cool completely.
5. Once cool, lift out using the parchment paper sling and cut into squares.

LEARNING WITH
BROWNIES

THE PART AND AMOUNT OF EGGS USED

Each part of the egg plays a distinct role in baking. While the egg whites contain much of the liquid and protein of an egg, the egg yolks contain the majority of the fats and emulsifiers. With a higher ratio of yolks to whites in a recipe, these fats from the yolk help create a baked good that not only has a richer flavor but also a chewier texture. A higher percentage of egg whites, on the other hand, allows for a brownie with more structure and an airier interior. In addition to altering the ratio of egg whites to egg yolks, it can also prove beneficial to adjust the total amount of eggs added to a recipe. Increasing the amount of eggs and, as a result, the amount of liquid leads to a fluffier and puffier final result. Decrease the amount of egg for a final product that is denser and fudgier.

CHOCOLATE VS. COCOA POWDER

Cocoa butter, the fat found in chocolate, is firm at room temperature. Because there is more cocoa butter in a bar of chocolate than in cocoa powder, brownies made with a higher percentage of melted chocolate will be firmer than those made with cocoa powder alone. Cocoa powder, on the other hand, introduces extra starch into the brownie batter. This starch, along with the protein in the flour and eggs, helps provide structure in your baked goods.

DISSOLVED SUGAR (SEE PHOTO)

The characteristic shine that adorns so many brownies now is a result of a set percentage of dissolved sugar in the recipe. When the amount of sugar relative to the amount of water in a recipe is just right, a shiny layer of crystallized sugar forms on top of the brownies. This dissolved sugar can come from melted chocolate and/or added granulated sugar mixed into the liquid ingredients in the recipe. In order to make sure that the sugar dissolves, I prefer to use superfine sugar. The smaller crystals will more readily dissolve and create the ideal conditions for a shiny top. Finally, it is worth noting that the type of sugar used makes a difference in creating this glossy crust. Too high a proportion of brown sugar can interrupt the granulated sugar's tendency to crystallize and once again leave a matte top.

SUGAR COOKIES

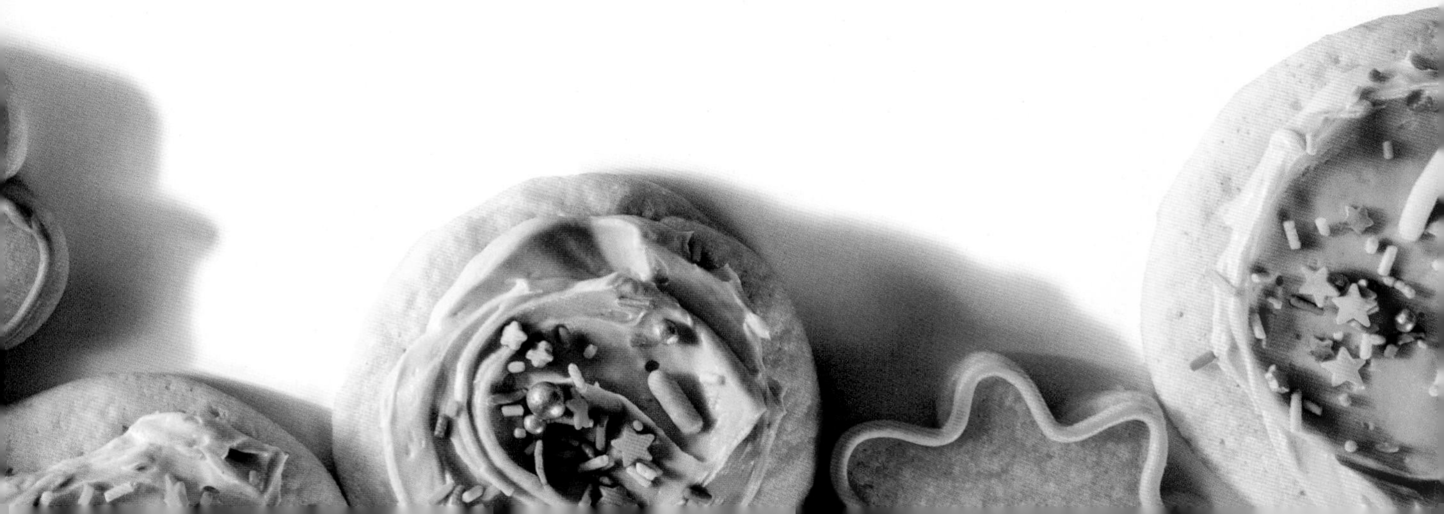

A CLOSER LOOK AT SUGAR COOKIES

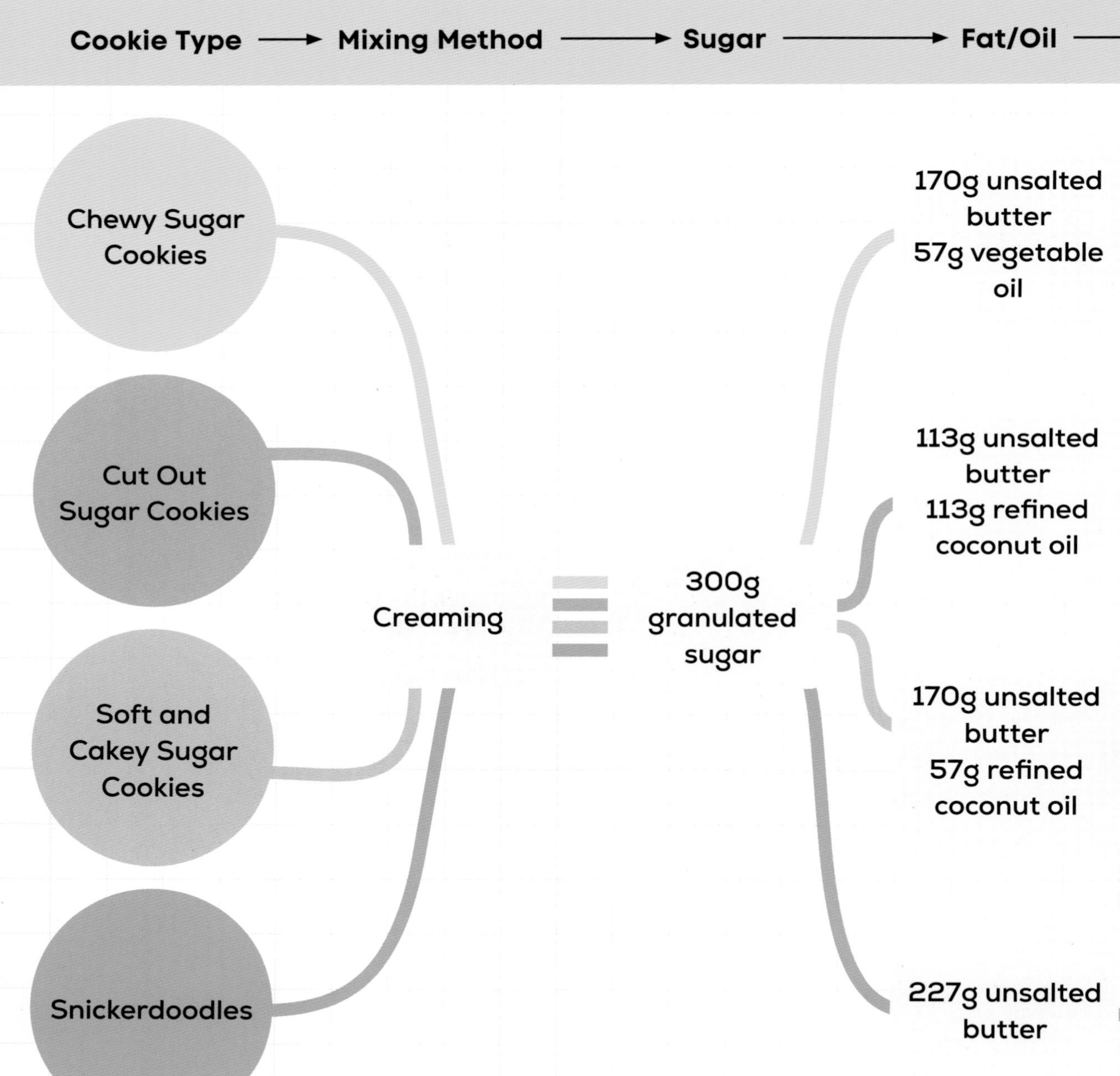

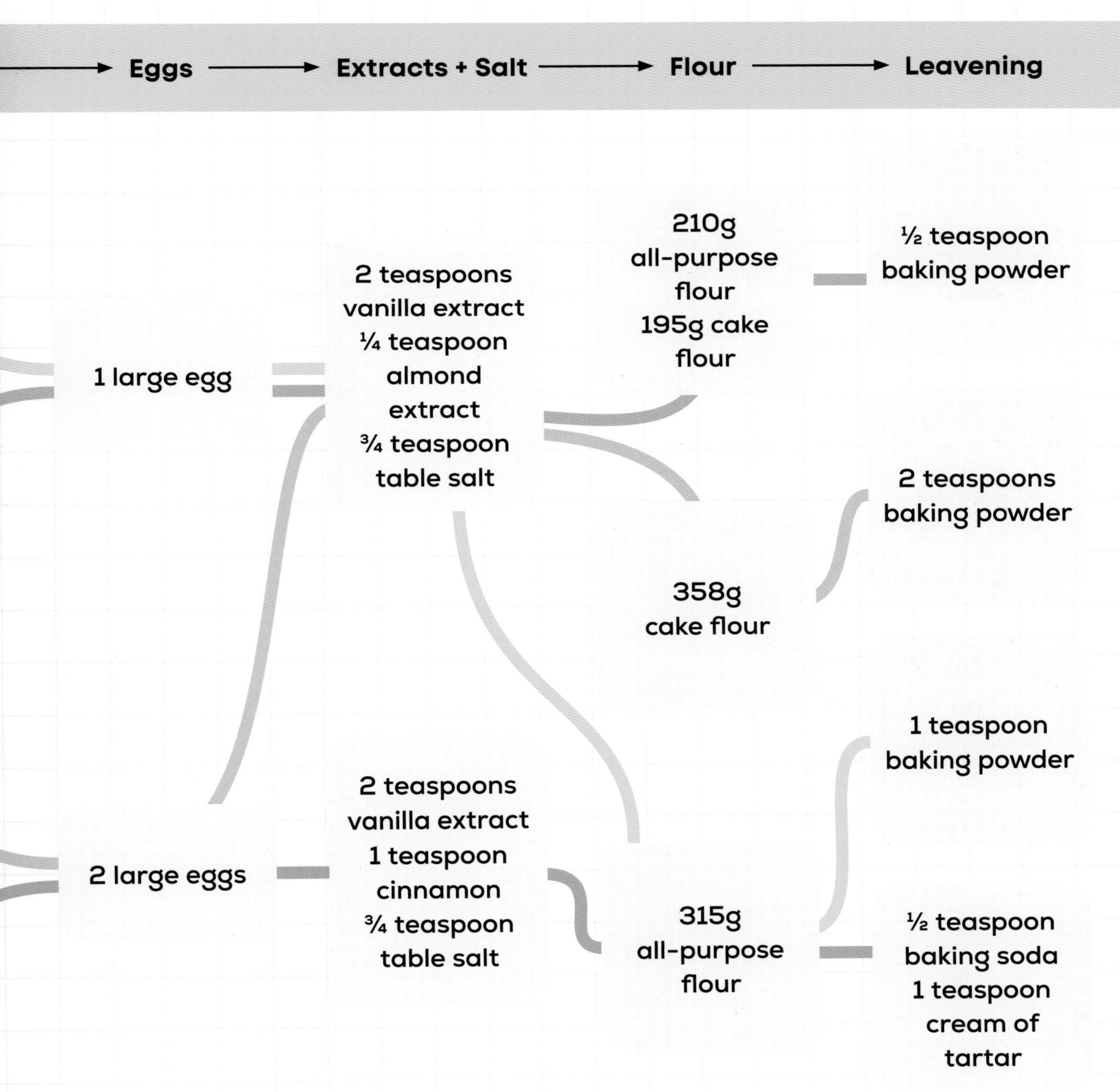

Eggs
Extracts + Salt
Flour
Leavening
1 large egg
2 teaspoons vanilla extract ¼ teaspoon almond extract ¾ teaspoon table salt
210g all-purpose flour 195g cake flour
½ teaspoon baking powder
358g cake flour
2 teaspoons baking powder
2 large eggs
2 teaspoons vanilla extract 1 teaspoon cinnamon ¾ teaspoon table salt
315g all-purpose flour
1 teaspoon baking powder
½ teaspoon baking soda 1 teaspoon cream of tartar

CHEWY SUGAR COOKIES

Mixing Method: Classic Creaming

Yield: 14 to 16 cookies
Prep Time: 20 minutes
Bake Time: 14 to 16 minutes

Special Equipment

Stand mixer with the paddle attachment

#20 scoop

Half sheet pans

Ingredients

1½ cups (300g) granulated sugar

1½ sticks (170g) unsalted butter, softened

¼ cup (57g) vegetable oil

1 large egg

2 teaspoons vanilla extract

¼ teaspoon almond extract

2¼ cups (315g) all-purpose flour

1 teaspoon baking powder

¾ teaspoon table salt

Method

1. Follow the Classic Creaming Method outlined on page 36, including the vegetable oil with the sugar and butter in the first step.
2. Optionally, cover the cookie dough and chill in the refrigerator for 30 minutes or up to overnight. Preheat the oven to 375°F (190°C) 30 minutes before baking.
3. Divide the dough into cookies, each about the size of 3 tablespoons or measuring 60g. For the quickest and easiest portioning, use a #20 size scoop.
4. Arrange 6 cookies on each half sheet pan lined with parchment paper.
5. Bake for 14 to 16 minutes or until the edge just begins to turn golden but is still soft.
6. Remove from the oven and let cool on the pan for 5 to 10 minutes before moving to a baking rack to cool completely.

CUT-OUT SUGAR COOKIES

Mixing Method: Classic Creaming

Yield: 12 to 24 cookies, depending on the size of your cookie cutters

Prep Time: 20 minutes

Inactive Time: 1 hour

Bake Time: 14 to 16 minutes

Special Equipment

Stand mixer with the paddle attachment

Cookie cutters (whatever shape you like)

Half sheet pans

Ingredients

1½ cups (300g) granulated sugar

1 stick (113g) unsalted butter, softened

½ cup (114g) refined coconut oil

1 large egg

2 teaspoons vanilla extract

¼ teaspoon almond extract

1½ cups (210g) all-purpose flour

1½ cups (195g) cake flour, sifted

½ teaspoon baking powder

¾ teaspoon table salt

1 batch Royal Icing (page 205)

Method

1. Follow the Classic Creaming Method outlined on page 36, including the coconut oil with the sugar and butter in the first step.
2. Place the cookie dough between two sheets of parchment paper and roll to roughly ¼ inch (6mm) thick. Place the cookie dough and parchment paper together on a sheet pan and place in the fridge for 1 hour.
3. In the final 30 minutes of chill time, preheat the oven to 350°F (180°C).
4. Remove the cookie dough from the fridge and let sit at room temperature for 5 minutes to soften slightly. Leaving the dough between the sheets of parchment, roll to a final thickness of ⅛ inch (3mm).
5. Use your desired cookie cutters to cut cookies and place roughly 1 inch (2.5cm) apart on a parchment paper–lined half sheet pan,
6. Push the scraps of the cookie dough together and re-roll one more time to a thickness of ⅛ inch (3mm).
7. Bake for 14 to 16 minutes or until the edge just begins to turn golden and just set.
8. Remove from the oven and let cool on the pan for 5 to 10 minutes before moving to a baking rack to cool completely.
9. Once completely cool, decorate with Royal Icing.

SOFT AND CAKEY SUGAR COOKIES

Mixing Method: Classic Creaming

Yield: 16 to 18 cookies
Prep Time: 20 minutes
Inactive Time: 1 hour
Bake Time: 16 to 18 minutes

Special Equipment

Stand mixer with the paddle attachment

#20 scoop

Half sheet pans

Ingredients

1½ cups (300g) granulated sugar

1½ sticks (170g) unsalted butter, softened

¼ cup (57g) refined coconut oil

2 large eggs

2 teaspoons vanilla extract

¼ teaspoon almond extract

2¾ cups (358g) cake flour, sifted

2 teaspoons baking powder

¾ teaspoon table salt

1 batch American Buttercream (page 212)

Method

1 Follow the Classic Creaming Method outlined on page 36, including the coconut oil with the sugar and butter in the irst step.

2 Cover the cookie dough and let chill in the refrigerator for 1 hour. In the meantime, preheat the oven to 350°F (180°C).

3 Divide the dough into cookies, each about the size of 3 tablespoons or measuring 60g. For the quickest and easiest portioning, use a #20 size scoop.

4 Arrange 6 cookies on each half sheet pan lined with parchment paper.

5 Bake for 16 to 18 minutes or until the edge just begins to turn golden but is still soft.

6 Remove from the oven and let cool on the pan for 5 to 10 minutes before moving to a baking rack to cool completely.

7 Once completely cool, decorate with American Buttercream.

SNICKERDOODLES

Mixing Method: Classic Creaming

Yield: 22 to 24 cookies
Prep Time: 20 minutes
Bake Time: 14 to 16 minutes

Special Equipment

Stand mixer with the paddle attachment

#30 scoop

Half sheet pans

Ingredients

1½ cups (300g) granulated sugar, plus ½ cup (100g) for the rolling sugar

2 sticks (227g) unsalted butter, softened

2 large eggs

2 teaspoons vanilla extract

2¼ cups (315g) all-purpose flour

½ teaspoon baking soda

1 teaspoon cream of tartar

1 teaspoon cinnamon, plus one tablespoon for the rolling sugar

¾ teaspoon table salt

Method

1. Follow the Classic Creaming Method outlined on page 36.
2. Optionally, cover the cookie dough and chill in the refrigerator for 30 minutes or up to overnight. Preheat the oven to 375°F (190°C) 30 minutes before baking.
3. Divide the dough into cookies, each about the size of 2 tablespoons or measuring 40g. For the quickest and easiest portioning, use a #30 size scoop.
4. Mix the reserved ½ cup (100g) of sugar and 1 tablespoon of cinnamon. Roll each cookie dough ball in the cinnamon sugar before arranging 8 cookies on each half sheet pan lined with parchment paper.
5. Bake for 14 to 16 minutes or until the edge just begins to turn golden but is still soft.
6. Remove from the oven and let cool on the pan for 5 to 10 minutes before moving to a baking rack to cool completely.

ALL
BUTTER
BUTTER +
VEGETABLE
OIL
BUTTER +
COCONUT
OIL

LEARNING WITH
SUGAR COOKIES

THE TYPE OF FAT USED (SEE PHOTO, PAGE 114)

Each fat comes with its own properties: melting point, amount of liquid, and level of unsaturated vs. saturated fat, to name a few. Butter, with its water content around 15 to 20%, will cause a cookie to spread more than one made with all coconut oil. Coconut oil, being a pure fat, does not introduce extra moisture into the cookie. Oils such as vegetable oil (and peanut oil from the peanut butter in the peanut butter cookie section) contain more unsaturated than saturated fats. Balancing these two types of fats can also impact the texture and chew of the final product.

CAKE FLOUR VS. ALL-PURPOSE FLOUR

One of the key differences between different types, and even different brands, of flour is protein content. Specifically, we are talking about the proteins that form gluten. All-purpose flour, named for its use in a wide range of baked goods, has a moderate protein content of around 9 to 11%. Cake flour, on the other hand, sits right in between the 6 to 8% range. This low protein content in conjunction with a high starch content helps create a lighter final product with a softer and finer interior texture.

BAKING POWDER VS ITS SUBSTITUTES

One of the most important ingredients to a classic snickerdoodle cookie is cream of tartar, a powdered acid. The combination of cream of tartar and baking soda is designed to give a quick and powerful reaction all at once. This means a snickerdoodle that quickly spreads in the oven and then flattens out as it cools for a crisp edge and chewy center. Baking powder, on the other hand, is formulated with baking soda and different powdered acids that are designed to react gradually. Adding liquid this time starts a slow reaction that steadily continues as the cookie dough is heated and the baking powder continues to dissolve. Cookies made with baking powder spread less and puff more for a rounded cookie with a thicker and doughier interior.

HOW TO TELL WHEN COOKIES ARE DONE BAKING

To tell when your cookies are done baking, keep an eye on the edge. For sugar cookies, if you take them out just before the outside starts to brown and while the edge offers no resistance you'll get a cookie that is soft all throughout. Bake a few more minutes until the edge turns a light golden brown and springs back slightly when pressed for a cookie with a crispy edge and a still soft center. And finally, when the entire outside turns a dark golden brown and the edge doesn't move when gently pushed, the cookie will be crunchy without being burnt.

SPICED COOKIES

A CLOSER LOOK AT SPICED COOKIES

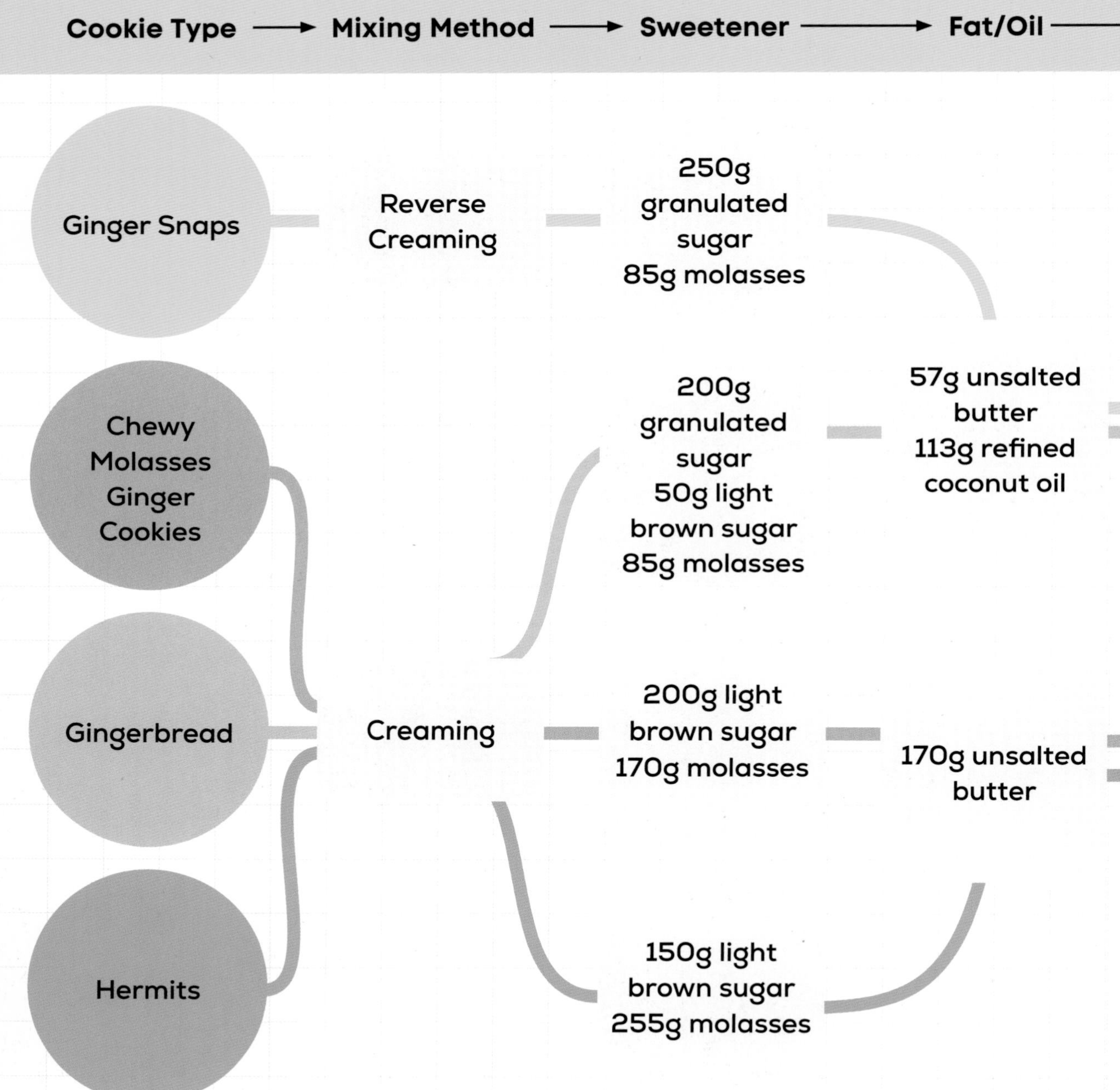

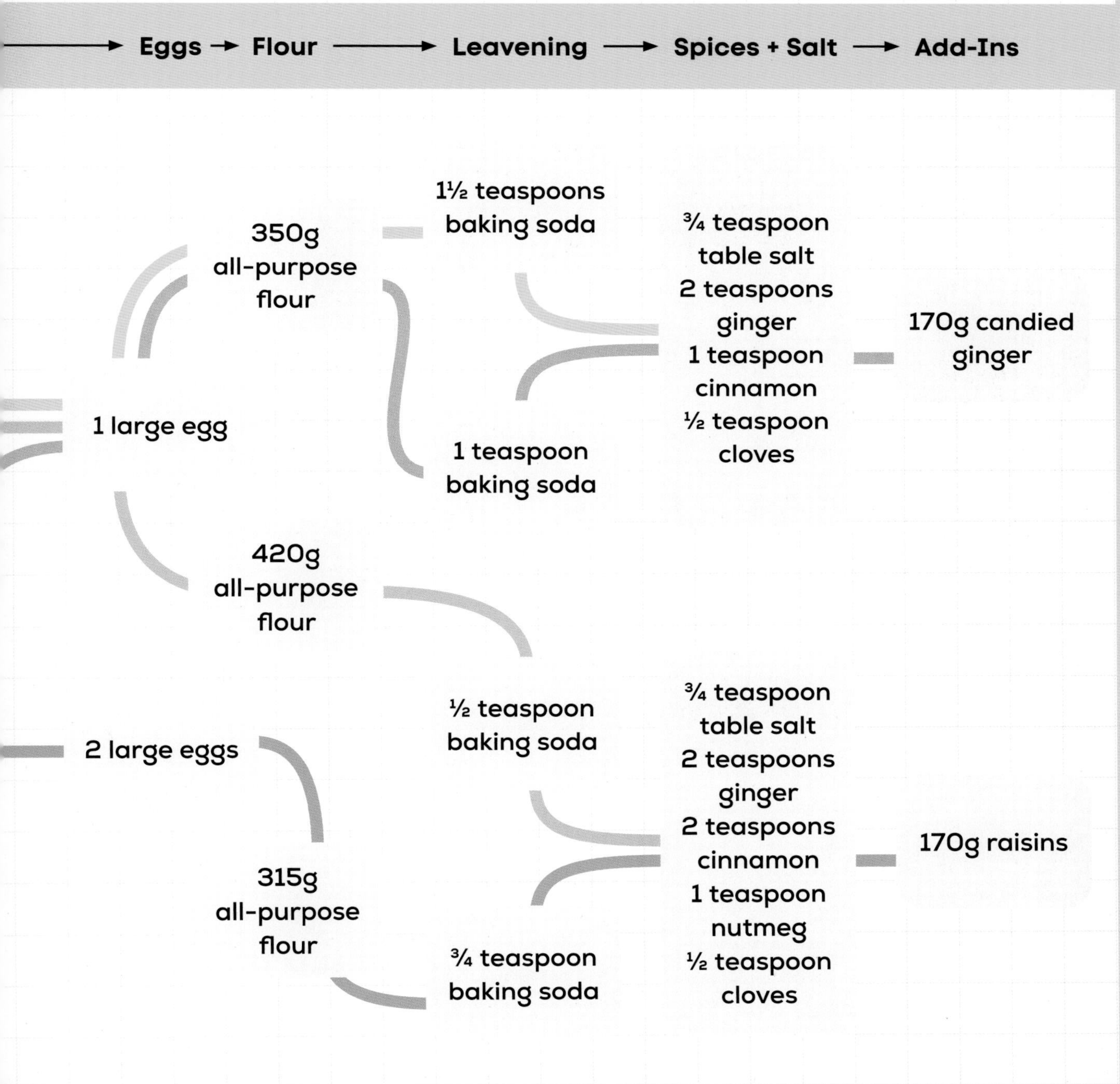

→ Eggs → Flour → Leavening → Spices + Salt → Add-Ins

1 large egg

350g all-purpose flour

1½ teaspoons baking soda

1 teaspoon baking soda

¾ teaspoon table salt
2 teaspoons ginger
1 teaspoon cinnamon
½ teaspoon cloves

170g candied ginger

420g all-purpose flour

½ teaspoon baking soda

2 large eggs

315g all-purpose flour

¾ teaspoon baking soda

¾ teaspoon table salt
2 teaspoons ginger
2 teaspoons cinnamon
1 teaspoon nutmeg
½ teaspoon cloves

170g raisins

GINGER SNAPS

Mixing Method: Reverse Creaming

Yield: 22 to 24 cookies
Prep Time: 20 minutes
Bake Time: 18 to 20 minutes

Special Equipment

Stand mixer with the paddle attachment

#30 scoop

Half sheet pans

Ingredients

1¼ cups (250g) granulated sugar

2½ cups (350g) all-purpose flour

1½ teaspoons baking soda

¾ teaspoon table salt

2 teaspoons ginger

1 teaspoon cinnamon

½ teaspoon cloves

4 tablespoons (57g) unsalted butter, softened

½ cup (113g) refined coconut oil

¼ cup (85g) molasses

1 large egg

Method

1. Preheat the oven to 350°F (180°C).
2. Follow the Reverse Creaming Method outlined on page 37, adding the molasses with the eggs at the end.
3. Divide the dough into cookies, each about the size of 2 tablespoons or measuring 40g. For the quickest and easiest portioning, use a #30 size scoop.
4. Arrange 8 cookies on each half sheet pan lined with parchment paper.
5. Bake for 18 to 20 minutes or until the edge is completely set.
6. Remove from the oven and let cool on the pan for 5 to 10 minutes before moving to a baking rack to cool completely.

CHEWY MOLASSES GINGER COOKIES

Mixing Method: Classic Creaming

Yield: 18 to 20 cookies
Prep Time: 20 minutes
Inactive Time: 1 hour
Bake Time: 14 to 16 minutes

Special Equipment

Stand mixer with the paddle attachment

#20 scoop

Half sheet pans

Ingredients

1 cup (200g) light brown sugar

1½ sticks (170g) unsalted butter, softened

½ cup (170g) molasses

1 large egg

2½ cups (350g) all-purpose flour

1 teaspoon baking soda

¾ teaspoon table salt

2 teaspoons ginger

1 teaspoon cinnamon

½ teaspoon cloves

1 cup (170g) candied ginger, chopped

Method

1. Follow the Classic Creaming Method outlined on page 36, adding the molasses in between creaming the sugar and butter and adding the eggs.
2. Cover the cookie dough and let rest in the refrigerator for 1 hour. In the meantime, preheat the oven to 375°F (190°C).
3. Divide the dough into cookies, each about the size of 3 tablespoons or weighing 60g. For the quickest and easiest portioning, use a #20 size scoop.
4. Arrange 6 cookies on each half sheet pan lined with parchment paper.
5. Bake for 14 to 16 minutes or until the edge is just beginning to set.
6. Remove from the oven and let cool on the pan for 5 to 10 minutes before moving to a baking rack to cool completely.

GINGERBREAD

Mixing Method: Classic Creaming

Yield: 20 to 24 cookies
Prep Time: 20 minutes
Inactive Time: 1 hour
Bake Time: 14 to 16 minutes

Special Equipment

Stand mixer with the paddle attachment

Cookie cutters (whatever shape you like)

Half sheet pans

Ingredients

1 cup (200g) granulated sugar

¼ cup (50g) light brown sugar

4 tablespoons (57g) unsalted butter, softened

½ cup (113g) refined coconut oil

¼ cup (85g) molasses

1 large eggs

3 cups (420g) all-purpose flour

½ teaspoon baking soda

¾ teaspoon table salt

2 teaspoons ginger

2 teaspoons cinnamon

1 teaspoon nutmeg

½ teaspoon cloves

1 batch Royal Icing (page 205)

Method

1 Follow the Classic Creaming Method outlined on page 36, adding the molasses in between creaming the sugar and butter and adding the eggs.

2 Place the cookie dough between two sheets of parchment paper and roll to roughly ¼ inch (6mm) thick. Place the cookie dough and parchment paper together on a sheet pan and place in the fridge for 1 hour.

3 In the final 30 minutes of chill time, preheat the oven to 350°F (180°C).

4 Remove the cookie dough from the fridge and let sit at room temperature for 5 minutes to soften slightly. Leaving the dough between the sheets of parchment, roll to a final thickness of ⅛ inch (3mm).

5 Use your desired cookie cutters to cut cookies and place roughly 1 inch (2.5cm) apart on a parchment paper–lined half sheet pan,

6 Push the scraps of the cookie dough together and re-roll one more time to a thickness of ⅛ inch (3mm).

7 Bake for 14 to 16 minutes or until the edge just begins to set.

8 Remove from the oven and let cool on the pan for 5 to 10 minutes before moving to a baking rack to cool completely.

9 Once completely cool, decorate with Royal Icing.

HERMITS

Mixing Method: Classic Creaming

Yield: 20 to 24 cookies
Prep Time: 20 minutes
Inactive Time: 2 hours
Bake Time: 16 to 18 minutes

Special Equipment

Stand mixer with the paddle attachment

Half sheet pans

Ingredients

¾ cup (150g) light brown sugar

1½ sticks (170g) unsalted butter, softened

¾ cup (255g) molasses

2 large eggs

3 cups (315g) all-purpose flour

¾ teaspoon baking soda

¾ teaspoon table salt

2 teaspoons ginger

2 teaspoons cinnamon

1 teaspoon nutmeg

½ teaspoon cloves

1 cup (170g) raisins

1 batch Flat Icing (page 204)

Method

1. Follow the Classic Creaming Method outlined on page 36, adding the molasses in between creaming the sugar and butter and adding the eggs.
2. Cover the cookie dough and let chill in the refrigerator for 2 hours. In the final 30 minutes of chill time, preheat the oven to 375°F (190°C).
3. Remove the dough from the fridge and empty onto a lightly floured work surface. Divide the dough into 4 equal pieces and roll each piece into a log roughly 12 inches (30cm) long. Place two logs on each parchment lined half sheet pan.
4. Brush off any excess flour and bake for 16 to 18 minutes or until the edge is just beginning to set.
5. Remove from the oven and let cool on the pan for 5 to 10 minutes before moving to a baking rack to cool completely.
6. Once cool, cut each log on an angle to make the individual cookie bars and drizzle Flat Icing over the top.

NONE
1½ tsp
1 tbsp

LEARNING WITH SPICED COOKIES

USING A LIQUID SUGAR

In addition to providing extra acidity that can react with the baking soda in the batter of dough, molasses also introduces a very hygroscopic sugar to the mix. Cookies, bars, and desserts made with molasses will hold onto moisture much better than those made with just granulated or brown sugar. The result is a final cookie with a soft texture and distinct taste.

AMOUNT OF BAKING SODA

Increased amounts of baking soda, with an unequal amount of acidic ingredients to balance it out, leads to a dough or batter that leans toward the alkaline side of the pH scale. As seen earlier on page 78, this alkalinity encourages cookies to spread out and brown more. The more browning a cookie undergoes, the deeper its flavor, but only to a certain point. Just as with adding too much baking powder, adding too much baking soda can lead to a final product that falls flat. Even worse, excessive amounts of baking soda lend a chemical and burnt taste to your baked goods.

THE IMPORTANCE OF SCRAPING THE BOWL

One of the most important steps in making cookies is scraping the bowl. Forgoing this step leads to a misshapen cookie with some parts that are underdone and others that are extra crispy. This is especially true for cookies that include a liquid sugar. Without scraping, some of the butter and sugar mixture never gets incorporated into the rest of the dough. This is exactly the part that quickly melts in the oven and causes inconsistencies in how the cookies bake. On the other hand, by periodically scraping the bowl and the paddle, the dough mixes uniformly and in the end you get a perfectly shaped cookie with your desired texture.

CRUMB CRUSTS AND TOPPINGS

A CLOSER LOOK AT CRUMB CRUSTS & TOPPINGS

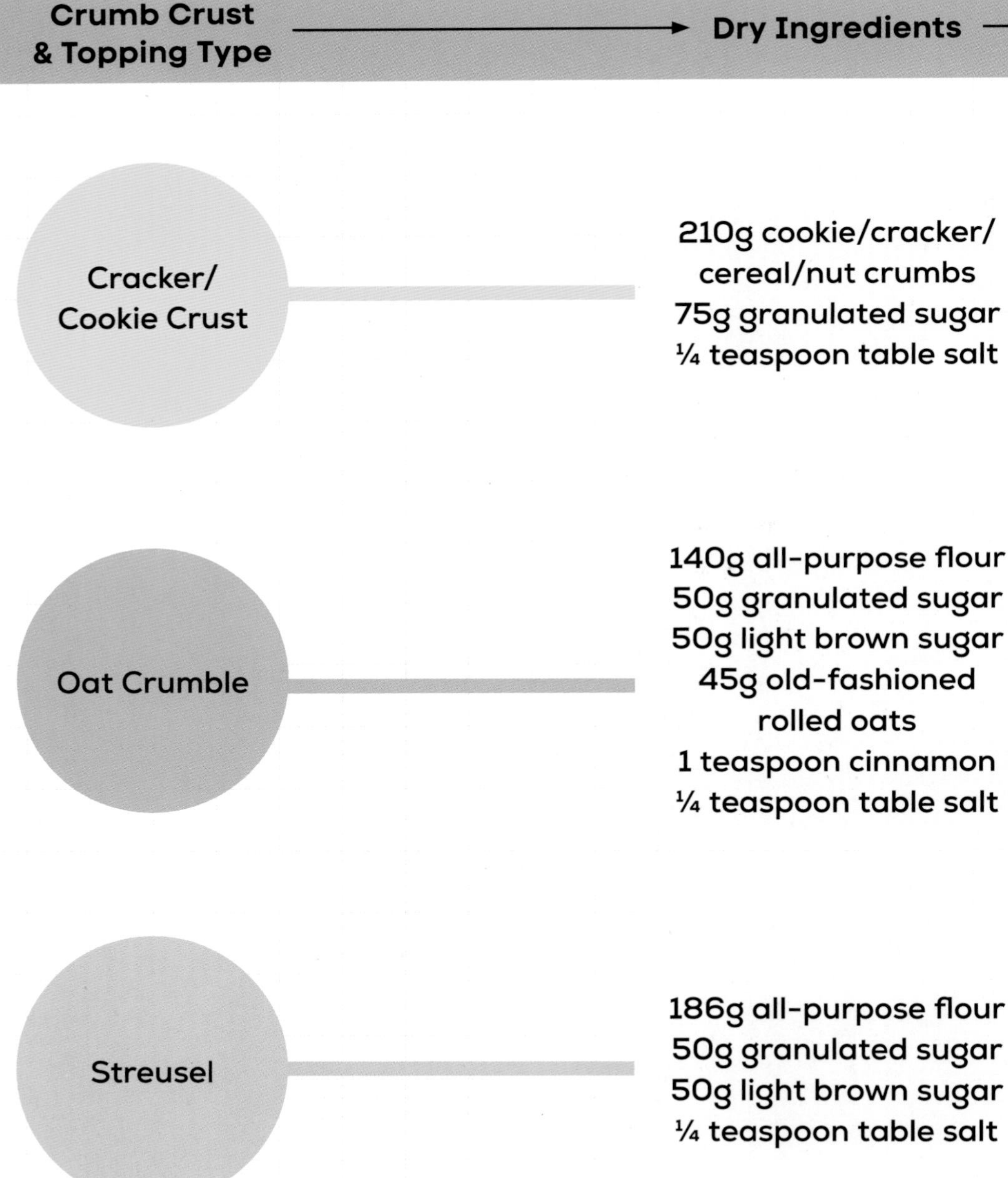

Fat

113g unsalted butter, melted

113g unsalted butter, cold and cut into ½ inch (1cm) cubes

CRUMB CRUST

Mixing Method: All in One

Yield: One 9-inch (23cm) pie crust
Prep Time: 10 minutes
Bake Time: 10 to 15 minutes

Special Equipment

9-inch (23cm) pie pan (at least 2 inches (5cm) deep)

Ingredients

1½ cups (211g) fine crumbs from crackers, cookies, cereal, and/or nuts

2 to 6 tablespoons (25 to 75g) granulated sugar

0 to ¼ teaspoon table salt

4 to 8 tablespoons (57 to 113g) unsalted butter, melted and cooled

Method

1. Preheat the oven to 325°F (160°C).
2. Mix the finely ground crumbs with a portion of the granulated sugar and/or salt depending on the type of crumb being used. For example, if using a sweet cookie, add just 2 tablespoons of the sugar and all the salt. If using a salty cracker, add the full 6 tablespoons of sugar and omit the added salt.
3. Start by adding 4 tablespoons of melted butter to the crumb mixture and mix together. Continue adding melted butter until the crumbs just hold together when compacted.
4. Firmly press the crumbs into the sides and bottom of the pie pan.
5. Bake for 10 to 15 minutes or until the crust is firm and set.

STREUSEL

Mixing Method: All in One

Yield: Approximately 1½ cups
Prep Time: 15 minutes

Ingredients

1⅓ cups (186g) all-purpose flour

¼ cup (50g) granulated sugar

¼ cup (50g) light brown sugar

¼ teaspoon table salt

1 stick (113g) unsalted butter, cold and cut into ½-inch (1cm) cubes

Method

1. Combine the flour, sugars, and salt together in a medium bowl.
2. Add the cubes of cold butter and, using your fingertips, a pastry blender, or a fork, work the butter into the dry ingredients. Continue working the butter into the flour mixture until completely incorporated and the mixture holds together when compacted.

OAT CRUMBLE

Mixing Method: All in One

Yield: Approximately 1½ cups
Prep Time: 15 minutes

Ingredients

1 cup (140g) all-purpose flour

¼ cup (50g) granulated sugar

¼ cup (50g) light brown sugar

½ cup (46g) old-fashioned rolled oats

1 teaspoon cinnamon

¼ teaspoon table salt

1 stick (113g) unsalted butter, melted and cooled

Method

1 Combine the flour, sugars, oats, cinnamon, and salt together in a medium bowl.

2 Pour the melted butter over the dry ingredients and mix until combined, crumbly, and no streaks of dry ingredients remain.

LEARNING WITH

CRUMB CRUSTS AND TOPPINGS

MELTED BUTTER VS. SOFTENED BUTTER

Both melted and softened butter accomplish the goal of moistening the flour, sugar, and other dry ingredients to make a crumbly topping to use on top of muffins, cakes, pies, and pastries. The state of the butter when adding to the dry ingredients, though, helps determine the resulting texture of the crumble after baking. Using melted butter creates a more compact and dense crumb that hardens to a crisp final texture. Softened butter more evenly distributes into the dry ingredients and makes a relatively softer and more aerated topping.

BLIND BAKED PIE DOUGH (SEE PHOTO)

In many cream and custard pies, my preference is to have a crumb crust that can be quickly assembled and baked to provide a firm base for the pie. Because classic pie dough is designed to puff and be flaky, blind baking (baking without a filling inside) requires extra equipment and care. My preferred method omits the pie weights, dried beans, or any ingredient designed to control the pie dough's puff. After lining the pie dish with pie dough, add another pie pan on top to weigh it down. Now, flip both pans over and bake inverted on a sheet pan with another couple sheet pans on top to weigh it down. This time, gravity does the work of controlling the expanding and slippery dough. (Note: This works best with deep, disposable aluminum pie plates.) (See illustration below).

FRUIT PIES

A CLOSER LOOK AT FRUIT PIES

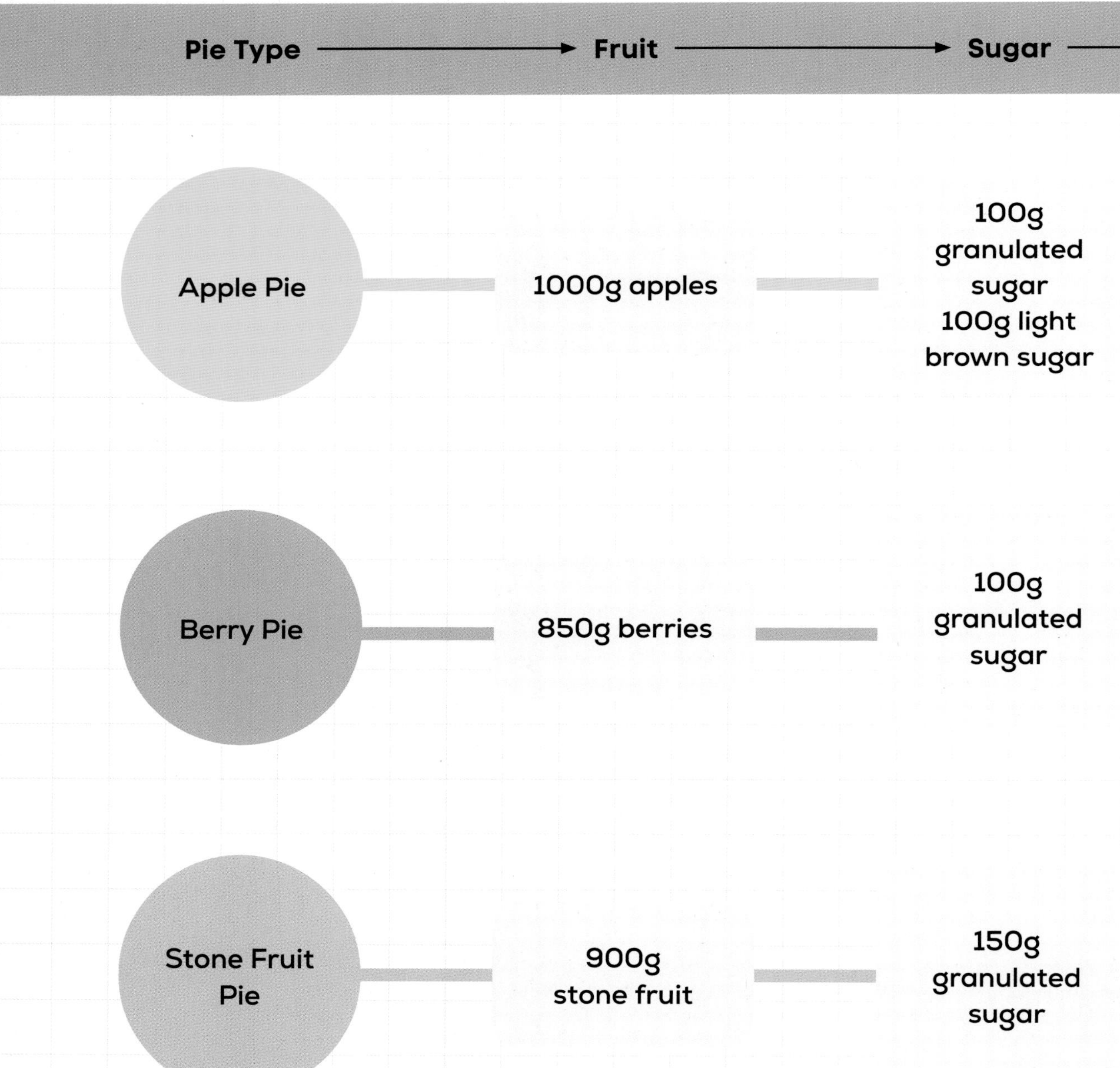

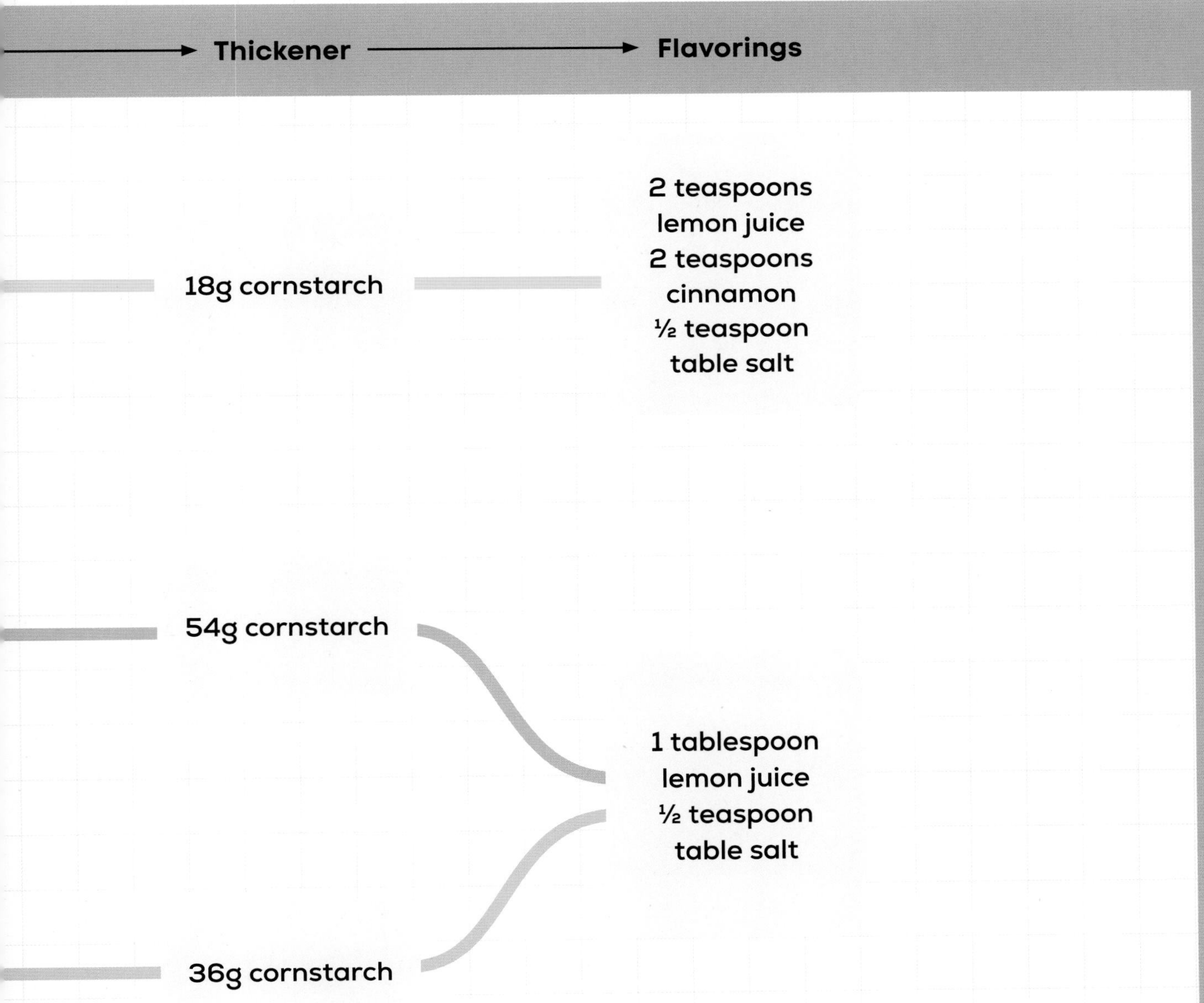

Thickener → Flavorings

18g cornstarch

2 teaspoons lemon juice
2 teaspoons cinnamon
½ teaspoon table salt

54g cornstarch

36g cornstarch

1 tablespoon lemon juice
½ teaspoon table salt

APPLE PIE

Mixing Method: Wet and Dry

Yield: One 9-inch (23cm) pie
Prep Time: 30 minutes
Inactive Time: 3 hours
Cook Time: 50 to 60 minutes

Special Equipment

9-inch (23cm) pie pan

Saucepan

Ingredients

1 batch Pie Dough (page 56)

9 cups (1,000g) apples peeled and sliced into ½-inch (1cm) wedges, from about 3 pounds (1.3kg) of apples (I prefer a combination of a tart apple like Granny Smith and a sweet apple like Honeycrisp)

2 teaspoons lemon juice

½ cup (100g) granulated sugar

½ cup (100g) light brown sugar

2 tablespoons (18g) cornstarch

2 teaspoons cinnamon

½ teaspoon table salt

1 large egg

2 tablespoons whole milk

½ cup (100g) turbinado sugar

Method

1. Toss the apples together with the lemon juice and granulated sugar (this is half of the overall sugar in the recipe) in a large bowl and leave to macerate for 1 to 2 hours or until the apples have given up much of their liquid.
2. Preheat the oven to 400°F (200°C).
3. Pour the liquid from the apples into a small saucepan set over medium-low heat. Leave to cook and reduce until thick and syrupy, around 10 minutes.
4. While the syrup reduces, roll out half of the pie dough and lay into the bottom of the pie dish, allowing for 1 to 2 inches of overhang.
5. Roll the other half of the pie dough into a circle the same diameter as the pie dish. Using a small cookie cutter, cut an opening into the center of the pie crust. Set aside.
6. Toss the apples with the brown sugar, cornstarch, cinnamon, and salt. Mix in the reduced syrup and toss to combine.
7. Cover the apples with the top pie crust so that it goes right to the edge of the pie dish.
8. Roll the top crust over the edge of the pie dish and crimp with your pressing the thumb of one hand in between the thumb and forefinger of the other (see illustration below).
9. Brush with an egg wash made from whisking together the egg and milk. Sprinkle the top with turbinado sugar and bake.
10. Bake for 50 to 60 minutes or until the pie crust is golden and the filling has slow, thick bubbles.
11. Remove from the oven and place on a baking rack to cool completely.

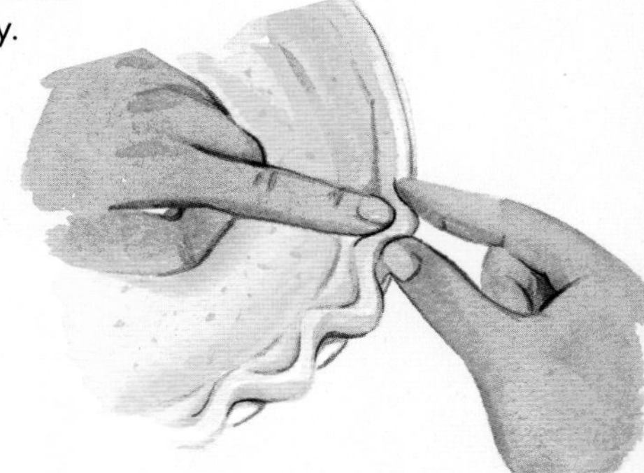

BERRY PIE

Mixing Method: Wet and Dry

Yield: One 9-inch (23cm) pie
Prep Time: 30 minutes
Inactive Time: 3 hours
Cook Time: 60 to 70 minutes

Special Equipment

9-inch (23cm) pie pan

Saucepan

Ingredients

½ batch Pie Dough (page 56)

6 cups (850g) berries (I prefer an equal split of halved strawberries, blackberries, and blueberries)

1 tablespoon lemon juice

½ cup (100g) granulated sugar

¼ cup plus 2 tablespoons (54g) cornstarch

½ teaspoon table salt

2 batches Oat Crumble (page 132)

Method

1. Preheat the oven to 375°F (190°C)
2. Follow the method outlined in the Apple Pie recipe on page 138. Roll the bottom crust just so that it meets the edge of the pie pan, cutting off any excess. Instead of topping the pie with a second layer of pie dough, sprinkle the oat crumble on right before baking.
3. Bake for 60 to 70 minutes or until the crumble is golden and the filling has slow, thick bubbles.
4. Remove from the oven and place on a baking rack to cool completely.

STONE FRUIT PIE

Mixing Method: Wet and Dry

Yield: One 9-inch (23cm) pie
Prep Time: 30 minutes
Inactive Time: 3 hours
Cook Time: 60 to 70 minutes

Special Equipment

9-inch (23cm) pie pan
Saucepan

Ingredients

1 batch Pie Dough (page 56)

8 cups (900g) stone fruit sliced into ½-inch (1cm) wedges (I prefer an equal mix of peaches and nectarines)

1 tablespoon lemon juice

¾ cup (150g) granulated sugar

¼ cup (36g) cornstarch

½ teaspoon table salt

1 large egg

2 tablespoons whole milk

½ cup (100g) turbinado sugar

Method

1 Follow the method outlined in the Apple Pie recipe on page 138.

2 Bake for 60 to 70 minutes or until the pie crust is golden and the filling has slow, thick bubbles

LEARNING WITH
FRUIT PIES

HOW TO TELL WHEN FRUIT PIES ARE DONE BAKING

To prevent a lake of fruit juices emerging after cutting into your freshly baked pie, it's important to monitor the doneness of the pie while baking. The crust color gives an indication of how it is baking, but it doesn't tell us much about the filling. To know when the fruit filling inside is done, look for slow, thick bubbles emerging through the crust. These bubbles indicate that the starch and pectin inside the filling are fully thickening up. Equally as important is letting the pie cool once removed from the oven. This allows the starch structure to fully set. If the crust browns before the filling is ready, turn down the oven temperature. I prefer this method to wrapping the pie in foil and running the risk of steaming the once-crisp crust. Bake it too long, on the other hand, and the filling inside turns to mush.

DIFFERENT STYLES OF EGG WASH (SEE PHOTO)

The name "egg wash" implies a whole egg brushed (or washed) on top of a pie or pastry before baking. To achieve different looks when egg washing, use different parts of the egg and/ or add some dairy into the mix. Different shades of golden brown and different degrees of shine come from using different parts of the egg and dairy proteins.

CREAM PIES

A CLOSER LOOK AT CREAM PIES

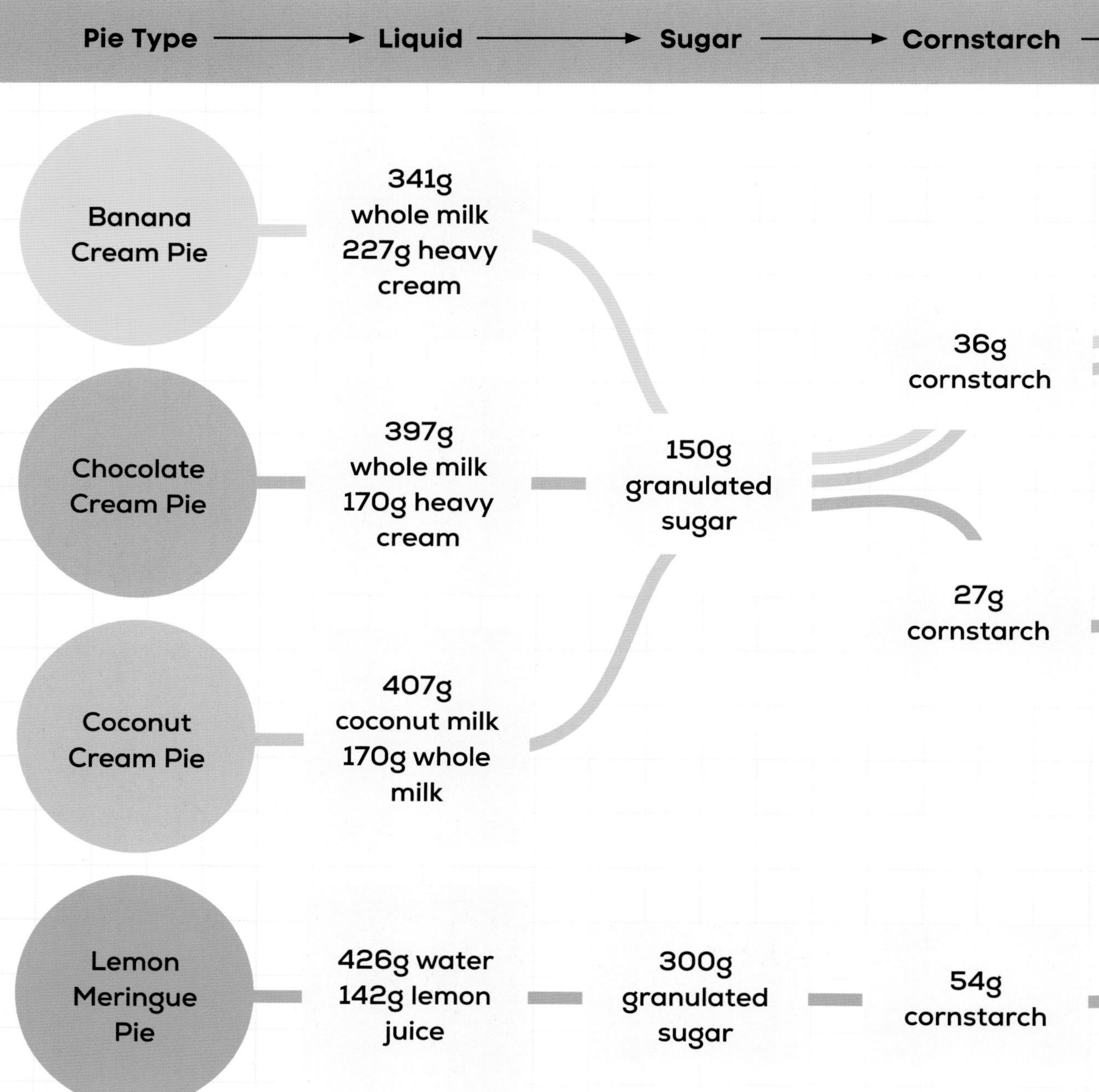

Egg Yolks → Butter + Salt → Flavorings

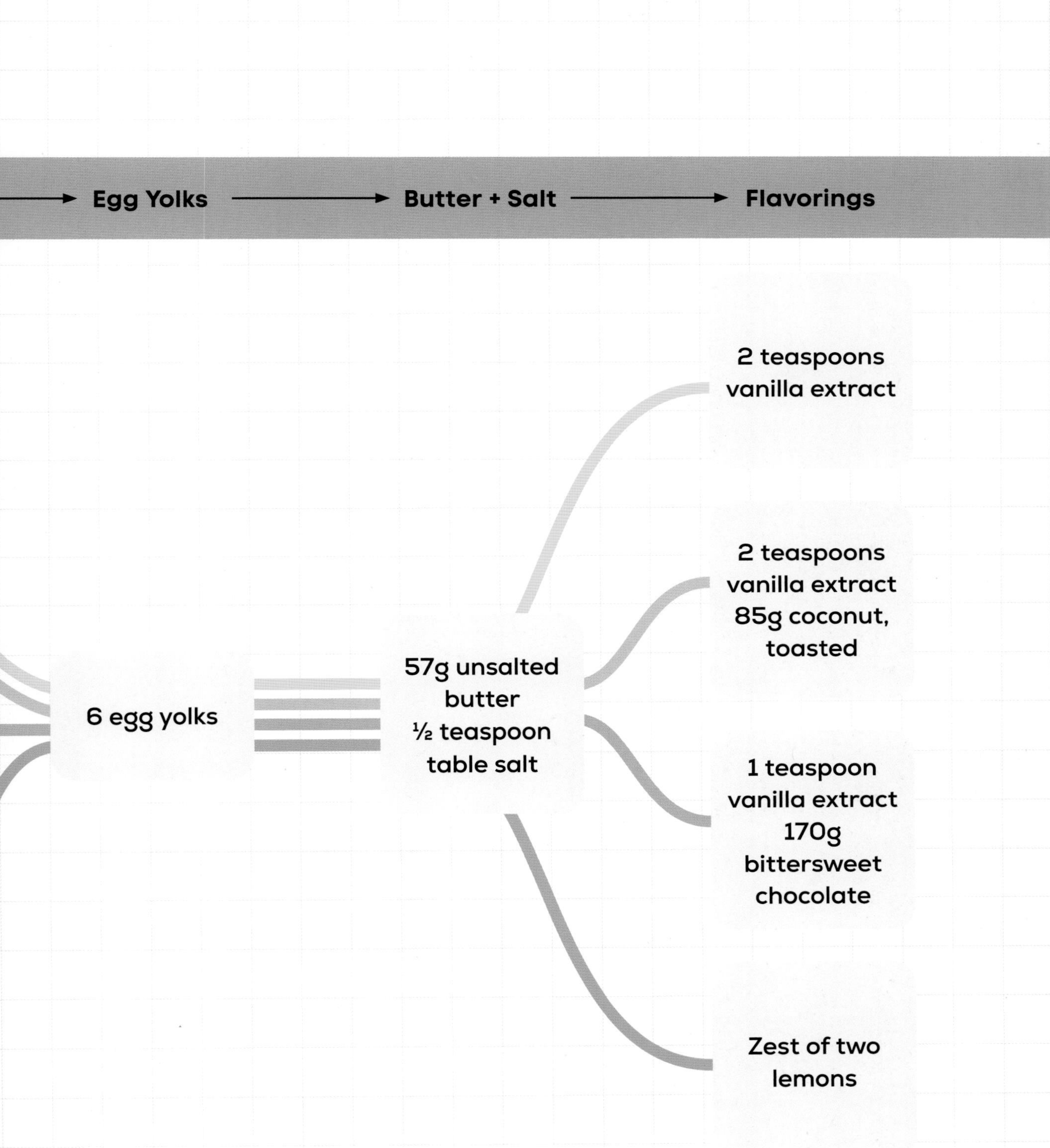

BANANA CREAM PIE

Mixing Method: All in One

Yield: One 9-inch (23cm) pie
Prep Time: 20 minutes
Cook Time: 20 minutes

Special Equipment

Saucepan
Sieve
9-inch (23cm) pie pan

Ingredients

1 batch Crumb Crust (page 130), recommended crumbs to try: vanilla wafer cookies or peanuts

1½ cups (341g) whole milk

1 cup (227g) heavy cream

¾ cup (150g) granulated sugar

½ teaspoon table salt

6 egg yolks

4 tablespoons (36g) cornstarch

4 tablespoons (57g) unsalted butter, softened

2 teaspoons vanilla extract

4 medium bananas (340g), sliced into ¼-inch (6mm) thick coins

1 to 2 batches Stabilized Whipped Cream (page 277), depending on preference

¼ cup (35g) cookie, cracker, or nut crumbs (the same crumbs as used to make the crust)

Method

1. Add the milk, cream, ½ cup (100g) of the sugar, and the salt to a saucepan set over medium heat. Whisk briefly to combine and heat until the mixture just comes to a simmer.
2. In a medium bowl, whisk together the remaining ¼ cup (50g) of sugar with the egg yolks and cornstarch.
3. Once the milk/cream comes to a simmer, remove from the heat and whisk a few tablespoons of the mixture into the egg yolk mixture. Continue slowly adding the hot milk/cream into the egg yolks while whisking continuously until roughly ¾ of the liquid has been incorporated.
4. Pour the mixture that now contains the egg yolks and most of the milk/cream back into the saucepan and set over medium low heat.
5. Whisk continuously until the custard thickens and you see large bubbles break the surface of the liquid.
6. Continue cooking for 1 more minute.
7. Remove from the heat and add the butter and vanilla. Whisk to combine.
8. Layer the bottom of the pie crust with half of the banana slices. Pour half of the vanilla custard through a sieve into the bananas and repeat with the remaining bananas and custard.
9. Press a piece of plastic wrap onto the top of the custard and let cool in the fridge for at least 4 hours.
10. Once cool, top with stabilized whipped cream (1 batch for an even layer and 2 batches for a mounded appearance) and optionally sprinkle the same crumbs used to make the crust around the edge of the pie for decoration.

CHOCOLATE CREAM PIE

Mixing Method: All in One

Yield: One 9-inch (23cm) pie
Prep Time: 20 minutes
Cook Time: 25 minutes

Special Equipment

Saucepan
Sieve
Peeler
9-inch (23cm) pie pan

Ingredients

- 1 batch Crumb Crust (page 130), recommended crumbs to try: graham crackers, chocolate cookies or peanut butter cereal
- 1¾ cups (398g) whole milk
- ¾ cup (170g) heavy cream
- ¾ cup (150g) granulated sugar
- ½ teaspoon table salt
- 6 egg yolks
- 3 tablespoons (27g) cornstarch
- 4 tablespoons (57g) unsalted butter, softened and cut into small cubes
- 1 teaspoon vanilla extract
- 6 ounces (170g) bittersweet chocolate (60–70%), chopped into fine pieces
- 1 to 2 batches Stabilized Whipped Cream (page 277), depending on preference
- 1 bittersweet chocolate bar

Method

1. Follow the method for the Banana Cream Pie recipe (page 146), adding the bittersweet chocolate at the end with the butter and vanilla.
2. Pour the chocolate custard through a sieve into the prepared pie crust, press a piece of plastic wrap onto the top of the pie and let cool in the fridge for at least 4 hours.
3. Once completely cool, top with the stabilized whipped cream (1 batch for an even layer and 2 batches for a mounded appearance) and finish by peeling the sides of a chocolate bar to create chocolate shavings to go around the edge of the pie.

COCONUT CREAM PIE

Mixing Method: All in One

Yield: One 9-inch (23cm) pie
Prep Time: 20 minutes
Cook Time: 25 minutes

Special Equipment

Saucepan
Sieve
9-inch (23cm) pie pan

Ingredients

1 batch Crumb Crust (page 130), recommended crumbs to try: almond shortbread cookies

13.5 ounces (407g) coconut milk

⅔ cup plus 1 tablespoon (161g) whole milk

¾ cup (150g) granulated sugar

½ teaspoon table salt

6 egg yolks

4 tablespoons (36g) cornstarch

4 tablespoons (57g) unsalted butter, softened

2 teaspoons vanilla extract

1 cup (85g) coconut, toasted*

1 to 2 batches Stabilized Whipped Cream (page 277), depending on preference

¼ cup (21g) coconut, toasted for sprinkling on top*

Method

1 Follow the method for the Banana Cream Pie recipe, adding the toasted coconut after passing the fully cooked coconut custard through a sieve into a separate bowl.

2 Press a piece of plastic wrap onto the top of the pie and let cool in the fridge for at least 4 hours.

3 Once completely cool, top with the stabilized whipped cream (1 batch for an even layer and 2 batches for a mounded appearance) and extra toasted coconut around the edge of the pie.

*Toast the coconut by placing in a thin layer on a sheet pan and bake at 325°F (160°C) for 5 to 10 minutes or until golden around the edges.

LEMON MERINGUE PIE

Mixing Method: All in One

Yield: One 9-inch (23cm) pie
Prep Time: 20 minutes
Cook Time: 20 minutes

Special Equipment

Saucepan
Sieve
Stand mixer with the whisk attachment
9-inch (23cm) pie pan
Torch

Ingredients

½ batch Pie Dough (page 56), blind baked (page 133)

For the filling:

1¾ cups plus 2 tablespoons (426g) water
Zest of two lemons
1½ cups (300g) granulated sugar
½ teaspoon table salt
6 tablespoons (54g) cornstarch
6 egg yolks
4 tablespoons (57g) unsalted butter, softened
½ cup plus 2 tablespoons (142g) lemon juice, from approximately 4 medium lemons

For the topping:

4 egg whites
1¼ cups (250g) granulated sugar
¼ teaspoon table salt

Method

1 Add the water, lemon zest, 1 cup (200g) of the sugar, salt, and cornstarch to a saucepan set over medium heat.

2 Whisk continuously until the mixture becomes translucent and thickens.

3 In a separate bowl, whisk together the remaining ½ cup (100g) of sugar with the egg yolks.

4 Once the water and cornstarch mixture is ready, whisk a few tablespoons of the liquid into the egg yolks. Continue slowly adding the hot mixture into the egg yolks while whisking continuously until roughly ¾ of the liquid has been incorporated.

5 Pour the mixture that now contains the egg yolks and most of the liquid back into the saucepan and set over medium low heat.

6 Whisk continuously until the filling thickens and you see large bubbles break the surface of the liquid.

7 Continue cooking for 1 more minute.

8 Remove from the heat and add the butter and lemon juice. Whisk to combine.

9 Pour the lemon filling through a sieve into the prepared crust.

10 Press a piece of plastic wrap onto the top of the pie and let cool in the fridge for at least 4 hours.

11 Once cool, make a Swiss meringue by adding the egg whites, sugar, and salt to a medium bowl set atop a pot of barely simmering water. Continue whisking until the egg white and sugar mixture reaches 160 to 165°F (70 to 75°C).

12 Pour into the bowl of a stand mixer and whisk until stiff peaks form.

13 Spread all over the top of the pie, creating peaks and swirls for decoration and finish by torching.

UNDER
COOKED
COOKED
OVER
COOKED

LEARNING WITH CREAM PIES

THE PURPOSE OF TEMPERING

Mixing hot and cold ingredients can be a dangerous proposition. Especially when dealing with eggs, the risk of cooking a portion of the eggs and ending up with scrambled egg filling is high. In order to minimize this risk, first mix the eggs with a portion of the sugar and other ingredients. This dilutes the egg proteins and raises the temperature at which they will begin coagulating. Second, slowly add some of the hot to the cold while whisking constantly. Increase the speed of your pour and continue adding the hot to the cold until most of the liquid has been added. Then, reverse course and add the now warm mixture back into the remaining hot liquid.

HOW TO TELL WHEN THE CUSTARD IS DONE COOKING (SEE PHOTO, PAGE 150)

At one point I am telling you to be careful about cooking the eggs when adding them to the hot liquid, and now I am going to tell you the importance of bringing the cooked custard to a full boil. Luckily, the starch in the filling, now diluted with swollen starch granules, will help prevent the eggs from cooking, but it is exactly this starch that is at risk if we don't cook the filling enough. Egg yolks have an enzyme (amylase) that when left to its own devices will break down starch over time. In order to deactivate this enzyme and make sure that the pie filling doesn't turn into soup, bring the custard to boil where thick bubbles break the surface and continue cooking for another full minute. Stop the cooking at this point because going too far can have the opposite effect and will leave a thick and rubbery filling.

CORNSTARCH AND BOILING

In the following sections you will see me talk about the importance of not heating custards to too high of a temperature. In those cases, a water bath is extremely valuable in maintaining a gentle heat. Here, on the other hand, it is important to bring the mixture to a boil. The key ingredient that allows each of the fillings in this section to boil without overcooked eggs dotting the mixture is cornstarch.

CORNSTARCH AND ACID

You will notice that the lemon meringue pie filling follows a slightly different procedure than that of the other cream pies in this section. This is mainly due to the interaction between cornstarch and acidic ingredients. Including the acidic lemon juice too early on in the mixing procedure can prevent the filling from fully setting up. Letting the starch fully swell in water first helps ensure that the mixture stays properly set after the lemon juice is added towards the end.

CUSTARD PIES

A CLOSER LOOK AT CUSTARD PIES

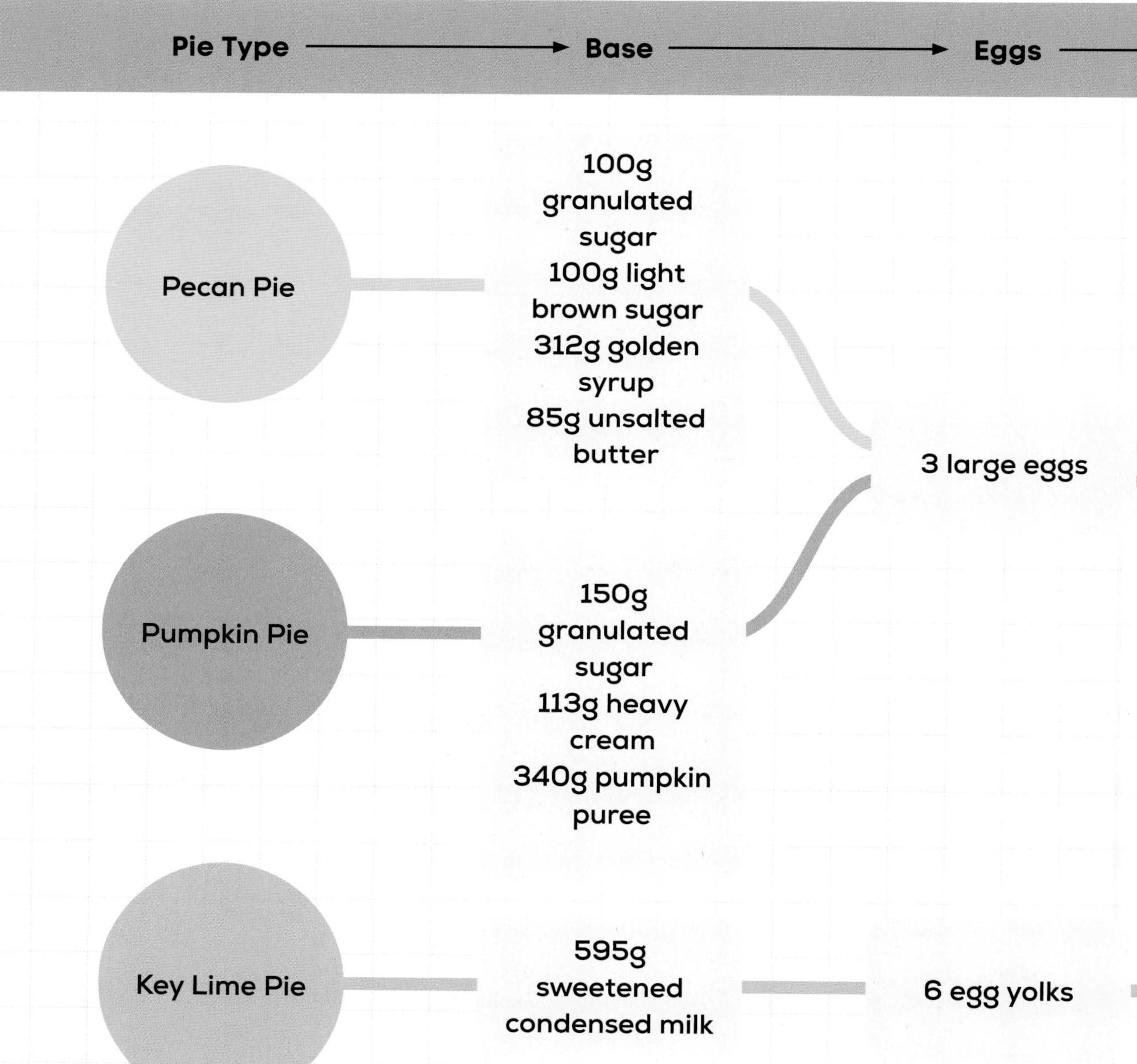

Finishing	Flavorings
227 pecans	2 teaspoons vanilla extract ½ teaspoon table salt
227g whole milk	1 teaspoon vanilla extract 1½ teaspoons cinnamon 1 teaspoon ground ginger ½ teaspoon table salt ½ teaspoon ground nutmeg ¼ teaspoon ground cloves
227g lime juice	½ teaspoon table salt

PECAN PIE

Mixing Method: All in One

Yield: One 9-inch (23cm) pie
Prep Time: 30 minutes
Bake Time: 40 to 45 minutes

Special Equipment

Saucepan
9-inch (23cm) pie pan

Ingredients

1 batch Crumb Crust (page 130), recommended crumbs to try: butter crackers

½ cup (100g) granulated sugar

½ cup (100g) light brown sugar

1 cup (310g) golden syrup (substitute light corn syrup if you can't find golden syrup)

6 tablespoons (85g) unsalted butter

3 large eggs

2 cups (227g) pecans, chopped

2 teaspoons vanilla extract

½ teaspoon table salt

Method

1. Preheat the oven to 325°F (160°C).
2. Add the sugars, golden syrup, and butter to a saucepan set over medium heat. Cook until the butter has melted and most of the sugar has dissolved. Remove from the heat and let cool for 5 minutes.
3. Once cool, whisk in the eggs and finish by adding the pecans, vanilla, and salt.
4. Pour into the prepared pie crust and bake for 40 to 45 minutes or until the edge is set but the center wobbles slightly when the pan is nudged.
5. Remove from the oven and allow to cool completely on a baking rack.

PUMPKIN PIE

Mixing Method: All in One

Yield: One 9-inch (23cm) pie
Prep Time: 30 minutes
Bake Time: 30 to 35 minutes

Special Equipment

Saucepan
9-inch (23cm) pie pan

Ingredients

1 batch Crumb Crust (page 130), recommended crumbs to try: gingersnaps, oatmeal cookies, or snickerdoodle cookies

¾ cup (150g) granulated sugar

¼ cup (57g) water

½ cup (113g) heavy cream

1½ cups (332g) pumpkin puree

3 large eggs

1 cup (227g) whole milk

1 teaspoon vanilla extract

1½ teaspoons cinnamon

1 teaspoon ground ginger

½ teaspoon table salt

½ teaspoon ground nutmeg

¼ teaspoon ground cloves

1 batch Classic Whipped Cream (page 276)

Method

1. Preheat the oven to 325°F (160°C).
2. Add the sugar and water to the saucepan set over medium heat. Let cook until the sugar caramelizes and turns an amber color.
3. Remove from the heat and carefully whisk in the heavy cream and pumpkin puree. The mixture will bubble up so add the cream only a little at a time to prevent spilling over.
4. Let the pumpkin caramel cool for 10 minutes before whisking in the eggs.
5. Finish by adding the milk, vanilla, and spices, and whisking to combine.
6. Pour into the prepared crust and bake for 30 to 35 minutes or until the edge is set but the center wobbles slightly when the pan is nudged.
7. Remove from the oven and allow to cool completely on a baking rack.
8. Serve with whipped cream dolloped onto each slice.

KEY LIME PIE

Mixing Method: All in One

Yield: One 9-inch (23cm) pie
Prep Time: 30 minutes
Bake Time: 30 to 35 minutes

Special Equipment

One 9-inch (23cm) pie pan

Ingredients

1 batch Crumb Crust (page 130), recommended crumbs to try: graham crackers

21 ounces (595g) sweetened condensed milk

6 egg yolks

1 cup (227g) lime juice

¼ teaspoon table salt

1 batch Stabilized Whipped Cream (page 277)

Method

1. Preheat the oven to 325°F (160°C).
2. Mix together the sweetened condensed milk and egg yolks with a spatula.
3. Pour in the lime juice and salt and mix until combined.
4. Pour into the prepared crust and bake for 20 to 25 minutes or until the edge is set but the center wobbles slightly when the pan is nudged.
5. Remove from the oven and allow to cool on a baking rack for 15 minutes before moving to the fridge.
6. Serve cold with whipped cream dolloped onto each slice.

LEARNING WITH
CUSTARD PIES

HOW TO TELL WHEN CUSTARDS ARE DONE BAKING (SEE PHOTO)

A custard pie, baked custard, and classic cheesecake all rely on the power of eggs to coagulate and help set their structure. Unlike the starch and proteins in flour, the proteins in eggs are much more sensitive to overheating, which can create a grainy custard. The first tool used to prevent over-coagulation is a low oven temperature, sometimes aided with the help of a water bath (more about that in the next section). The second tool is making sure to take the custard out at the right time. The custard will go from a thin liquid that ripples across the entire surface of the dessert to one that wobbles only in the center. This is the time to remove it from the oven. Outside of the oven, the filling will carry over and continue to cook. Beyond this point, the filling will begin to puff and crack on the outside and curdle within.

COMBINING ACID AND DAIRY

You will notice that the Key Lime Pie uses relatively less egg proteins when compared to the other custard pies. This is because there is another combination of ingredients working together to help set the pie. The combination of dairy and acid can help set a dessert without any eggs or flour and minimal baking. Some key lime pies take advantage of this fact and include extra ingredients like sour cream for extra acidic and dairy ingredients. Other desserts like lemon posset are a perfect example of the combination of heavy cream and lemon juice to make a custard-like filling that is silky smooth without the addition of eggs. Still, I prefer the richness and creaminess that the egg yolks provide to the heavier dairy flavors of the alternative fillings.

CHEESECAKES

A CLOSER LOOK AT CHEESECAKES

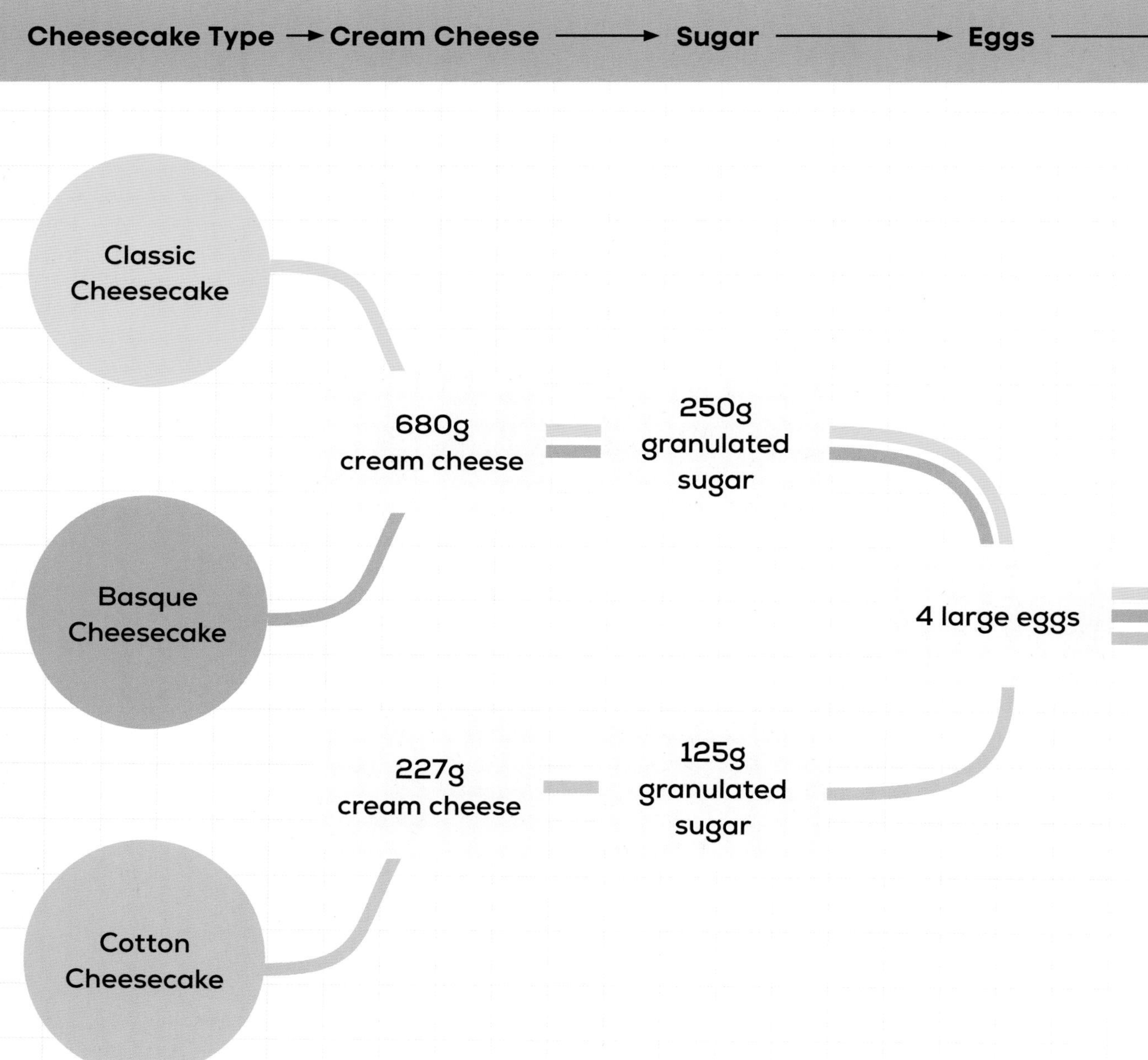

→ Cream → Dry Ingredients → Flavorings

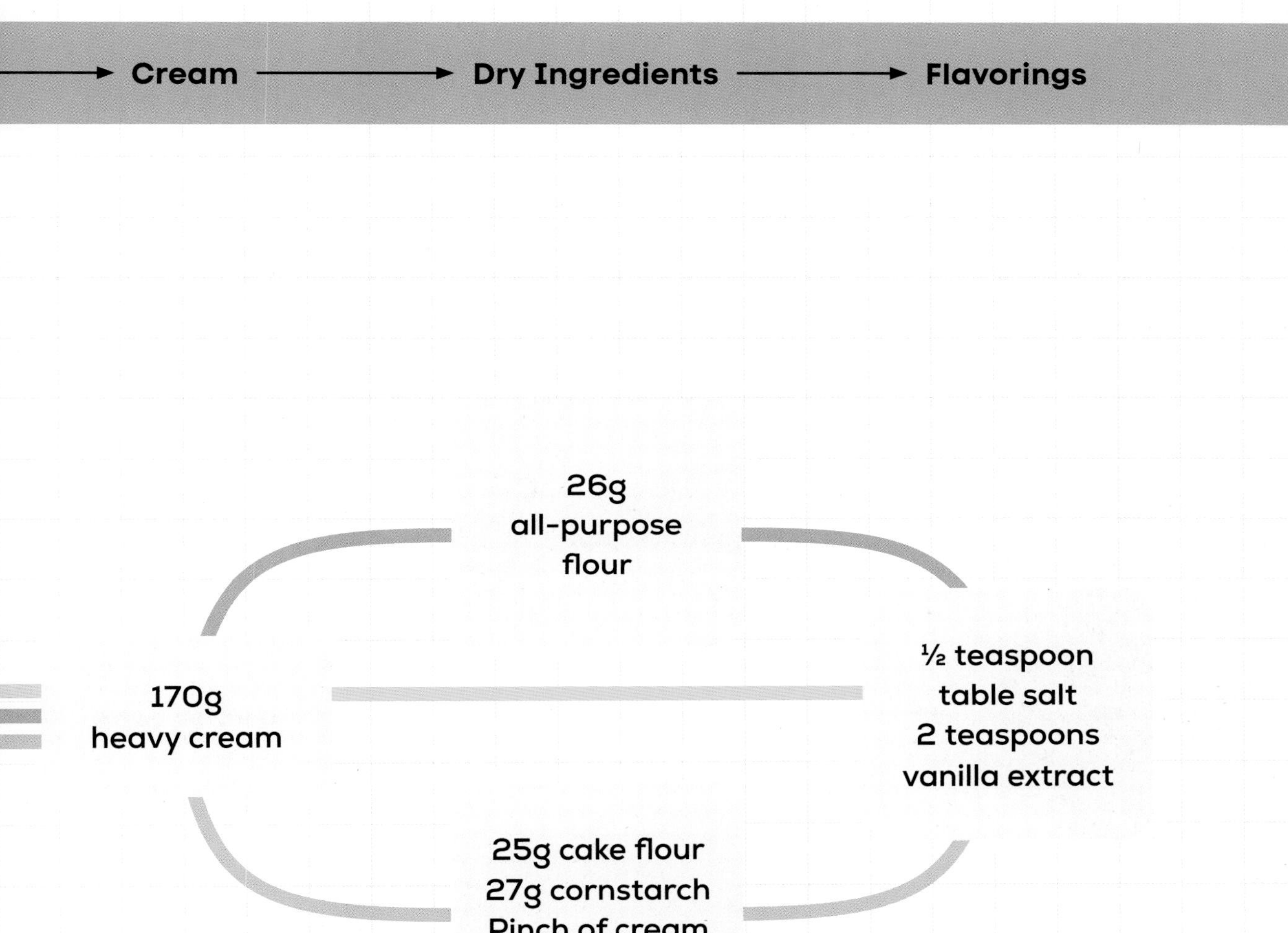

CLASSIC CHEESECAKE

Mixing Method: Classic Creaming

Yield: One 9×2-inch (23×5cm) cheesecake

Prep Time: 20 minutes

Bake Time: 55 to 65 minutes

Special Equipment

Stand mixer with the paddle attachment

9×2-inch (23×5cm) round cake pan

Roasting pan

Torch

Ingredients

1 batch Crumb Crust (page 130), recommended crumbs to try: cinnamon cereal

24 ounces (680g) cream cheese, softened

1¼ cups (250g) granulated sugar

4 large eggs

¾ cup (170g) heavy cream

¼ teaspoon fine salt

2 teaspoons vanilla extract

Method

1. Preheat the oven to 325°F (160°C).
2. Add the cream cheese and sugar to the bowl of a stand mixer. Mix on medium-low speed until completely smooth (approximately 4 to 5 minutes), stopping the mixer to scrape the bowl and paddle every minute.
3. With the mixer running, add the eggs one at a time, waiting until the previous one is completely incorporated before adding the next. Once all the eggs have been incorporated, stop the mixer one more time to scrape the bowl and paddle attachment.
4. Finish by adding the heavy cream, salt, and vanilla.
5. Pour into the prepared crust and set the cake pan into the roasting pan.
6. Place into the oven and fill the roasting pan about a third of the way with hot water.
7. Bake for 55 to 65 minutes or until the edge of the cheesecake is set but the center wobbles slightly when the pan is tapped.
8. Remove from the oven and let cool for 20 minutes before placing in the fridge for at least 4 hours.
9. When ready to unmold, heat the sides and bottom of the cake pan with a torch or over a very low flame. Once hot, invert the cheesecake onto a cake board or a plate. Gently tap the cake pan to loosen the cheesecake and then grab the cake pan with towels or oven mitts and lift off. Invert one more time to present the cheesecake right-side up.

BASQUE CHEESECAKE

Mixing Method: Classic Creaming

Yield: One 8×3-inch (20×8cm) cheesecake

Prep Time: 20 minutes

Bake Time: 35 to 40 minutes

Special Equipment

Stand mixer with the paddle attachment

8×3-inch (20×8cm) cake pan

Ingredients

24 ounces (680g) cream cheese, softened

1¼ cups (250g) granulated sugar

4 large eggs

¾ cup (170g) heavy cream

¼ teaspoon fine salt

2 teaspoons vanilla extract

3 tablespoons (26g) all-purpose flour

Method

1. Preheat the oven to 400°F (200°C).
2. Prepare the cake pan by taking a piece of parchment paper larger than the pan and crumpling it up. Uncrumple and press into the bottom and sides of the cake pan.
3. Follow the instructions for the Classic Cheesecake (page 164), adding the flour at the end with the cream, salt, and vanilla.
4. Pour the cheesecake into the prepared pan and set in the oven without a water bath.
5. Bake for 35 to 40 minutes or until the top is a deep caramel color and the center wobbles when tapped.
6. Remove from the oven and place on a baking rack until cool.
7. Lift the parchment out and serve slightly warm or at room temperature.

COTTON CHEESECAKE

Mixing Method: Sponge (Separated Egg)

Yield: One 8×3-inch (20×8cm) cheesecake

Prep Time: 20 minutes

Bake Time: 60 to 70 minutes

Special Equipment

Saucepan

Stand mixer with the whisk attachment

8×3-inch (20×8cm) cake pan

Roasting pan

Ingredients

8 ounces (227g) cream cheese

¾ cup (170g) heavy cream

4 large eggs, separated

3 tablespoons (25g) cake flour, sifted

3 tablespoons (27g) cornstarch, sifted

¼ teaspoon table salt

2 teaspoons vanilla extract

Pinch of cream of tartar

½ cup plus 2 tablespoons (125g) granulated sugar

Method

1. Preheat the oven to 325°F (160°C).
2. Prepare the cake pan by spraying with a light layer of nonstick baking spray, then covering the bottom with a circle of parchment paper and the sides with a rectangle that wraps all the way around the inside walls.
3. Add the cream cheese and heavy cream to the saucepan set over medium-low heat. Stir with a spatula until the cream cheese has melted.
4. Remove from the heat and let cool for 5 minutes before mixing in the egg yolks, cake flour, cornstarch, salt, and vanilla.
5. Add the egg whites to the bowl of a stand mixer along with the cream of tartar.
6. Whisk on medium-low speed until foamy and then increase the speed to medium.
7. Slowly add the sugar one tablespoon at a time. Once all the sugar has been added, continue mixing until medium to stiff peaks form.
8. Gently fold the meringue into the cream cheese mixture and pour into the prepared cake pan.
9. Set the cake pan in a roasting pan and place in the oven. Fill the roasting pan a third of the way up with hot water and bake for 60 to 70 minutes or until the top of the cheesecake is golden brown and filling is firm.
10. Remove from the oven and place on a baking rack until completely cool.
11. Once cool, invert onto a cake board or plate, remove the parchment paper, and invert one more time to present right-side up.
12. Serve immediately at room temperature or refrigerate and serve cold.

LEARNING WITH
CHEESECAKES

USING STARCH IN A CUSTARD

Many custards are set only with the proteins present in eggs. These custards bake at low temperatures and have a smooth and creamy filling. More structure is required to allow for a faster bake at a higher temperature or to set a light and delicate filling. In each case, adding more starch ensures that the eggs in the filling do not overcook. The resulting baked good will have a solid and set structure when removed from the oven.

THE PURPOSE OF A WATER BATH (SEE PHOTO)

When overbaked, cheesecakes and other custards curdle on the inside and crack on the outside. This happens quickly at high oven temperatures and is even a dangerous proposition at moderate oven temperatures. While you could turn the oven temperature down to very low levels (275°F/135°C or below), an even safer bet would be to take advantage of a water bath. The hot water in the water bath settles just below boiling temperatures and helps ensure a gentle and even heating of the outside of the pan. In a water bath, heating occurs much more gradually, which allows you to remove your custard from the oven at just the right time.

BAKED CUSTARDS

A CLOSER LOOK AT BAKED CUSTARDS

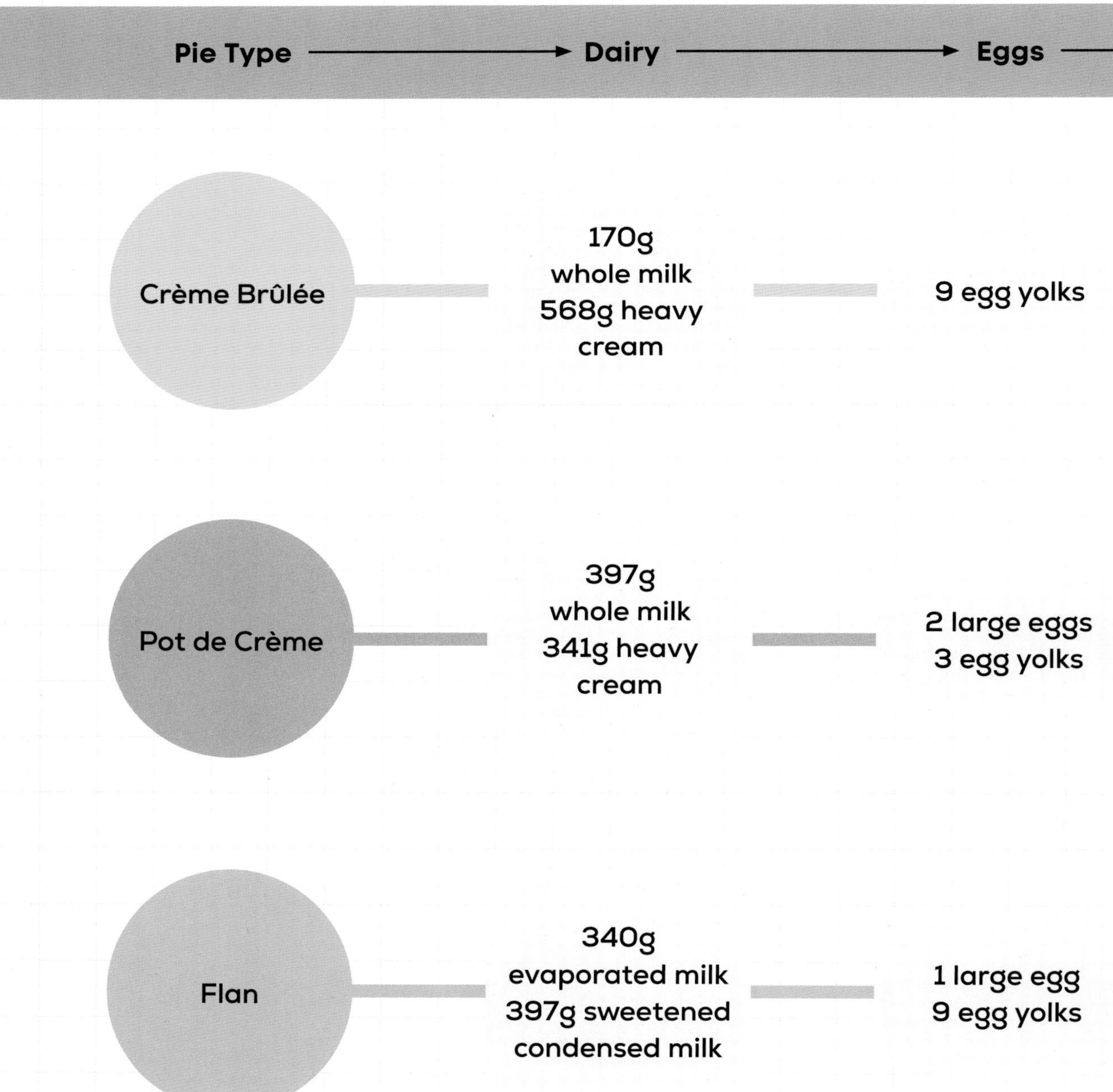

150g granulated sugar

1 vanilla bean
¼ teaspoon table salt

284g bittersweet chocolate
1 teaspoon vanilla extract
¼ teaspoon table salt

2 teaspoons vanilla extract
¼ teaspoon salt

CRÈME BRÛLÉE

Mixing Method: All in One

Yield: Six 4-ounce ramekins
Prep Time: 25 minutes
Bake Time: 30 to 35 minutes

Special Equipment

Saucepan

Sieve

Six 4-ounce ramekins

9×13-inch (23×33 cm) baking pan

Torch

Ingredients

1 vanilla bean

¾ cup (170g) whole milk

2½ cups (567g) heavy cream

¾ cup (150g) granulated sugar

¼ teaspoon table salt

9 egg yolks

½ cup (100g) granulated sugar for brûléeing

Method

1. Preheat the oven to 325°F (160°C).
2. Cut the vanilla bean in half and scrape out the seeds. Add both the seeds and the pod to the saucepan with the milk, cream, ½ cup (100g) of the sugar, and salt. Set over medium heat and bring to just below a boil. Cover and let steep for 30 minutes.
3. Add the egg yolks and remaining ¼ cup (50g) of sugar to a medium bowl and whisk together until combined.
4. Slowly pour the hot milk/cream mixture into the egg yolks.
5. Pour the custard through a sieve into a large measuring cup.
6. Divide between the ramekins set in the baking pan.
7. Place the baking pan into the oven and fill about a third of the way with hot water.
8. Bake for 30 to 35 minutes or until the custard wobbles slightly in the center when tapped.
9. Remove from the oven, let cool on the counter for 20 minutes, and then at least 4 hours in the fridge.
10. Once completely cool, top each custard with a thin layer of sugar and use the torch to brûlée until the sugar caramelizes and turns a deep amber color.

CHOCOLATE POT DE CRÈME

Mixing Method: All in One

Yield: Six 4-ounce ramekins
Prep Time: 25 minutes
Bake Time: 20 to 25 minutes

Special Equipment

Saucepan

Sieve

Six 4-ounce ramekins

9×13-inch (23×33cm) baking pan

Ingredients

1¾ cups (397g) whole milk

1½ cups (340g) heavy cream

¾ cup (150g) granulated sugar

¼ teaspoon table salt

10 ounces (284g) bittersweet chocolate (60 to 70%), finely chopped

2 large eggs

3 egg yolks

1 teaspoon vanilla extract

1 batch Classic Whipped Cream (page 276)

Method

1. Preheat the oven to 325°F (160°C).
2. Add the milk, cream, ½ cup (100g) of the sugar, and salt to a saucepan set over medium heat.
3. When the milk/cream mixture comes to just below a boil, pour over the bittersweet chocolate. Let sit for 2 minutes and then stir to combine.
4. Mix together the eggs, yolks, and remaining ¼ cup (50g) of sugar.
5. Slowly pour the chocolate mixture into the eggs and sugar. Finish with the vanilla extract.
6. Pour the custard through a sieve into a large measuring cup.
7. Divide between the ramekins set in the baking pan.
8. Place the baking pan into the oven and fill about a third of the way with hot water.
9. Bake for 20 to 25 minutes or until the custard wobbles slightly in the center when tapped.
10. Remove from the oven, let cool on the counter for 20 minutes, and then at least 4 hours in the fridge.
11. Serve cold topped with whipped cream.

FLAN

Mixing Method: All in One

Yield: Six 4-ounce ramekins

Prep Time: 25 minutes

Bake Time: 40 to 45 minutes

Special Equipment

Saucepan

Sieve

Six 4-ounce ramekins

9×13-inch (23×33cm) baking pan

Ingredients

¾ cup (150g) granulated sugar

¼ cup (57g) water

12 ounces (340g) evaporated milk

14 ounces (397g) sweetened condensed milk

1 large egg

9 egg yolks

¼ teaspoon table salt

2 teaspoons vanilla extract

Method

1. Preheat the oven to 325°F (160°C).
2. Add the sugar and water to a saucepan and set over medium heat. Leave the sugar undisturbed until it reaches a medium amber color. Immediately distribute evenly between the ramekins and set aside.
3. Mix the milks, egg, yolks, salt, and vanilla together with a spatula until combined.
4. Pour the custard through a sieve into a large measuring cup.
5. Divide the custard evenly between the ramekins set in the baking pan.
6. Place the baking pan into the oven and fill about a third of the way with hot water.
7. Bake for 40 to 45 minutes or until the custard wobbles slightly in the center when tapped.
8. Remove from the oven, let cool on the counter for 20 minutes, and then at least 4 hours in the fridge.
9. When ready to serve, run a knife around the edge of each flan and invert onto a plate.

LEARNING WITH
BAKED CUSTARDS

EGGS VS. YOLKS IN CUSTARDS (SEE PHOTO)

Alter the texture of your custards by adjusting the ratio of egg white to egg yolk in the recipe. The proteins present in egg whites contribute to a custard that sets firm and holds its shape. Egg yolks, on the other hand, offer a richer flavor and silky final texture. In addition to the flavor and textural differences when using eggs vs egg yolks, it is also important to note the differences in rates of coagulation. Egg yolks coagulate at a higher temperature than egg whites or whole eggs. This means there is a slightly lower chance of over coagulation and curdling when using only egg yolks.

THE EFFECT OF THE TYPE OF DAIRY USED

One important factor affecting the taste and texture of your custard is the kind of dairy you use. Whole milk is roughly 87% water and between 3 and 4% fat. Using only whole milk creates a thin custard with a light flavor that emphasizes the taste of the other added ingredients. Cream, on the other hand, is around 57% water and 36% fat. Using only cream gives a strong dairy flavor and the texture is super silky and dense. Combinations of these two dairy options and/or the incorporation of other varieties (e.g., evaporated milk with twice the fat of whole milk) balance the water and fat contents to give a light and creamy custard.

QUICK CAKES

A CLOSER LOOK AT QUICK CAKES

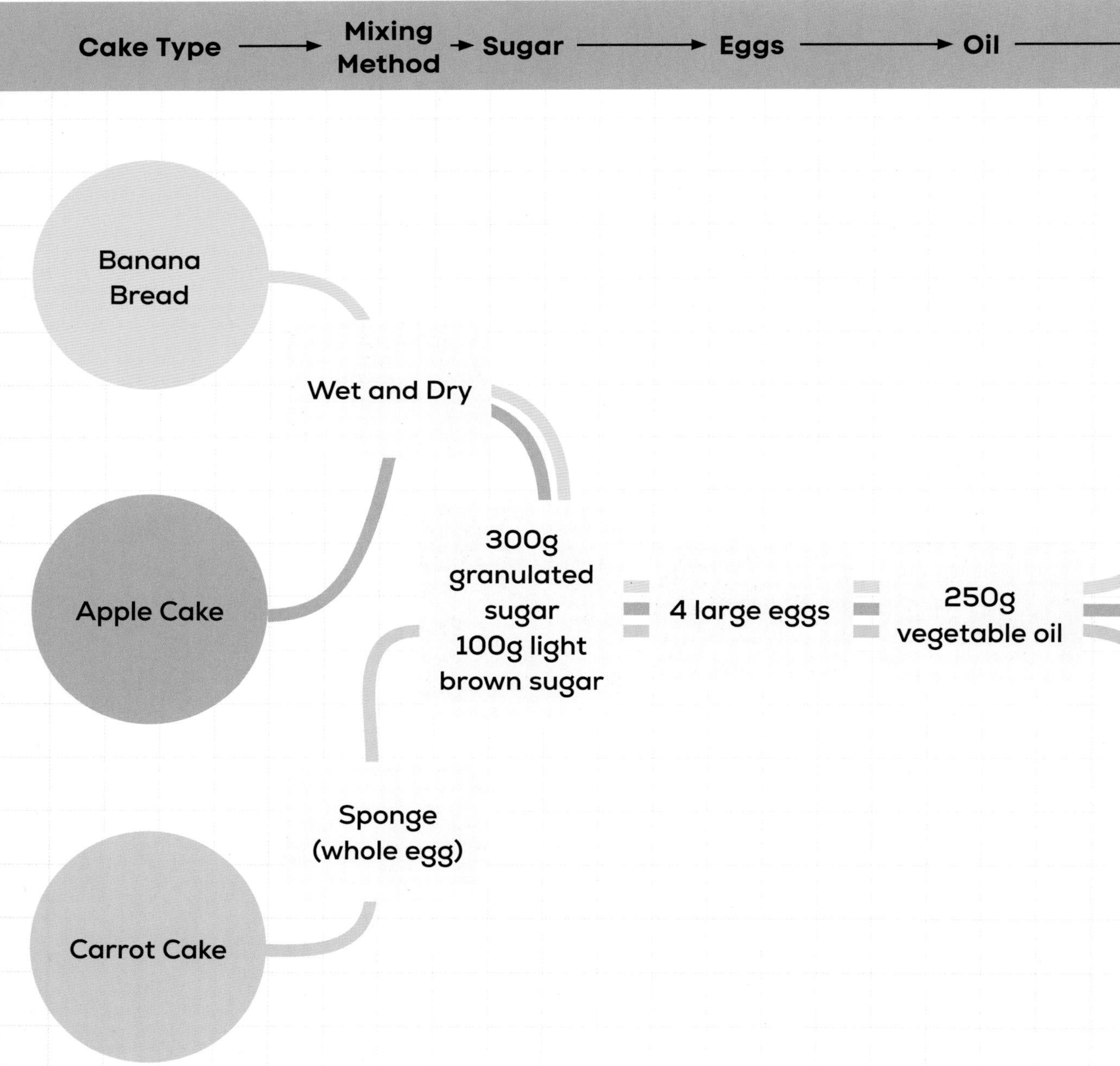

Liquid/Fruit/Vegetable → Flour → Leaveners + Salt → Add-Ins

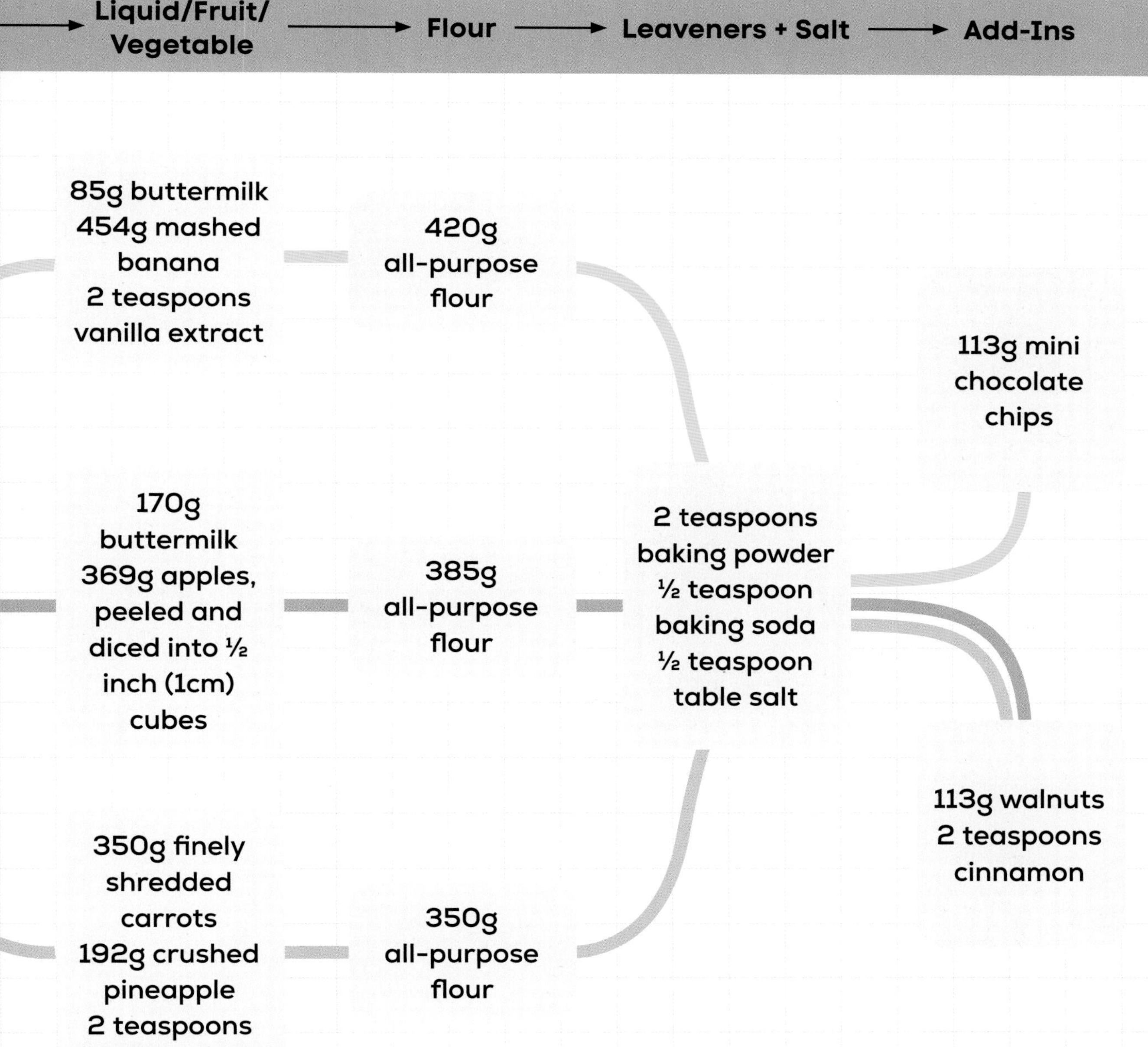

BANANA BREAD

Mixing Method: Wet and Dry

Yield: Two 9×5-inch (23×13cm) loaves

Prep Time: 15 minutes

Bake Time: 50 to 55 minutes

Special Equipment

Two 9×5-inch (23×13cm) loaf pans

Ingredients

3 cups (420g) all-purpose flour

2 teaspoons baking powder

½ teaspoon baking soda

½ teaspoon table salt

1½ cups (300g) granulated sugar

½ cup (100g) light brown sugar

4 large eggs

1¼ cups (250g) vegetable oil

2 teaspoons vanilla extract

¼ cup plus 2 tablespoons (85g) buttermilk

2 cups (454g) mashed banana (from approximately 5 medium bananas)

⅔ cup (113g) mini chocolate chips

Method

1. Preheat the oven to 350°F (180°C) and prepare two loaf pans with nonstick baking spray and a parchment sling that covers the bottom and two long sides of each loaf pan.
2. Follow the Wet and Dry Method on page 31, adding the mini chocolate chips after mixing the wet and dry ingredients together.
3. Divide the batter evenly between the two loaf pans and bake for 50 to 55 minutes or until a toothpick inserted in the center comes out with a few moist crumbs attached.
4. Remove from the oven and cool in the pan for 10 minutes before lifting each loaf out of the pan with the parchment sling and placing on a baking rack to cool completely.

CARROT CAKE

Mixing Method: Sponge (whole egg)

Yield: Two 8-inch (20cm) round cake layers

Prep Time: 20 minutes

Bake Time: 40 to 45 minutes

Special Equipment

Two 8×3-inch (20×8cm) round cake pans

Stand mixer with the whisk and paddle attachments

Ingredients

1½ cups (300g) granulated sugar

½ cup (100g) light brown sugar

4 large eggs, room temperature

1¼ cups (250g) vegetable oil

2 teaspoons vanilla extract

3½ cups (350g) finely shredded carrots (from approximately 1 pound of carrots)

¾ cup (189g) crushed pineapple, strained

2½ cups (350g) all-purpose flour

2 teaspoons baking powder

½ teaspoon baking soda

½ teaspoon table salt

2 teaspoons cinnamon

1 cup (113g) walnuts, chopped and toasted*

1 batch Cream Cheese Frosting (page 213)

1 batch Vanilla Swiss Buttercream (page 220)

Method

1. Preheat the oven to 350°F (180°C) and prepare the cake pans with nonstick baking spray and a circle of parchment paper on the bottom.
2. Follow the Sponge (Whole Egg) Method on page 42, including the carrots and pineapple with the liquid ingredients in step 2 and adding the toasted walnuts at the end.
3. Divide evenly between the two cake pans and bake for 40 to 45 minutes or until a toothpick inserted in the center comes out with a few moist crumbs attached.
4. Remove from the oven and let cool in the pan for 10 minutes before flipping out onto a baking rack to cool completely.
5. Once cool, level the top of each cake and then cut each cake in half to create 4 layers.
6. Alternate each layer with a layer of cream cheese frosting.
7. Go around the sides and top of the cake with a very thin layer of Swiss buttercream, removing any excess so that the cake is barely covered.
8. Place the cake in the fridge for 30 to 60 minutes to firm up.
9. Once cool, remove from the fridge and finish the cake by covering the sides and top with more of the Swiss buttercream.

*Toast walnuts by spreading them out in a thin layer on a sheet pan and baking at 350°F (180°C) for 5 to 10 minutes or until fragrant.

APPLE CAKE

Mixing Method: Wet and Dry

Yield: One 9×13-inch (23×33cm) cake

Prep Time: 20 minutes

Bake Time: 40 to 50 minutes

Special Equipment

9×13-inch (23×33cm) baking pan

Ingredients

2¾ cups (385g) all-purpose flour

2 teaspoons baking powder

½ teaspoon baking soda

½ teaspoon table salt

2 teaspoons cinnamon

1½ cups (300g) granulated sugar

½ cup (100g) light brown sugar

4 large eggs

1¼ cups (250g) vegetable oil

2 teaspoons vanilla extract

¾ cup (170g) buttermilk

3 cups (369g) apples, peeled and diced into ½-inch (1cm) cubes, from about 1 pound (454g) of apples (I prefer a tart apple like Granny Smith)

1 cup (113g) walnuts, chopped and toasted

1 batch Caramelized Honey Sauce (page 286)

Method

1. Preheat the oven to 350°F (180°C) and prepare the baking pan with nonstick baking spray and a parchment paper sling that covers the bottom and long sides of the rectangle (see page 38).
2. Follow the Wet and Dry Method on page 31, adding the apple cubes along with the buttermilk in the wet ingredients and finish the batter by adding the walnuts.
3. Spread the batter in the prepared baking pan and bake for 40 to 50 minutes or until a toothpick inserted in the center comes out with a few moist crumbs attached.
4. Remove from the oven and cool in the pan for 10 minutes before lifting each loaf out of the pan with the parchment sling and placing on a baking rack to cool completely.
5. Serve at room temperature with the hot Caramelized Honey Sauce.

LEARNING WITH
QUICK CAKES

AMOUNT OF FLOUR IN CAKES

One of the most important structure builders in all of baking is flour. When a cake has more liquid, there is a need for more structure to hold everything together. Often it is not as simple as just increasing the amount of flour, but with small alterations in the overall water content of a cake, a little added or subtracted flour can be the small difference needed for a tall and fluffy cake that is still moist.

OIL VS. BUTTER IN CAKES (SEE PHOTO)

Cakes that use the creaming method frequently rely on butter to aerate and lighten the cake. The flavor that butter brings to desserts is almost undeniably delicious. In cakes that already have a strong flavor independent of the fat used, though, it is often a better choice to use oil. Because oil is liquid at room temperature, it can easily be mixed into batters using the Wet and Dry or Sponge methods. The oil also helps keep the cake moist for longer than butter would, since butter is solid at room temperature. As shown in the next section, I have included a small amount of oil to create a cake that stays moist for longer, even for cakes that rely on butter.

BUTTER CAKES

A CLOSER LOOK AT BUTTER CAKES

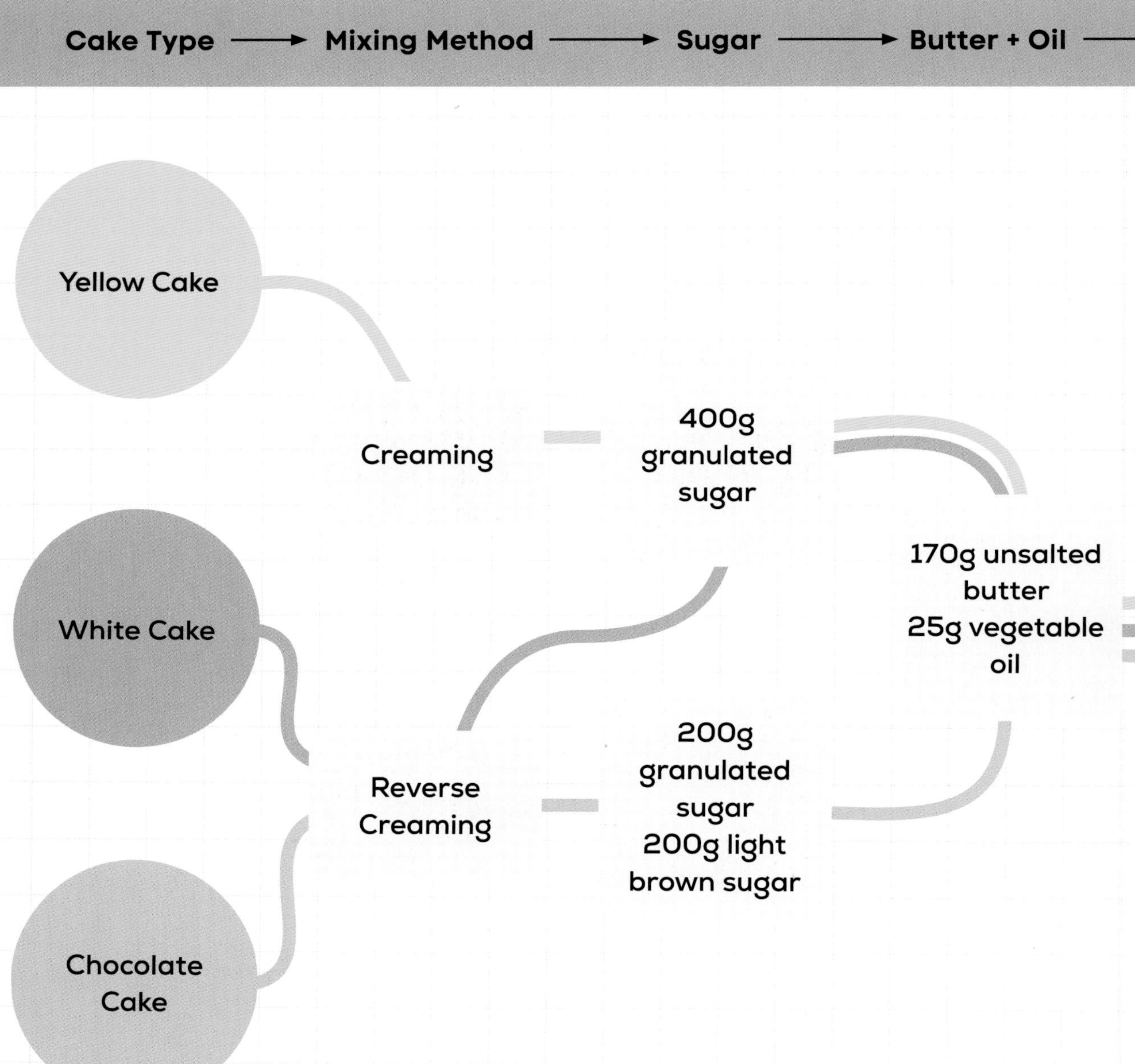

→ Eggs → Dry Ingredients → Leaveners + Salt → Liquid

2 large eggs
6 egg yolks

325g
cake flour

1½ teaspoons
baking powder
½ teaspoon
baking soda
1 teaspoon
table salt

227g
buttermilk
1 tablespoon
vanilla extract

227g
whole milk
2½ teaspoons
vanilla extract
½ teaspoon
almond
extract

6 egg whites

260g
cake flour
65g Dutch-
process cocoa
powder

4 teaspoons
baking powder
1 teaspoon
table salt

4 large eggs

227g water
2 teaspoons
vanilla extract

YELLOW CAKE

Mixing Method: Classic Creaming

Yield: Two 8-inch (20cm) cake layers

Prep Time: 25 minutes

Bake Time: 35 to 40 minutes

Special Equipment

Two 8×3-inch (20×8cm) round cake pans

Stand mixer with the paddle attachment

Ingredients

2 cups (400g) granulated sugar

1½ sticks (170g) unsalted butter, softened

2 large eggs

6 egg yolks

1 tablespoon vanilla extract

2½ cups (325g) cake flour, sifted

1½ teaspoons baking powder

½ teaspoon baking soda

1 teaspoon table salt

2 tablespoons (25g) vegetable oil

1 cup (227g) buttermilk, room temperature

Method

1. Preheat the oven to 350°F (180°C) and prepare the cake pans with nonstick baking spray and a circle of parchment paper on the bottom.
2. Follow the Classic Creaming Method on page 36.
3. Divide the cake batter evenly between the two cake pans and bake for 35 to 40 minutes or until a toothpick inserted in the center comes out with a few moist crumbs attached.
4. Let cool in the pan for 10 minutes and then flip out onto a baking rack to cool completely.
5. Once completely cool, level the top of each cake and then cut in half to end up with 4 layers.
6. Alternate the cake layers with your choice of filling and then go around the cake with a thin coat of your choice of frosting.
7. Let the cake chill in the fridge for 30 to 60 minutes to firm up before finishing the cake with a final coat of the frosting.

Recommended Cake + Filling + Frosting Combinations

Yellow Cake
+
Chocolate Fudge Frosting
+
Chocolate Swiss Buttercream

Yellow Cake
+
Banana Cream Pie Filling (with or without the bananas)
+
Vanilla Swiss Buttercream

Yellow Cake
+
Mascarpone Whipped Cream Butterscotch
+
Swiss Buttercream

WHITE CAKE

Mixing Method: Reverse Creaming

Yield: Two 8-inch (20cm) cake layers

Prep Time: 25 minutes

Bake Time: 35 to 40 minutes

Special Equipment

Two 8×3-inch (20×8cm) round cake pans

Stand mixer with the paddle attachment

Ingredients

2 cups (400g) granulated sugar

2½ cups (325g) cake flour, sifted

4 teaspoons baking powder

1 teaspoon table salt

1½ sticks (170g) unsalted butter, softened

2 tablespoons (25g) vegetable oil

1 cup (227g) whole milk, room temperature

6 egg whites

2½ teaspoons vanilla extract

½ teaspoon almond extract

Method

1. Preheat the oven to 350°F (180°C) and prepare the cake pans with nonstick baking spray and a circle of parchment paper on the bottom.
2. Follow the Reverse Creaming Method on page 37.
3. Divide the cake batter evenly between the two cake pans and bake for 35 to 40 minutes or until a toothpick inserted in the center comes out with a few moist crumbs attached.
4. Let cool in the pan for 10 minutes and then flip out onto a baking rack to cool completely.
5. Once completely cool, level the top of each cake and then cut in half to end up with 4 layers.
6. Alternate the cake layers with your choice of filling and then go around the cake with a thin coat of your choice of frosting.
7. Let the cake chill in the fridge for 30 to 60 minutes to firm up before finishing the cake with a final coat of the frosting.

Recommended Cake + Filling + Frosting Combinations

White Cake
+
Cream Cheese Frosting
+
Vanilla Swiss Buttercream

White Cake
+
Coconut Cream Pie Filling
+
Butterscotch Swiss Buttercream

White Cake
+
Lemon Meringue Pie Filling
+
1.5× batch of Swiss Meringue from the Lemon Meringue Pie

CHOCOLATE CAKE

Mixing Method: Reverse Creaming

Yield: Two 8-inch (20cm) cake layers
Prep Time: 25 minutes
Bake Time: 35 to 40 minutes

Special Equipment

Two 8×3-inch (20×8cm) round cake pans

Stand mixer with the paddle attachment

Ingredients

1 cup (227g) water

¾ cup (65g) Dutch-process cocoa powder, sifted

1 cup (200g) granulated sugar

1 cup (200g) light brown sugar

2 cups (260g) cake flour, sifted

4 teaspoons baking powder

1 teaspoon table salt

1½ sticks (170g) unsalted butter, softened

2 tablespoons (25g) vegetable oil

4 large eggs

2 teaspoons vanilla extract

Method

1. Preheat the oven to 350°F (180°C) and prepare the cake pans with nonstick baking spray and a circle of parchment paper on the bottom.
2. Bring the water to a boil and immediately pour over the cocoa powder. Whisk until there are no clumps of cocoa powder and set aside to use as the liquid in step 3 of the Reverse Creaming Method.
3. Follow the Reverse Creaming Method on page 37.
4. Divide the cake batter evenly between the two cake pans and bake for 35 to 40 minutes or until a toothpick inserted in the center comes out with a few moist crumbs attached.
5. Let cool in the pan for 10 minutes and then flip out onto a baking rack to cool completely.
6. Once completely cool, level the top of each cake and then cut in half to end up with 4 layers.
7. Alternate the cake layers with your choice of filling and then go around the cake with a thin coat of your choice of frosting.
8. Let the cake chill in the fridge for 30 to 60 minutes to firm up before finishing the cake with a final coat of the frosting.

Recommended Cake + Filling + Frosting Combinations

Chocolate Cake	**Chocolate Cake**	**Chocolate Cake**
+	+	+
Cream Cheese Frosting	**Chocolate Cream Pie Filling**	**Mascarpone Whipped Cream**
+	+	+
Chocolate Swiss Buttercream	**Butterscotch Swiss Buttercream**	**American Buttercream**

LEARNING WITH

BUTTER CAKES

WHOLE EGGS VS. EGG YOLKS VS. EGG WHITES IN CAKES

One factor impacting a cake's final height and texture is the part of the egg used. Using the whole egg gives a balance of moisture, structure, and richness that comes from both the yolk and white. This leads to a traditional cake with a semi-open crumb and tender interior texture. Leaving out the yolks, though, and only using egg whites creates a classic white cake. This time, the cake is slightly denser because it lacks the fat from the yolks, but it has a super soft and velvety interior. Finally, when making a yellow cake by using a higher ratio of egg yolks compared to egg whites, the cake will have a richer flavor. However, the texture will be slightly coarser due to a decrease in moisture from leaving out the egg whites.

THE EFFECT OF THE CAKE PAN YOU USE (SEE PHOTO)

Beyond ingredients and technique, the pan itself can have an impact on how your cake bakes. Cakes bake via conduction, convection, and radiation. Conduction is affected by the material of the pan and radiation is affected by the finish of the pan. Pans with a darker finish will absorb more heat upon being put in the oven. The result is a baked good with edges that darken more readily. On the other hand, pans with a reflective finish will reflect more of this radiant heat. The final baked good this time has a crust with a lighter color.

SPONGE CAKES

A CLOSER LOOK AT SPONGE CAKES

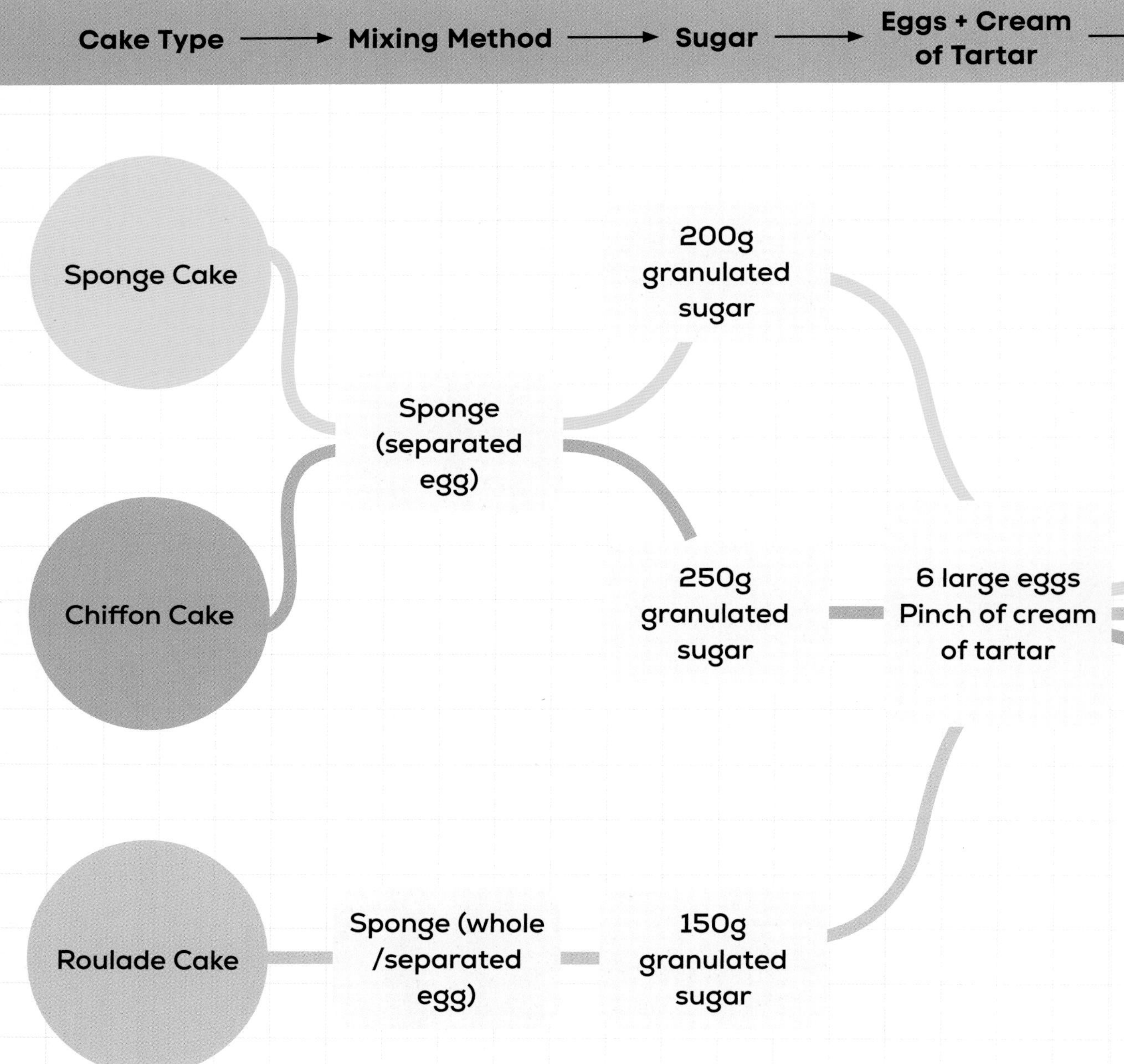

Flour → Liquid → Leaveners + Salt → Flavorings

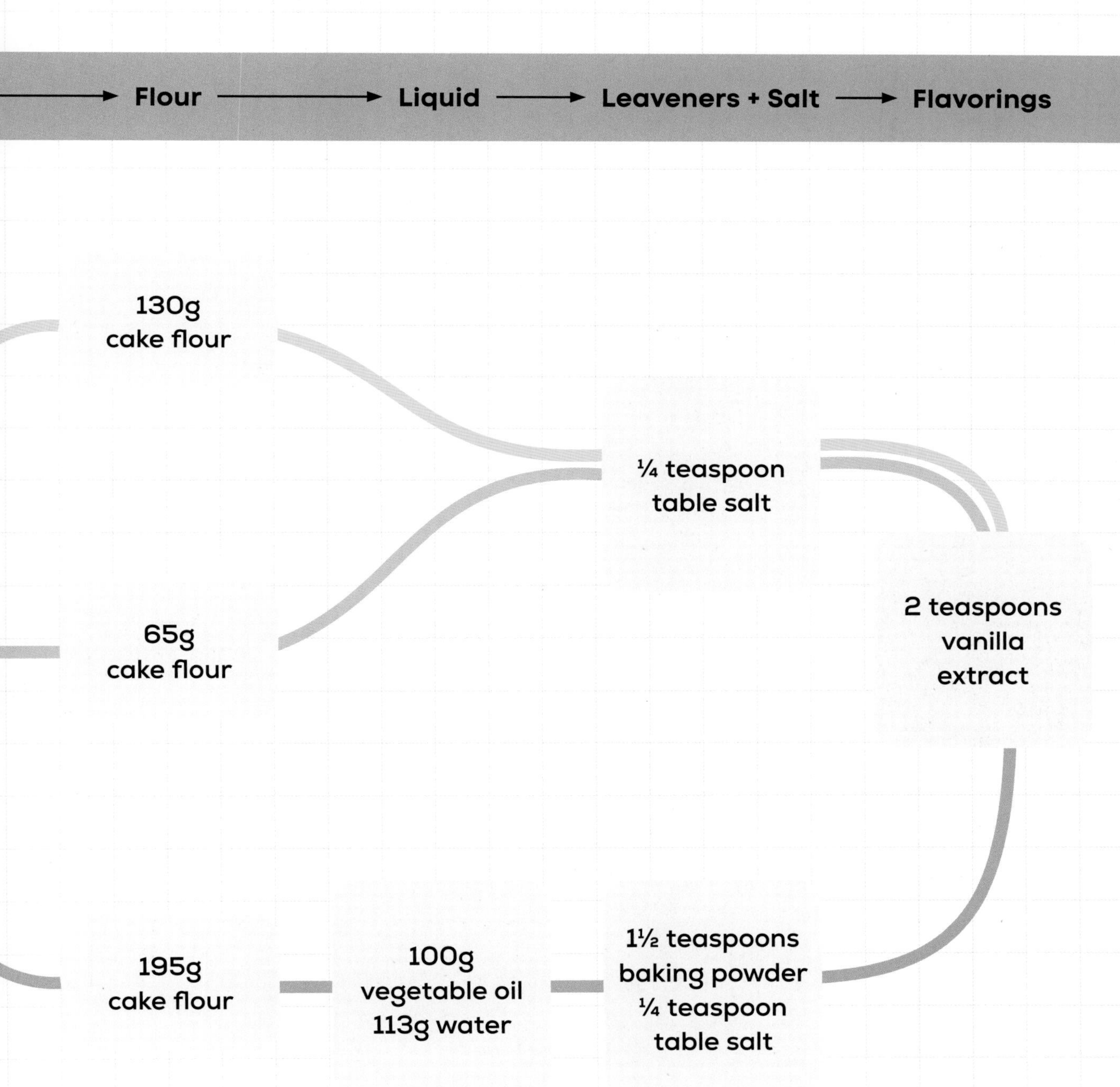

SPONGE CAKE

Mixing Method: Sponge (Separated Egg)

Yield: Two 8-inch (20cm) cake layers
Prep Time: 30 minutes
Bake Time: 30 to 35 minutes

Special Equipment

Two 8×3-inch (20×8cm) round cake pans

Stand mixer with the whisk attachment

Ingredients

1 cup (200g) granulated sugar

6 large eggs, separated and at room temperature

Pinch of cream of tartar

1 cup (130g) cake flour, sifted

¼ teaspoon table salt

2 teaspoons vanilla extract

Method

1 Preheat the oven to 350°F (180°C) and prepare the cake pans with a circle of parchment paper on the bottom (do not grease the pan).

2 Follow the Sponge (Separated Egg) method on page 43, using half of the sugar with the egg yolks and half when creating the meringue with the egg whites.

3 Divide the cake batter evenly between the two prepared cake pans and bake for 30 to 35 minutes or until golden and the cake springs back when gently pressed.

4 Remove from the oven and immediately flip each pan upside down to cool on a baking rack. Let cool completely before running an offset spatula around the edge of the pan and allowing the cake to fall out.

5 Level each cake by cutting a thin layer off the top and then cutting each cake in half to end up with 4 layers.

6 Layer the cakes with your choice of syrup, filling, and final exterior.

Recommended Cake – Syrup – Filling – Exterior Combinations

Sponge Cake
+
Strawberry Fruit Syrup
+
Mascarpone Whipped Cream and sliced strawberries
+
N/A

Sponge Cake
+
Honey Syrup
+
Stabilized Whipped Cream with cinnamon
+
Vanilla Swiss Buttercream

Sponge Cake
+
Simple Syrup
+
Whipped Milk Chocolate Ganache
+
Dark Chocolate Ganache

CHIFFON CAKE

Mixing Method: Sponge (Separated Egg)

Yield: Two 8-inch (20cm) cake layers

Prep Time: 30 minutes

Bake Time: 30 to 35 minutes

Special Equipment

Two 8×3-inch (20×8cm) round cake pans

Stand mixer with the whisk attachment

Ingredients

6 large eggs, separated and at room temperature

1¼ cups (250g) granulated sugar

Pinch of cream of tartar

½ cup (100g) vegetable oil

½ cup (113g) water

2 teaspoons vanilla extract

1½ cups (195) cake flour, sifted

1½ teaspoons baking powder

¼ teaspoon table salt

Method

1 Preheat the oven to 350°F (180°C) and prepare the cake pans with a circle of parchment paper on the bottom (do not grease the pan).

2 Follow the Sponge (separated egg) method on page 43, using half of the sugar with the egg yolks and half when creating the meringue with the egg whites.

3 Divide the cake batter evenly between the two prepared cake pans and bake for 30 to 35 minutes or until golden and the cake springs back when gently pressed.

4 Remove from the oven and immediately flip each pan upside down to cool on a baking rack. Let cool completely before running an offset spatula around the edge of the pan and allowing the cake to fall out.

5 Level each cake by cutting a thin layer off the top and then cutting each cake in half to end up with 4 layers.

6 Layer the cakes with your choice of syrup, filling, and final exterior.

Recommended Cake – Syrup – Filling – Exterior Combinations

Chiffon Cake	**Chiffon Cake**	**Chiffon Cake**
+	+	+
Simple Syrup	**Simple Syrup**	**Fruit Syrup**
+	+	+
Banana Cream Pie Filling (with or without the bananas)	**Butterscotch Swiss Buttercream**	**Cream Cheese Frosting**
+	+	+
Dark Chocolate Ganache	**Caramelized Honey Sauce**	**White Chocolate Ganache**

ROULADE CAKE

Mixing Method: Sponge (Whole/Separated egg)

Yield: One half sheet cake
Prep Time: 30 minutes
Bake Time: 10 to 15 minutes

Special Equipment

Half sheet pan

Stand mixer with the whisk attachment

Ingredients

6 large eggs (3 separated and 3 left whole), room temperature

¾ cup (150g) granulated sugar

¼ teaspoon table salt

Pinch of cream of tartar

½ cup (65g) cake flour

2 teaspoons vanilla extract

Method

1. Preheat the oven to 400°F (200°C) and prepare a half sheet pan with a rectangle of parchment paper on the bottom (do not grease the pan).
2. Add the 3 whole eggs and 3 egg yolks to the bowl of a stand mixer along with ½ cup (100g) of the sugar and the salt. Whisk on medium speed until lightened in color, thick, and approximately tripled in volume. Set the egg mixture aside and thoroughly clean out the mixing bowl.
3. Add the 3 egg whites to the mixture along with the cream of tartar and whisk on medium-low speed until foamy. Increase the speed to medium and add the remaining ¼ cup (50g) of sugar one tablespoon at a time. Continue whisking until medium to stiff peaks form.
4. Fold the meringue into the egg mixture from before and finish by gently folding in the cake flour and vanilla extract.
5. Spread into the cake pan and bake for 10 to 15 minutes or until the cake springs back when gently pressed. Remove from the oven and immediately flip each pan upside down to cool on a baking rack.
6. Finish by brushing the cake with your choice of syrup and spread a filling over the cake before rolling up and topping with any final syrups or sauces.

Recommended Cake – Syrup – Filling – Exterior Combinations

Roulade Cake	Roulade Cake	Roulade Cake
+	+	+
Fruit Syrup	Simple Syrup	Simple Syrup
+	+	+
Lemon Meringue Pie Filling	Mascarpone Whipped Cream	Chocolate Fudge Frosting
+	+	+
N/A	Dark Chocolate Ganache	Milk Chocolate Ganache

LEARNING WITH
SPONGE CAKES

PREPPING A SPONGE CAKE PAN (SEE PHOTO)

Sponge cakes are designed to be light and airy. In order to achieve this texture, the cake pan must be prepared in a way that promotes rising. The cake batter must be able to cling and rise up the walls of the cake pan. Any grease on the inside of the pan would cause the cake to slip and fall. Relatedly, sponge cakes should be cooled upside down, as their delicate structure might collapse if gravity is left to push on the top of the cake.

ADDING A SYRUP SOAK TO SPONGE CAKES

Sponge cakes, with their heavy reliance on egg proteins to help set their structure, are the perfect for a syrup soak. Since sponge cakes are inherently dry, a syrup soak gives extra flavor without negatively affecting the structure of the cake. Butter cakes, on the other hand, include more fat and have a structure that is much softer, so trying to soak them will cause the cake to disintegrate and have an unpleasant waterlogged texture.

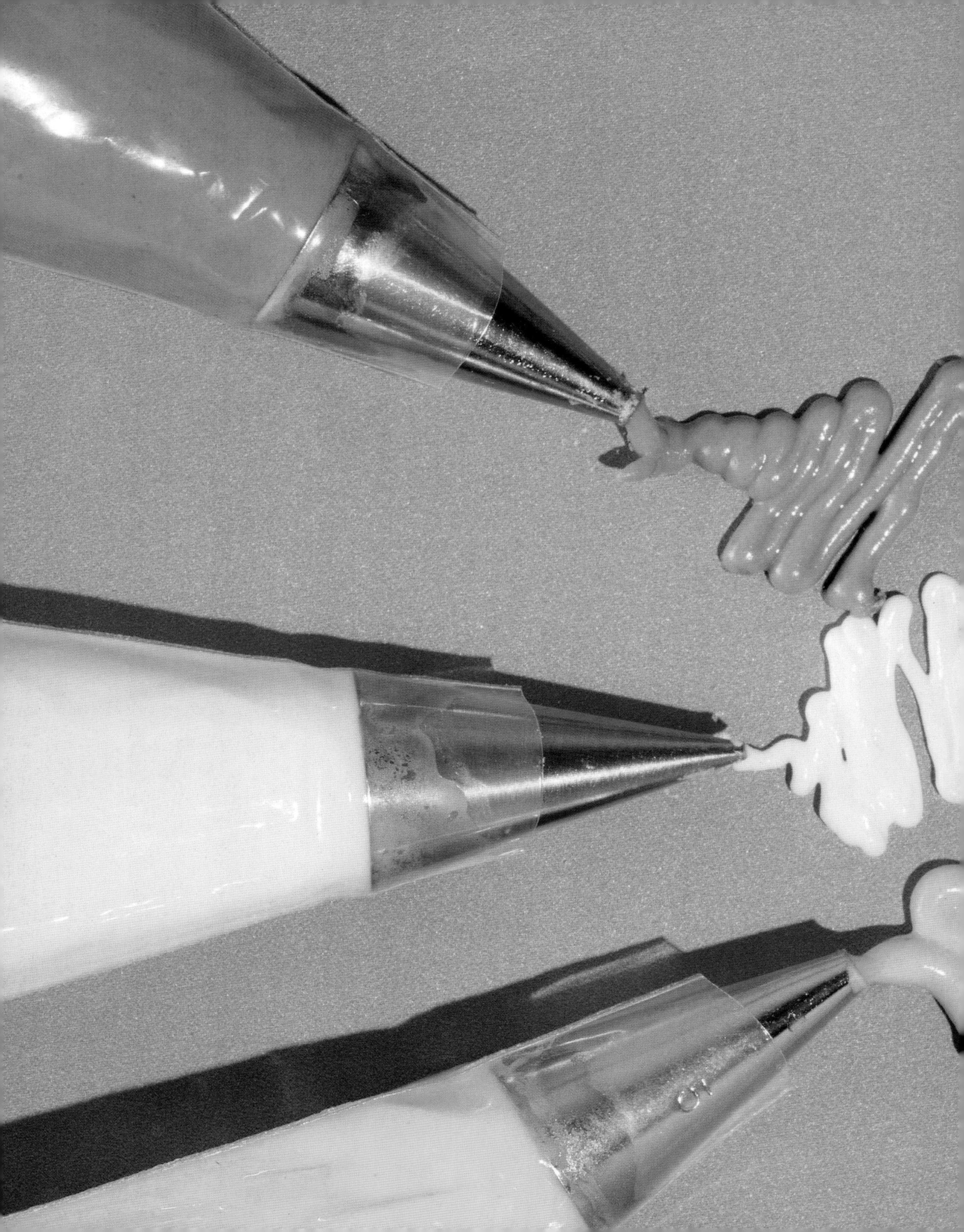

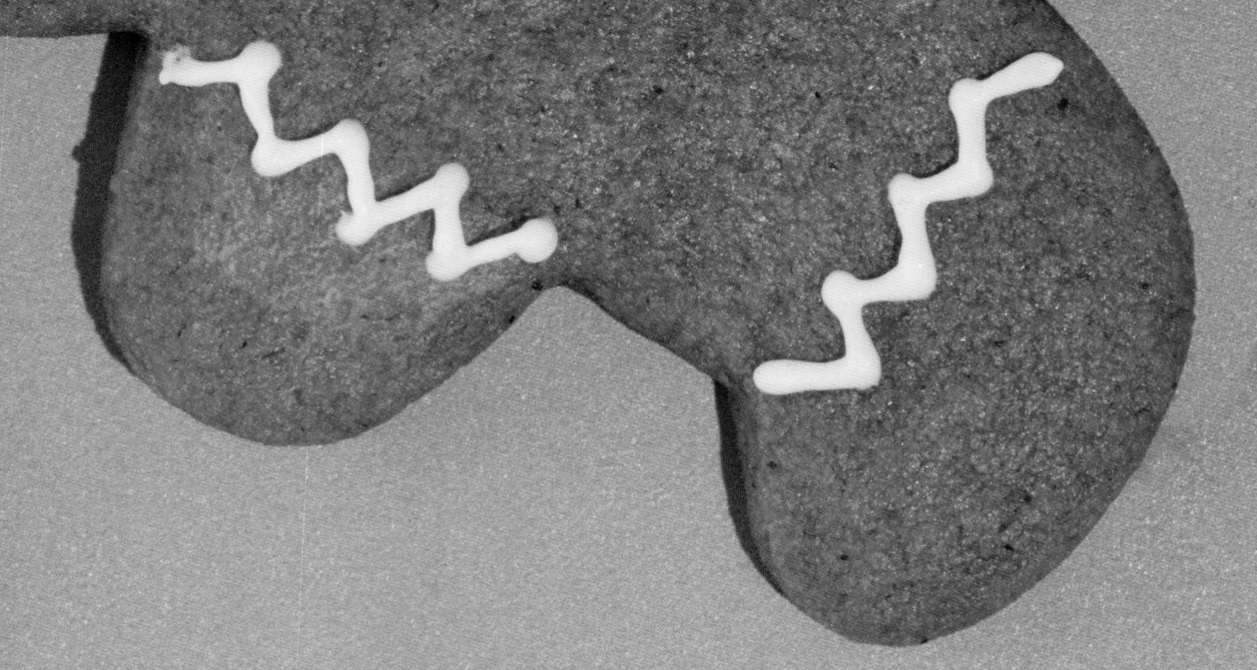

ICINGS

A CLOSER LOOK AT ICINGS

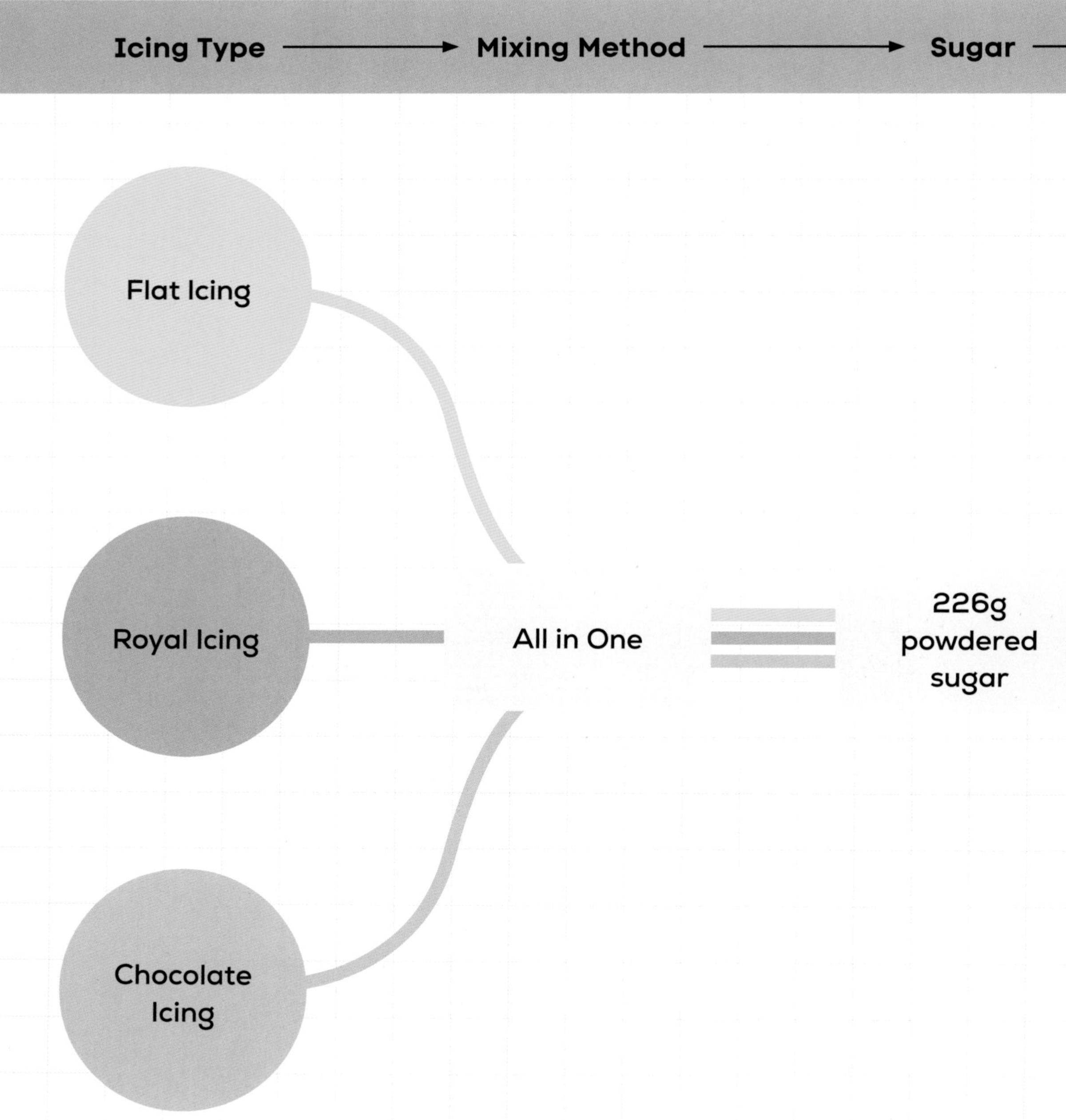

Liquid	Flavorings
28 to 56g water, milk, cream, or fruit juice	½ teaspoon vanilla extract Pinch of table salt
28 to 56g egg whites	½ teaspoon lemon juice Pinch of table salt
28 to 56g water	113g bittersweet chocolate 1 tablespoon cocoa powder (Dutch-process or natural) Pinch of table salt

FLAT ICING

Mixing Method: All in One

Yield: Approximately 1 cup
Prep Time: 10 minutes

Ingredients

2 cups (226g) powdered sugar, sifted

2 to 4 tablespoons (28 to 56g) water, milk, cream, or fruit juice

½ teaspoon vanilla extract

Pinch of table salt

Method

1. Whisk the powdered sugar, 2 tablespoons of the liquid, vanilla, and salt together.
2. If desired, add more liquid for a thinner consistency.

ROYAL ICING

Mixing Method: All in One

Yield: Approximately 1 cup
Prep Time: 10 minutes

Special Equipment

Stand mixer with the paddle attachment

Ingredients

2 cups (226g) powdered sugar, sifted

2 to 4 tablespoons (28 to 56g) pasteurized egg whites, from 1 to 2 large eggs

½ teaspoon lemon juice

Pinch of table salt

Method

1. Add the powdered sugar, 2 tablespoons of egg whites, lemon, and salt to the bowl of a stand mixer.
2. Mix on medium-high speed until the ingredients are combined and form a thick paste.
3. If desired, add more egg white for a thinner consistency.

CHOCOLATE ICING

Mixing Method: All in One

Yield: Approximately 1 cup
Prep Time: 10 minutes
Inactive Time: 10 minutes

Special Equipment

Saucepan

Ingredients

2 to 4 tablespoons (28 to 56g) water

4 ounces (113g) bittersweet chocolate (60 to 70%)

1 tablespoon cocoa powder (Dutch-process or natural)

Pinch of table salt

2 cups (226g) powdered sugar, sifted

Method

1. Add two tablespoons of the water, chocolate, cocoa powder, and salt to a bowl set over a pot of barely simmering water. Stir together until the chocolate has melted and the ingredients are combined. Let cool for 10 minutes.
2. Mix the powdered sugar together with the chocolate mixture.
3. If desired, add more water for a thinner consistency.

LEARNING WITH ICINGS

THE EFFECT OF THE TYPE OF LIQUID USED (SEE PHOTO)

The fundamental difference between a flat icing and a royal icing is the addition of egg whites. Using egg whites as the liquid creates a mixture that is part meringue and part sugar paste. This aeration from the egg white proteins helps royal icing hold its shape for piping. Ultimately, royal icing will set better than a simple icing made from other liquids.

GETTING A GLOSSY FINISH

In order to control the final appearance (whether matte or glossy) of your icing, one method is to monitor how the icing dries. This can be accomplished with devices like a dehydrator, fan, or an oven set at its lowest temperature. Another option is to include a tablespoon or two of corn syrup. Flat icing is named for its matte appearance when applied to the top of a baked good. A simple mixture of water or other liquid and powdered sugar creates an icing that dries and hardens. Corn syrup, when added to an icing, encourages moisture to stay in the icing. This extra moisture along with the sugar helps create a shiny overall appearance. The extra moisture also has the added benefit of creating an icing that dries to a softer consistency.

QUICK FROSTINGS

A CLOSER LOOK AT QUICK FROSTINGS

Frosting Type →	Fat →	Sugar →
American Buttercream	340g unsalted butter	339g powdered sugar
Cream Cheese Frosting	113g unsalted butter 227g cream cheese	339g powdered sugar
Chocolate Fudge Frosting	170g unsalted butter 84g cocoa powder (Dutch-process or natural)	339g powdered sugar

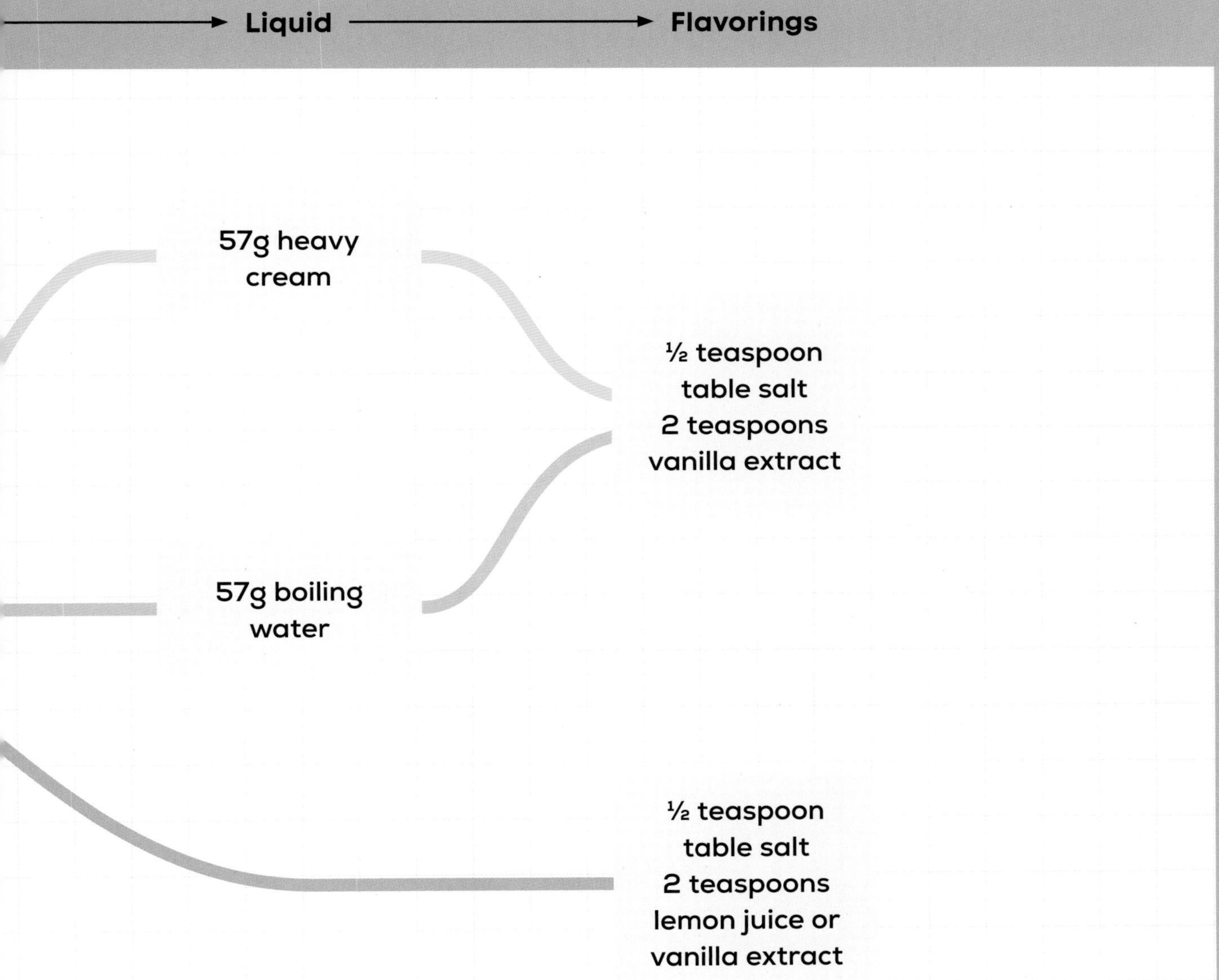

→ **Liquid** → **Flavorings**

57g heavy cream

½ teaspoon table salt
2 teaspoons vanilla extract

57g boiling water

½ teaspoon table salt
2 teaspoons lemon juice or vanilla extract

AMERICAN BUTTERCREAM

Mixing Method: Creaming

Yield: Approximately 2 cups
Prep Time: 20 minutes

Special Equipment

Stand mixer with the paddle attachment

Ingredients

3 sticks (340g) unsalted butter, softened

3 cups (339g) powdered sugar, sifted

½ teaspoon table salt

2 teaspoons vanilla extract

¼ cup (57g) heavy cream

Method

1. Add the butter to the bowl of a stand mixer and mix on medium speed until smooth.
2. Add half of the powdered sugar, mixing until incorporated. Stop and scrape the bowl and the paddle attachment.
3. Add the remaining powdered sugar along with the salt and vanilla.
4. With the mixer running, stream in the heavy cream and mix until combined and the frosting is fluffy.

CREAM CHEESE FROSTING

Mixing Method: Creaming

Yield: Approximately 2 cups
Prep Time: 20 minutes

Special Equipment

Stand mixer with the paddle attachment

Ingredients

8 ounces (227g) cream cheese

1 stick (113g) unsalted butter, softened

3 cups (339g) powdered sugar, sifted

½ teaspoon table salt

2 teaspoons lemon juice or vanilla extract

Method

1. Remove the cream cheese from the fridge and cut into small cubes. Let sit out while preparing the rest of the ingredients.
2. Add the butter to the bowl of a stand mixer and mix on medium speed until smooth.
3. Add half of the powdered sugar and mix until combined.
4. Add the second half of the powdered sugar and the salt and mix until you achieve a streusel-like texture.
5. With the mixer running, add the cubes of cream cheese one at a time.
6. Mix until the icing is smooth and there are no visible clumps of butter or cream cheese.
7. Finish by mixing in the lemon juice or vanilla extract.

CHOCOLATE FUDGE FROSTING

Mixing Method: All in One

Yield: Approximately 2 cups
Prep Time: 25 minutes

Special Equipment

Stand mixer with the paddle attachment

Ingredients

3 cups (339g) powdered sugar, sifted

1 cup (84g) cocoa powder, sifted (Dutch-process or natural)

¼ cup (57g) boiling water

1½ sticks (170g) unsalted butter, softened

½ teaspoon table salt

2 teaspoons vanilla extract

Method

1 Add 1 cup (113g) of the powdered sugar to the mixing bowl along with the cocoa powder. Pour the hot water over the sugar and cocoa powder and mix on low speed to combine.

2 Add all the remaining ingredients to the bowl of a mixer and mix on medium speed until the frosting comes together, stopping and scraping the bowl and paddle attachment as necessary.

LEARNING WITH
QUICK FROSTINGS

OVERMIXING CREAM CHEESE FROSTING (SEE PHOTO)

You will notice that I suggest adding the cream cheese to the frosting at the very end of the mixing procedure instead of mixing it with the butter at the beginning. Cream cheese is held together with stabilizers that can easily break with too much agitation. When they break, the resulting buttercream is thin and liquidy. This thin buttercream causes the cake layers to slide around and as a result the cake will bulge and fall apart.

CRUSTING BUTTERCREAM

Increasing the ratio of powdered sugar to fat in a buttercream creates a frosting that crusts once it sets on the cake. This happens when the extremely fine sugar crystals in powdered sugar don't completely dissolve in the frosting and come together to form a larger crystalline structure on the exterior of the cake. My recipe for American Buttercream (page 212) includes a nearly 1:1 ratio of powdered sugar to butter. Increase the amount of powdered sugar to achieve a ratio between 1.5:1 and 2:1 for a buttercream that crusts.

SWISS BUTTERCREAMS

A CLOSER LOOK AT SWISS BUTTERCREAMS

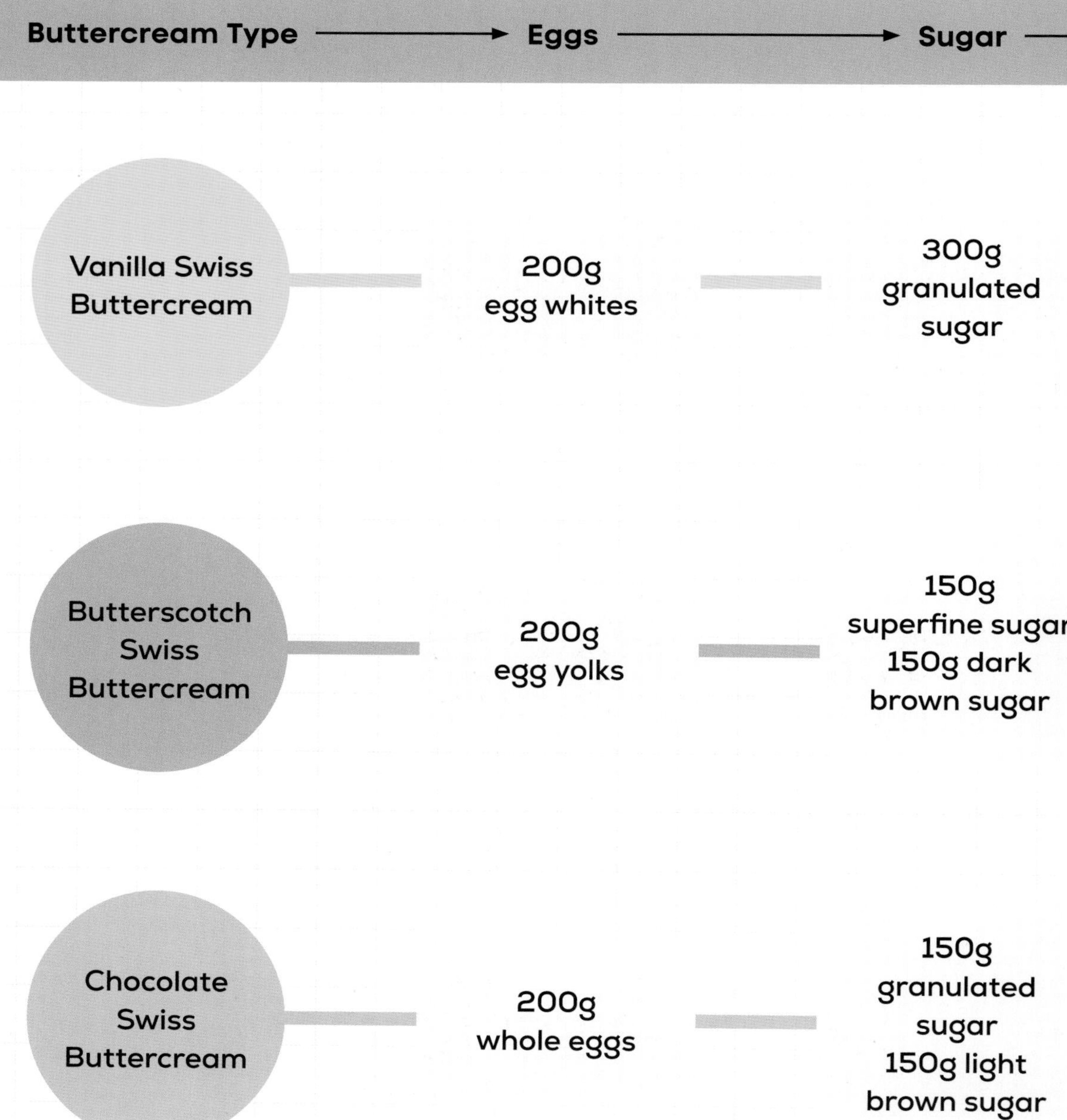

Butter	Flavorings
400g unsalted butter	½ teaspoon table salt 1 tablespoon vanilla extract
454g unsalted butter	½ teaspoon table salt 1 tablespoon vanilla extract 2 tablespoons toasted milk powder
340g unsalted butter	½ teaspoon table salt 2 teaspoons vanilla extract 227g bittersweet chocolate, melted

VANILLA SWISS BUTTERCREAM

Mixing Method: All in One

Yield: Approximately 4 cups
Prep Time: 25 minutes

Special Equipment

Stand mixer with the whisk attachment

Saucepan

Ingredients

6 egg whites (200g)

1½ cups (300g) granulated sugar

3½ sticks (400g) unsalted butter, cool but pliable

½ teaspoon table salt

1 tablespoon vanilla extract

Method

1. Add the egg whites and sugar to a heat-proof bowl and set over a pot of barely simmering water.
2. Whisk the egg whites and sugar until the sugar is dissolved and the mixture reaches a temperature between 160° to 165°F (71° to 74°C).
3. Pour the egg white and sugar mixture into the bowl of a stand mixer and whisk on medium-high speed.
4. Whisk the meringue until it reaches stiff peaks and the bowl is cool to the touch. Depending on your mixer, this will take anywhere from 7 to 12 minutes.
5. Once the bowl is cool, add the softened butter a tablespoon or two at a time.
6. Continue mixing until the buttercream comes together.
7. Finish with salt, vanilla, and any other extracts, spices, or flavorings to taste.

BUTTERSCOTCH SWISS BUTTERCREAM

Mixing Method: All in One

Yield: Approximately 3 cups
Prep Time: 25 minutes

Special Equipment

Stand mixer with the whisk attachment

Saucepan

Ingredients

12 egg yolks (200g)

2 tablespoons (28g) water

¾ cup (150g) superfine sugar

¾ cup (150g) dark brown sugar

2 tablespoons toasted milk powder (see page 79)

4 sticks (454g) unsalted butter, softened

½ teaspoon table salt

1 tablespoon vanilla extract

Method

1 Follow the method as in the Vanilla Swiss Buttercream on page 220, substituting the egg whites for egg yolks and adding the water and milk powder with the sugar in the first step. The buttercream may not reach stiff peaks in step 4, but should still increase in volume and become lighter in color.

CHOCOLATE SWISS BUTTERCREAM

Mixing Method: All in One

Yield: Approximately 3 cups
Prep Time: 25 minutes

Special Equipment

Stand mixer with the whisk attachment

Saucepan

Ingredients

4 large eggs

¾ cup (150g) granulated sugar

¾ cup (150g) light brown sugar

3 sticks (340g) unsalted butter, softened

½ teaspoon table salt

2 teaspoons vanilla extract

8 ounces (227g) bittersweet chocolate (60 to 70%), melted

Method

1 Follow the method as in the Vanilla Swiss Buttercream on page 220, substituting the egg whites for whole eggs and adding the melted chocolate at the end with the salt and vanilla. The buttercream may not reach stiff peaks in step 4, but should still increase in volume and become lighter in color.

LEARNING WITH SWISS BUTTERCREAMS

WHOLE EGGS VS. EGG YOLKS VS. EGG WHITES IN SWISS BUTTERCREAM (SEE PHOTO)

Using egg whites as the base for the frosting creates a light and airy buttercream with a simple flavor that can be easily enhanced with additional extracts and spices. As another option, switch out the egg whites for whole eggs. Because the fat in the yolks interrupts the egg white protein's ability to bond, the mixture is not able to trap the same amount of air. The result is a slightly denser buttercream but one that is also creamier thanks to the inclusion of the yolks. You can also try replacing all the egg whites with an equal weight of egg yolks. This time, the egg yolks form the base for a rich and silky buttercream with a pronounced custard-like flavor. Because there is less water in the egg yolks, I prefer to use superfine sugar and include a few tablespoons of water to help the sugar dissolve.

SAVING TOO HOT OR TOO COLD SWISS BUTTERCREAM

Like most emulsions, getting Swiss buttercream to the right texture relies on monitoring the temperature of each ingredient. Luckily, almost no matter what happens, the buttercream can be saved. If the meringue is too hot when incorporating the butter, the butter will immediately melt to a soupy mixture that never comes together. In this case, transfer the mixing bowl with the thin buttercream to the fridge for 15 minutes. Once cool, scrape the sides of the bowl and return to the mixer. Mix on medium speed and the buttercream should now come together to a thick and silky frosting. If, on the other hand, the butter is too cold, the resulting buttercream will be thick and chunky. In this case, some of the butter just needs to be melted into the buttercream. You can accomplish this by removing a small portion of the buttercream, melting it, and returning it to the mixing bowl and re-whipping. My preferred method, however, is to gently torch the outside of the mixing bowl while the mixer is running. Move the flame of the torch around the circumference of the bowl to evenly distribute the heat and continue mixing until the buttercream smooths out.

QUICK BREADS

A CLOSER LOOK AT QUICK BREADS

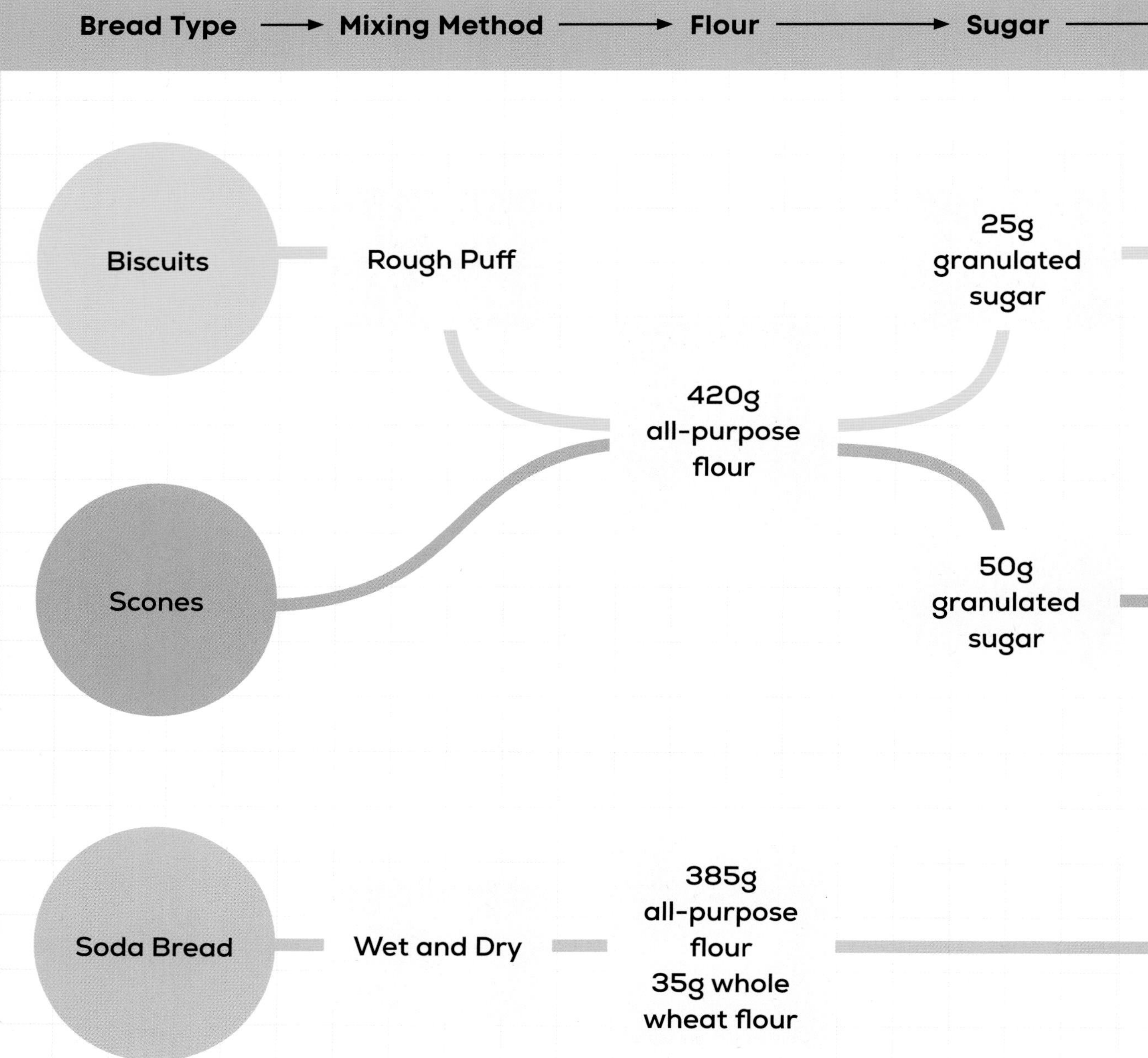

→ Leavening → Salt → Fat → Liquid → Add-Ins

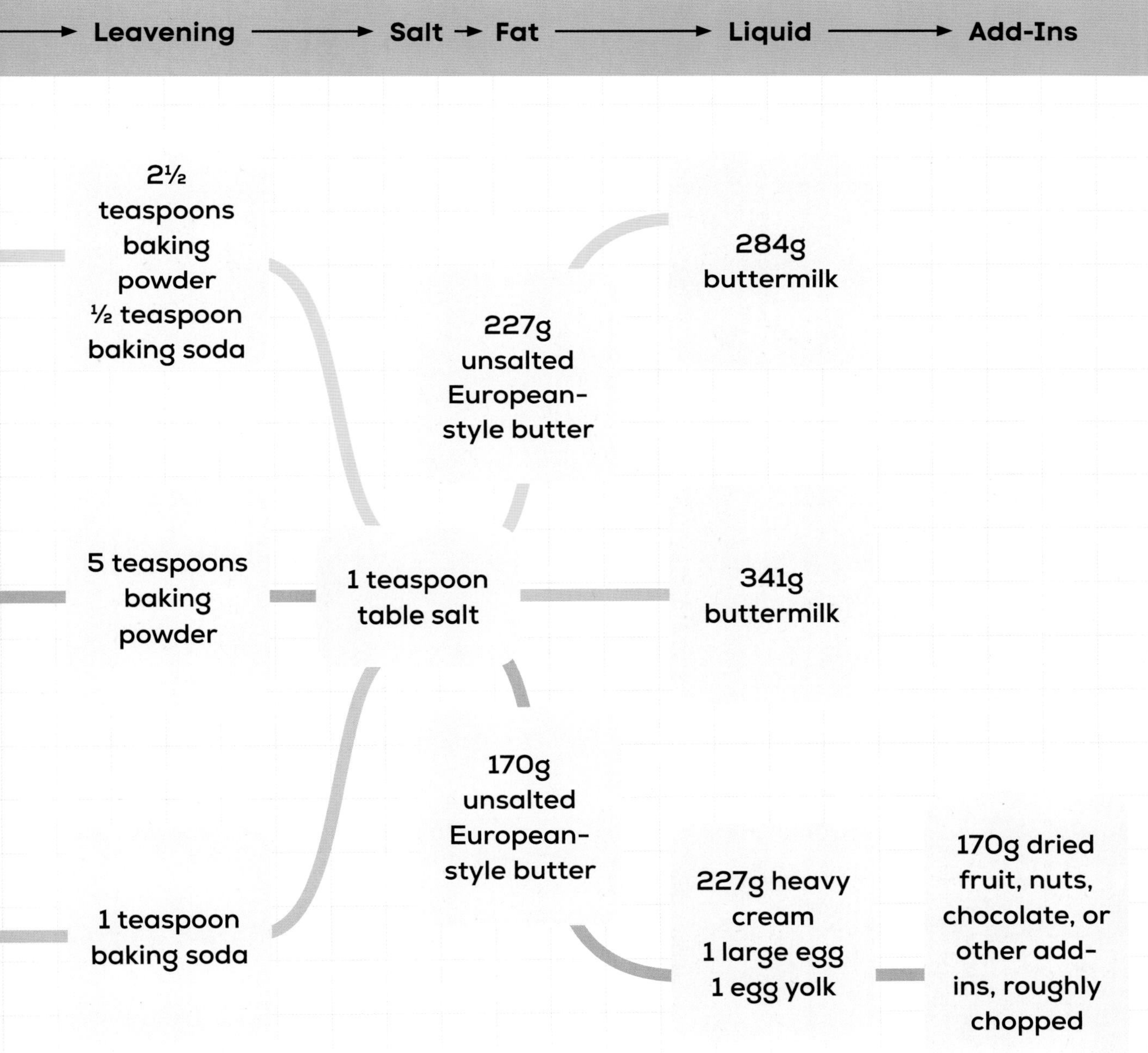

BISCUITS

Mixing Method: Rough Puff

Yield: 12 biscuits
Prep Time: 25 minutes
Bake Time: 15 to 20 minutes

Special Equipment

Rolling pin
Ruler
Half sheet pans

Ingredients

3 cups (420g) all-purpose flour

2 tablespoons (25g) granulated sugar

2½ teaspoons baking powder

½ teaspoon baking soda

1 teaspoon table salt

2 sticks (227g) unsalted European-style butter, cold and cut into ½-inch (1cm) cubes, plus 4 tablespoons (57g), melted for brushing

1¼ cups (284g) buttermilk

Method

1 Preheat the oven to 400°F (200°C). Line the sheet pans with a sheet of parchment paper.

2 Follow the Rough Puff method outlined on page 54, repeating the rolling and folding 4 times without refrigeration in between.

3 Roll the dough out one more time into a rectangle roughly ¾ inch (2cm) thick and cut into 12 biscuits.

4 Arrange the biscuits on the sheet pan and brush the tops with half the melted butter.

5 Bake for 15 to 20 minutes or until golden brown.

6 Remove from the oven and immediately brush with the remaining melted butter.

SCONES

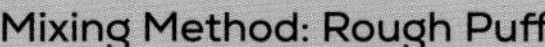

Mixing Method: Rough Puff

Yield: 12 scones
Prep Time: 30 minutes
Bake Time: 20 to 25 minutes

Special Equipment

Rolling pin
Ruler
Half sheet pans

Ingredients

3 cups (420g) all-purpose flour

4 tablespoons (50g) granulated sugar

5 teaspoons baking powder

1 teaspoon table salt

1½ sticks (170g) unsalted European-style butter, cold and cut into ½-inch (1cm) cubes

1 cup (227g) heavy cream, plus ¼ cup (57g) for brushing on top

1 large egg plus 1 egg yolk

8 ounces (227g) dried fruit, toasted nuts, chocolate, or other add-ins, roughly chopped

½ cup (100g) turbinado sugar

Method

1 Preheat the oven to 400°F (200°C). Line the sheet pans with a sheet of parchment paper.

2 Follow the Rough Puff Method outlined on page 54, adding the add-ins at the end. Repeat the rolling and folding 2 times without refrigeration in between.

3 Roll the dough out into a rectangle roughly ¾ inch (2cm) thick and cut into 6 rectangles. Then cut each rectangle along the diagonal to create triangles.

4 Arrange the scones on the sheet pans and brush the tops with heavy cream and sprinkle with turbinado sugar.

5 Bake for 20 to 25 minutes or until golden brown.

SODA BREAD

Mixing Method: Wet and Dry

Yield: One loaf
Prep Time: 15 minutes
Bake Time: 55 to 60 minutes

Special Equipment

10-inch (25cm) cast-iron skillet

Serrated knife or razor blade

Ingredients

2¾ cups (385g) all-purpose flour

¼ cup (35g) whole wheat flour

1 teaspoon baking soda

1 teaspoon table salt

1½ cups (341g) buttermilk

Method

1. Preheat the oven to 450°F (230°C). Line the skillet with a piece of parchment paper.
2. Follow the Wet and Dry Method on page 31.
3. Once the dough has come together (it will be sticky), turn out onto a lightly floured countertop and gently round into a circle.
4. Move the dough to the prepared pan and score the top by slicing an X across the top with a serrated knife or razor blade. Each cut should go roughly ¾ of the way down the dough.
5. Bake for 55 to 60 minutes or until golden brown and a thin, firm crust has formed around the outside.
6. Let cool on the pan for 10 minutes before moving to a baking rack to cool completely.

LEARNING WITH QUICK BREADS

WORKING THE DOUGH (SEE PHOTO)

For all the talk of gluten in this book, quick breads are a prime example of getting just the right amount. Work the dough too little and your final bread will be soft but squat. Work it too much and the result will be tall but dense and chewy. Giving the dough a few rolls and folds or a slight amount of work creates just enough structure for the dough to come together. In the case of biscuits and scones, this overlaps with the desire to create some flakiness in the final product.

ADDED SUGAR

In addition to its obvious role in providing sweetness, sugar also has a profound impact on the texture and browning of a dough. Sugar does a great job in retaining moisture in a dough for a softer and more tender final product. Leaving it out creates a baked good with a heartier and more coarse interior. Additionally, adding a little sugar to a dough can improve browning. Especially in doughs that may not include other browning ingredients (baking soda, egg wash, etc.), a little sugar can help create a deeper flavor that comes from a golden exterior.

LEAN BREADS

A CLOSER LOOK AT LEAN BREADS

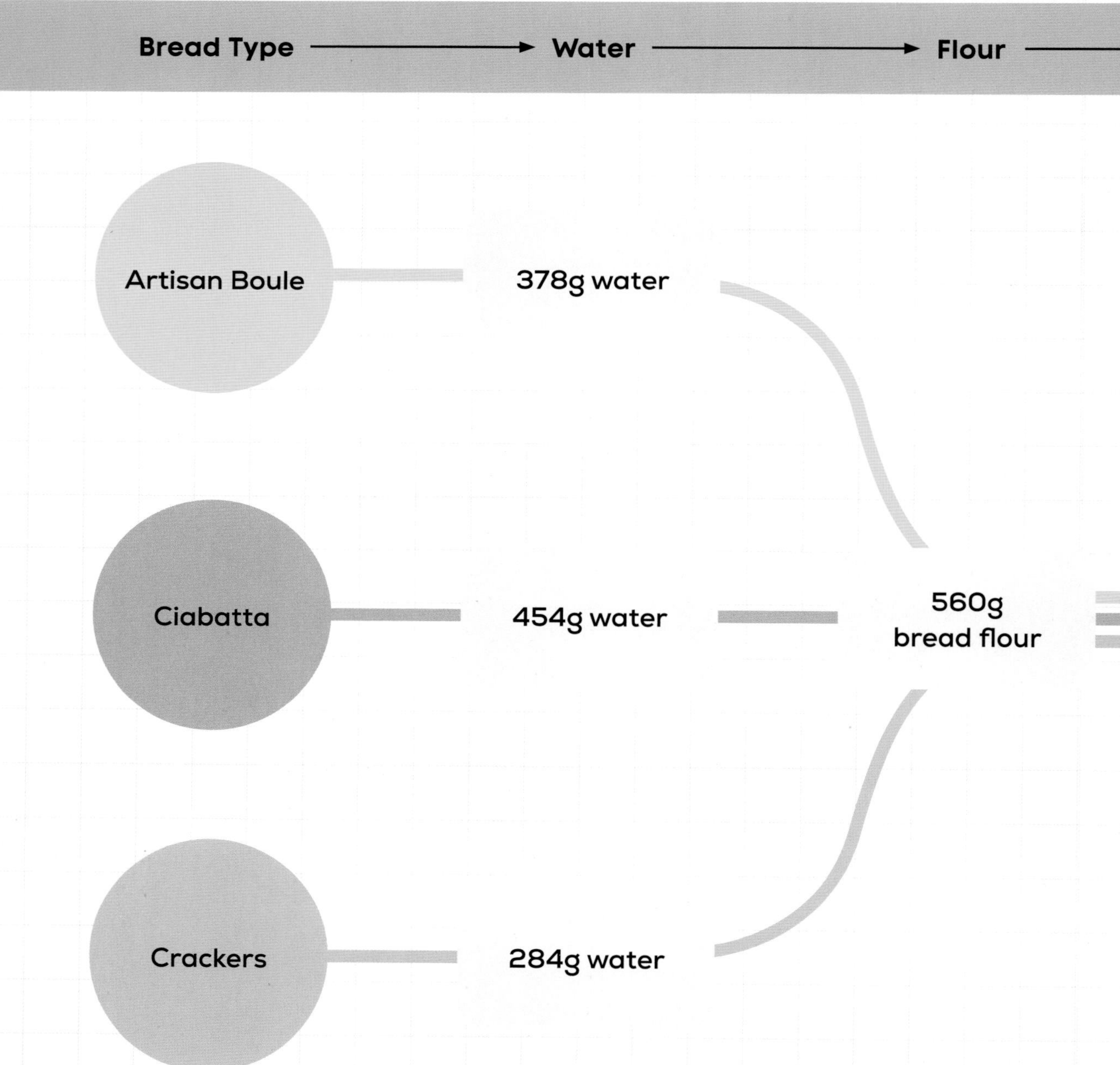

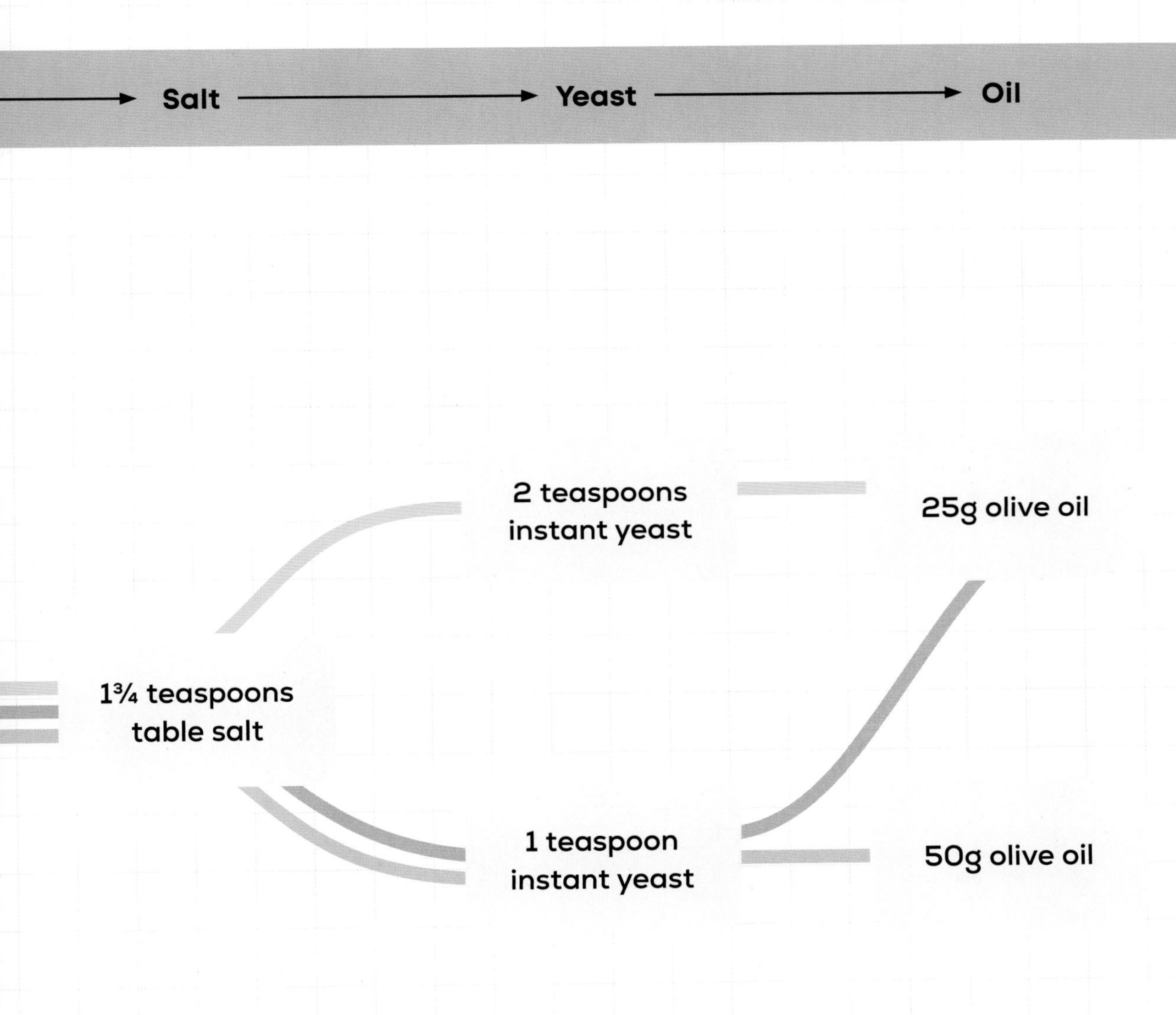
Salt
Yeast
Oil
2 teaspoons instant yeast
25g olive oil
1¾ teaspoons table salt
1 teaspoon instant yeast
50g olive oil

ARTISAN BOULE

Mixing Method: Low Knead

Yield: One loaf
Prep Time: 15 minutes
Inactive Time: 14 hours
Bake Time: 40 to 45 minutes

Special Equipment

Cast-iron combination cooker or Dutch oven

Serrated knife or razor blade

Ingredients

1⅔ cups (378g) water

2 teaspoons instant yeast

4 cups (560g) bread flour

2 tablespoons (25g) olive oil

1¾ teaspoons table salt

Method

1. Follow the Low Knead Method on page 49. In step 7 of the Low Knead Method, shape the dough into a round and let rise on a parchment paper circle just big enough to fit inside the bottom of your combination cooker.
2. Place the combination cooker in the oven and preheat the oven to 450°F (230°C).
3. Let the dough rise until puffy and about doubled in size (1 to 1½ hours).
4. Remove the combination cooker from the oven and carefully transfer the loaf and parchment into the bottom of the pan. Score an X pattern ½ inch (1cm) deep into the top of the loaf with a serrated knife or razor blade.
5. Place a few ice cubes in the bottom of the pan with the loaf and cover the top on the cooker. Place in the oven.
6. Bake for 30 minutes covered and then remove the top and bake for another 10 to 15 minutes or until golden brown.
7. Remove from the oven and place on a baking rack to cool completely.

CIABATTA

Mixing Method: Low Knead

Yield: 4 loaves
Prep Time: 15 minutes
Inactive Time: 14 hours
Bake Time: 25 to 30 minutes

Special Equipment

Two half sheet pans

Ingredients

2 cups (454g) water
1 teaspoon instant yeast
4 cups (560g) bread flour, plus extra for dusting
2 tablespoons (25g) olive oil
1¾ teaspoons table salt

Method

1. Follow the Low Knead Method outlined on page 49.
2. After removing the dough from the fridge, preheat the oven to 450°F (230°C). Prepare two baking sheets with a piece of parchment paper.
3. Turn the dough out onto a generously floured work surface. Sprinkle the top of the dough with flour and pat into a rectangle approximately 1 to 1½ inches (2 to 4cm) tall.
4. Using a bench scraper, cut the dough into four equal pieces by cutting across the middle lengthwise and widthwise.
5. Transfer 2 pieces to each prepared baking sheet and cover loosely with greased plastic wrap.
6. Let rise at room temperature until puffy and approximately one and half times their original size (1½ to 2 hours).
7. Bake for 25 to 30 minutes or until golden brown.
8. Remove from the oven and transfer to a baking rack to cool completely.

CRACKERS

Mixing Method: Full Knead

Yield: 2 pounds (900g) of crackers

Prep Time: 20 minutes

Inactive Time: 1½ hours

Bake Time: 15 to 20 minutes

Special Equipment

Rolling pin

Two half sheet pans

Ingredients

1¼ cups (284g) water

1 teaspoon instant yeast

4 cups (560g) bread flour

4 tablespoons (50g) olive oil

1¾ teaspoons table salt

1 large egg, beaten for egg wash

½ cup (70g) Everything seasoning

Method

1. Follow the Full Knead Method outlined on page 48. Because this is a stiff dough and the mixer may struggle, it is best to knead this dough by hand. In step 4 of the Full Knead Method, turn the dough out onto a lightly oiled work surface. Divide the dough in two and roll each half into a rough rectangle approximately ⅛ inch (3 mm) thick so that it fits on the half sheet pan.
2. Preheat the oven to 400°F (200°C). Line each baking sheet with a piece of parchment paper.
3. Place each piece of dough onto the prepared baking sheets, prick all over with a fork, and brush the top with egg wash. Then sprinkle with Everything seasoning.
4. Immediately bake for 15 to 20 minutes or until golden brown.
5. Remove from the oven and let cool before breaking the dough into individual crackers.

LEARNING WITH
LEAN BREADS

DOUGH HYDRATION

At low levels of hydration (the amount of liquid relative to the amount of flour), the resulting dough is stiff and dense. This is perfect when dealing with products such as crackers and bagels that are designed to be strong. For an open and airy interior, it is best to increase the amount of water and other liquids in the dough. These doughs take more time, patience, and gentleness, but the payoff of a light and airy dough with an open crumb is well worth it.

STEAMING (SEE PHOTO)

Professional bread ovens often come with built-in steam injectors. After loading the dough into the oven, a button is pushed that releases hot water onto metal plates to create steam. After some time, the steam is released and the bread finishes baking in a dry oven. At home, the best way to accomplish this is to bake your bread dough in a covered cooker. The vapor released from the dough is trapped and the loaf essentially steams itself. I also like to add a few ice cubes in with the loaf to bump up this amount of steam. The steam pre-gelatinized some of the starch on the exterior of the loaf for a shiny finish and creates a dough with a thin, crisp crust, rather than one that is thick and chewy.

ENRICHED BREADS

A CLOSER LOOK AT ENRICHED BREADS

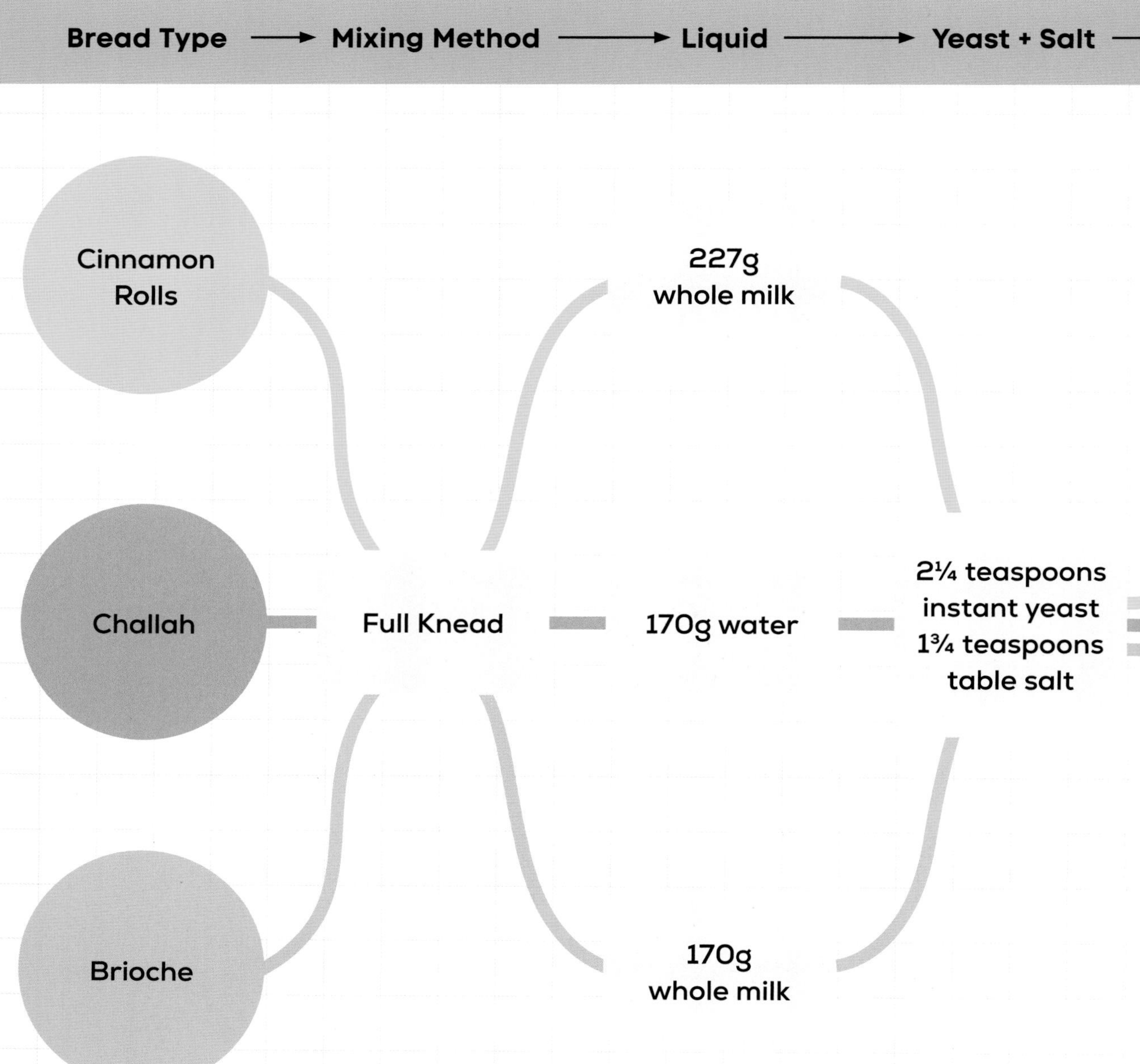

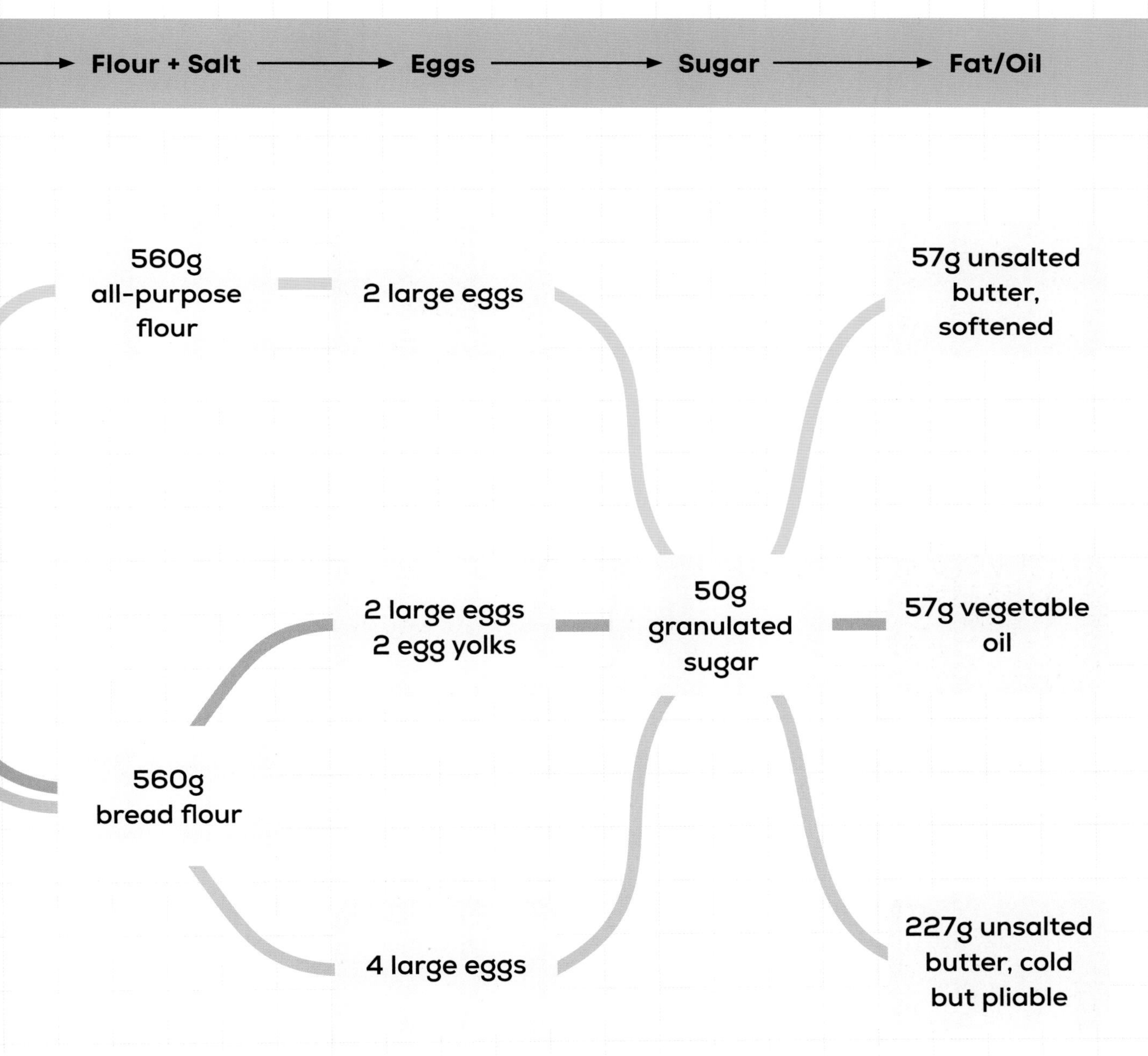
Flour + Salt
Eggs
Sugar
Fat/Oil
560g
all-purpose
flour
2 large eggs
57g unsalted
butter,
softened
2 large eggs
2 egg yolks
50g
granulated
sugar
57g vegetable
oil
560g
bread flour
4 large eggs
227g unsalted
butter, cold
but pliable

CINNAMON ROLLS

Mixing Method: Full Knead

Yield: 12 cinnamon rolls
Prep Time: 20 minutes
Inactive Time: 2½ hours
Bake Time: 30 to 35 minutes

Special Equipment

Stand mixer with the hook attachment

9×13-inch (23×33cm) baking pan

Ingredients

For the dough

1 cup (227g) whole milk

2¼ teaspoons instant yeast

4 cups (560g) all-purpose flour

2 large eggs

¼ cup (50g) granulated sugar

4 tablespoons (57g) unsalted butter, softened

1¾ teaspoons table salt

For the filling

¾ cup (150g) light brown sugar

1 stick (113g) unsalted butter, softened

1 tablespoon cinnamon

1 teaspoon vanilla extract

½ teaspoon table salt

For baking

⅔ cup (151g) heavy cream, warmed

1 batch Cream Cheese Frosting (page 213)

Method

1. Follow the Full Knead Method outlined on page 48. In step 4 of the Full Knead Method, roll out the sweet dough into a 12×16-inch (30×40cm) rectangle.
2. Combine all the cinnamon filling ingredients and mix until combined.
3. Spread the filling evenly over the dough and roll up along the long edge. Cut into 12 equal pieces and place each roll in a baking pan that has been lightly greased with nonstick baking spray and covered with a parchment paper sling (see page 38).
4. Cover the rolls loosely with plastic wrap and let rise at room temperature for 45 to 90 minutes or until puffy.
5. Preheat the oven to 350°F (180°C).
6. Right before going into the oven, pour the warm heavy cream over the rolls.
7. Bake for 30 to 35 minutes or until a light golden brown on top.
8. Remove from the oven and serve warm with the Cream Cheese Icing.

CHALLAH

Mixing Method: Full Knead

Yield: Two 6-strand loaves
Prep Time: 20 minutes
Inactive Time: 3 hours
Bake Time: 25 to 30 minutes

Special Equipment

Stand mixer with the hook attachment

Two half sheet pans

Ingredients

¾ cup (170g) water

2¼ teaspoons instant yeast

4 cups (560g) bread flour

2 large eggs

2 egg yolks

¼ cup (50g) granulated sugar

¼ cup plus 1½ teaspoons (57g) vegetable oil

1¾ teaspoons table salt

1 large egg plus 1 egg yolk, beaten for the egg wash

Method

1 Follow the Full Knead Method outlined on page 48. In step 4 of the full Knead method, divide the dough into 12 equal pieces (roughly 80g each) and roll each piece into a rough cylinder. Cover with a dish towel and let rest for 15 minutes before the final shape.

2 For the final shape, begin by rolling each cylinder into a longer cylinder that is tapered on the ends. Using 6 strands, braid into the final challah.*

3 Move each challah to their own half sheet pan lined with parchment paper. Cover with lightly greased plastic wrap and let rise at room temperature until a slight indent in the dough springs back slowly and halfway (about 1½ to 2 hours).

4 In the final hour of proofing time, preheat the oven to 375°F (190°C).

5 Before placing in the oven, brush each loaf with the egg wash. Bake for 25 to 30 minutes or golden brown.

6 Remove from the oven and set on a baking rack to cool completely.

*To braid a six-strand challah, begin by connecting the ends of each strand together in a point.

1 With the strands numbered 1 through 6 from left to right, start by bringing strand 5 all the way to the left of strand 1. Then move strand 6 so that it lies between the original strands 2 and 3.

2 Re-number all the strands 1 through six from left to right. Bring strand 2 all the way to the right of strand 6. Move strand 1 so that it lies in between strands 4 and 5.

3 Repeat steps 1 and 2 until you get to the end of the strands and tuck the excess underneath the loaf.

BRIOCHE

Mixing Method: Full Knead

Yield: Two 9-inch (23cm) loaves
Prep Time: 30 minutes
Inactive Time: 14 hours
Bake Time: 35 to 40 minutes

Special Equipment

Stand mixer with the hook attachment

Two 9×5-inch (23×13cm) loaf pans

Ingredients

¾ cup (170g) whole milk, cold

2¼ teaspoons instant yeast

4 cups (560g) bread flour

4 large eggs, cold

¼ cup (50g) granulated sugar

1¾ teaspoons table salt

2 sticks (227g) unsalted butter, cold but pliable

1 large egg plus 1 egg yolk, beaten for egg wash

Method

1 Add the milk and yeast to the bowl of a stand mixer. Let the yeast dissolve for one to two minutes before adding all the remaining ingredients except for the butter.

2 Mix the dough on low speed until it comes together.

3 Turn the speed up to medium-low and mix until the dough has medium gluten development (about 6 minutes).

4 Add chunks of butter one tablespoon or two at a time to the dough while mixing. Wait until the butter is incorporated before adding the next piece.

5 Once all the butter has been added, continue mixing until the dough reaches full gluten development and passes the windowpane test (see page 50). Remove the dough from the bowl and add to a lightly greased bowl.

6 Let the dough rise for 30 minutes before giving the dough a fold (bring the bottom of the dough to the middle, top to middle, left to middle, right to middle, and then flip over).

7 Let the dough rise 30 more minutes before wrapping in plastic and placing it in the fridge overnight.

8 The next day, preheat the oven to 375°F (190°C). Prepare the loaf pans with a light coat of nonstick baking spray.

9 Divide the brioche dough in half and pat each into a rectangle with a width of roughly 9 inches (23cm). Tightly roll up the dough so that you have a cylinder loaf and place in the prepared pans.

10 Cover each pan with lightly greased plastic wrap. Let rise at room temperature until a slight indent in the dough springs back slowly and halfway (about 1½ to 2 hours).

11 Brush with an egg wash made from whisking together 1 whole egg and 1 egg yolk. Bake for 35 to 40 minutes or until golden brown.

12 Remove from the oven and let cool in the pan for 10 minutes before moving to a baking rack to cool completely.

LEARNING WITH
ENRICHED BREADS

BREAD FLOUR VS. ALL-PURPOSE FLOUR IN BREAD DOUGHS

Try this simple experiment: create two doughs from the same amount of all-purpose and bread flours and enough water to fully hydrate the flours. Knead the dough by hand or in a mixer until it reaches full gluten development and then let it rest. Once rested, knead the dough underwater to wash away all the starches from the dough ball. What remains is a good visual estimation of the gluten-forming potential of each flour. Bread flour has much more gluten-forming protein present. This means it is able to create a stronger dough. This strength is crucial when the number of enrichments in the dough increases. At modest amounts, however, all-purpose flour is nice for a softer and more tender final product.

THE EFFECT OF FAT ON BREAD DOUGH (SEE PHOTO)

In addition to fat offering an unbeatable flavor to bread doughs, it alters the texture of the final loaf. Because fat weakens or shortens (as in shortbread) the gluten strands in the dough, a loaf made with an increased amount of fat will be shorter in height. As long as there is enough protein coming from high-gluten flour and eggs present in the dough, a dough with more fat will be much softer than those with more modest amounts of fat. As the amount of fat increases (in some breads all the way up to an equal weight of flour in the recipe), the importance of developing a strong gluten network before adding the fat is crucial. This is why while the butter is added directly to the Cinnamon Roll dough, its addition is delayed in the Brioche dough.

BOILED AND STEAMED BREADS

A CLOSER LOOK AT BOILED AND STEAMED BREADS

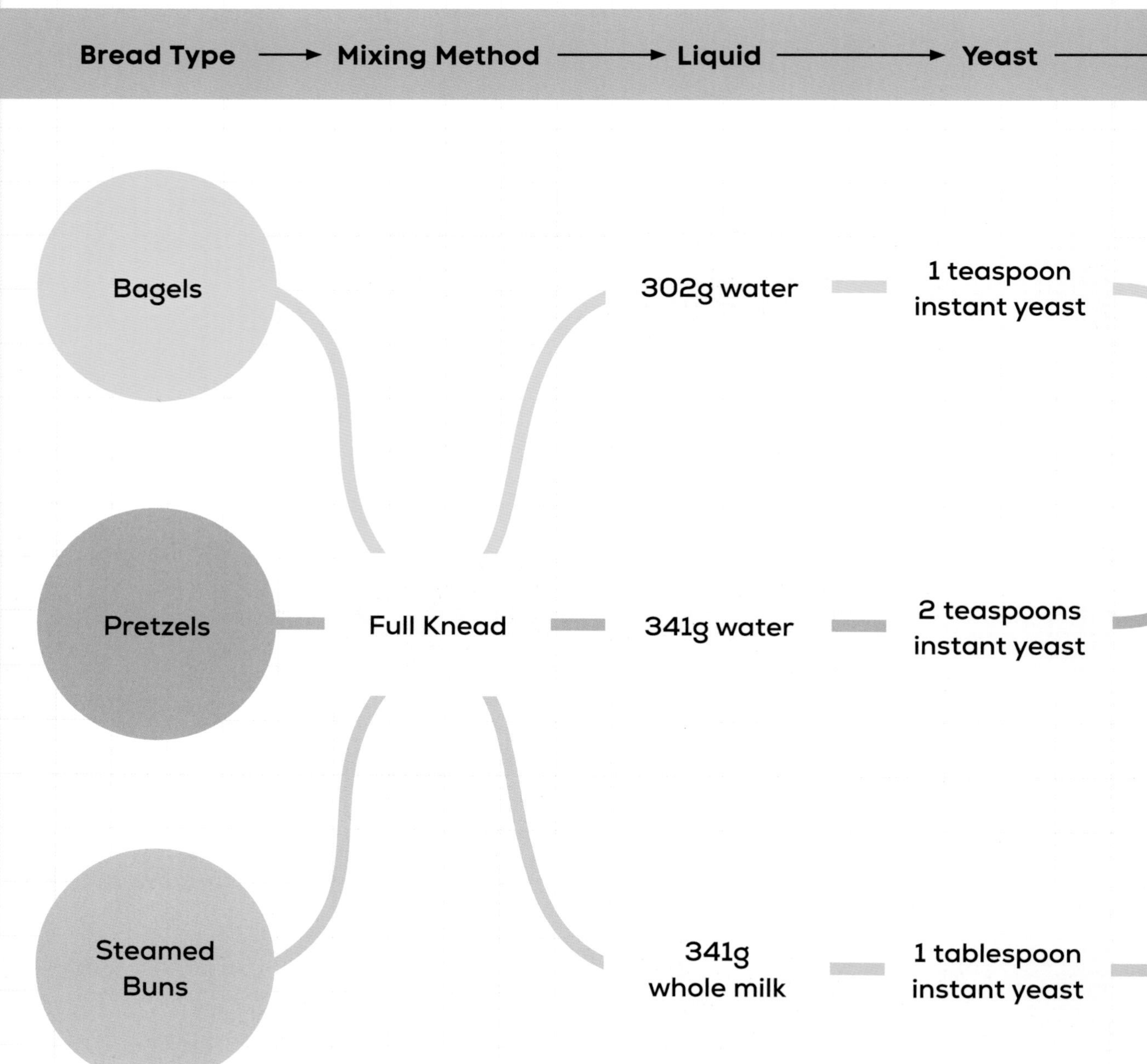

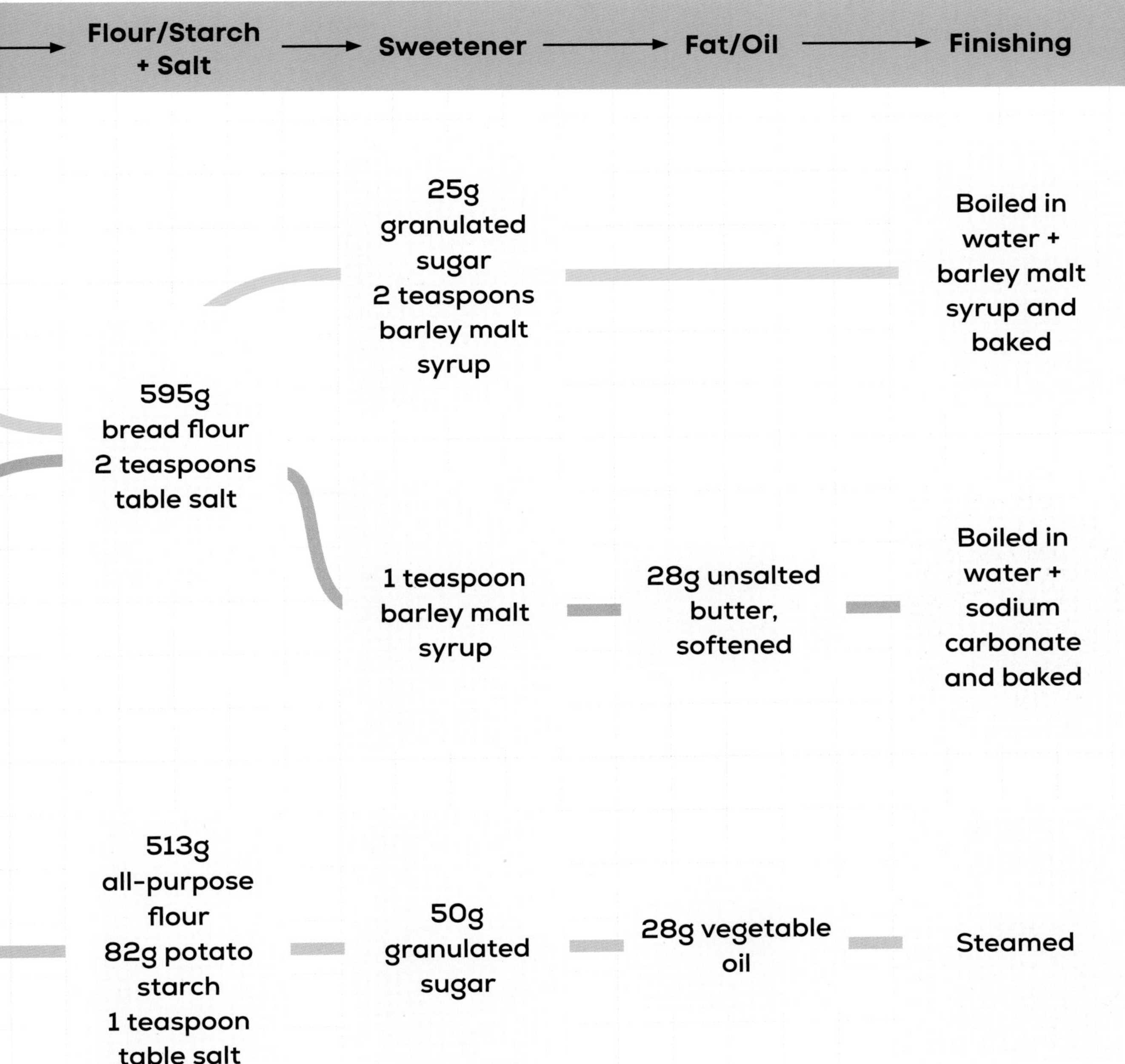
Flour/Starch + Salt
Sweetener
Fat/Oil
Finishing
25g granulated sugar
2 teaspoons barley malt syrup
Boiled in water + barley malt syrup and baked
595g bread flour
2 teaspoons table salt
1 teaspoon barley malt syrup
28g unsalted butter, softened
Boiled in water + sodium carbonate and baked
513g all-purpose flour
82g potato starch
1 teaspoon table salt
50g granulated sugar
28g vegetable oil
Steamed

BAGELS

Mixing Method: Full Knead

Yield: 8 bagels
Prep Time: 30 minutes
Inactive Time: 12 hours
Bake Time: 15 to 20 minutes

Special Equipment

Wide saute pan or Dutch oven

Half sheet pans

Ingredients

1⅓ cups (302g) water

1 teaspoon instant yeast

4¼ cups (595g) bread flour

2 tablespoons (25g) granulated sugar

2 teaspoons barley malt syrup, plus ¼ cup (84g) barley malt syrup for the boiling water

2 teaspoons table salt

½ cup (70g) everything seasoning

Method

1 Follow the Full Knead Method outlined on page 48. Because this is a stiff dough and the mixer may struggle, it is best to knead this dough by hand. In step 4 of the Full Knead Method, divide the dough into 8 equal pieces (approximately 115g each) and shape each piece into a round. Cover with a dish towel and let rest for 15 minutes before the final shape.

2 For the final shape, poke through the center of each round and slowly work your way out to end up with a donut shape.

3 Add 4 bagels to each sheet pan lined with parchment paper and place in the fridge overnight.

4 The next day, preheat the oven to 450°F (230°C) and bring a large pot with 3 quarts of water to a boil. Once the water comes to a boil, whisk in the remaining barley malt syrup and hold the water at a simmer.

5 Working 3 to 4 at a time depending on the size of your pot, add the bagels to the simmering water and cook for 1 minute on each side.

6 Remove from the water, immediately dip into the everything seasoning, and place onto a sheet pan lined with parchment paper that has been sprayed with nonstick baking spray. Space 4 bagels on each half sheet.

7 Bake for 15 to 20 minutes or until golden brown.

8 Remove from the oven and place on a baking rack to cool completely.

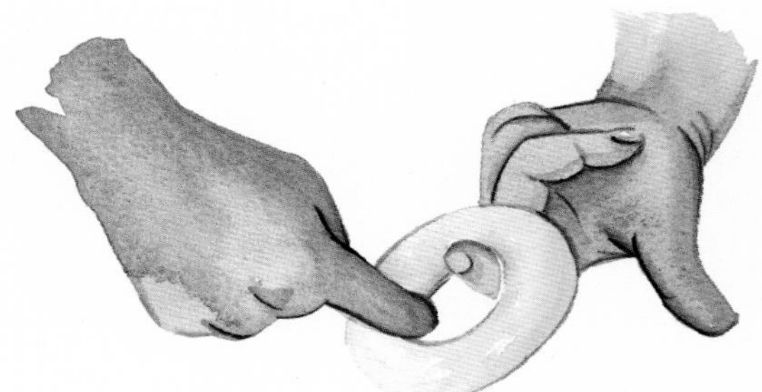

PRETZELS

Mixing Method: Full Knead

Yield: 10 pretzels
Prep Time: 1 hour
Inactive Time: 12 hours
Bake Time: 15 to 20 minutes

Special Equipment

Stand mixer with the hook attachment, optional

Wide saute pan or Dutch oven

Half sheet pans

Ingredients

1½ cups (341g) water

2 teaspoons instant yeast

4¼ cups (595g) bread flour

2 tablespoons (28g) unsalted butter, softened

1 teaspoon barley malt syrup

2 teaspoons table salt

½ cup (32g) baking soda, baked*

Coarse salt for sprinkling on top

Method

1. Make the dough following the Full Knead Method outlined on page 48. Perform step 3 of the Full Knead Method in the refrigerator overnight.
2. The next day, remove the dough from the fridge, deflate, and divide into 10 equal portions (approximately 95g each). Shape into a pretzel.
3. Cover the pretzels loosely with greased plastic wrap and let rise for 1 to 1½ hours or until puffy (they will not double in size).
4. While the pretzels rise, preheat the oven to 450°F (230°C) and bring a large pot with 3 quarts of water to a boil. Once the water comes to a boil, whisk in the baked baking soda and hold the water at a simmer.
5. Working three to four at a time depending on the size of your pot, add the pretzels to the simmering water and cook for one minute on each side.
6. Move the pretzels to a half sheet pan lined with parchment paper that has been sprayed with nonstick baking spray. Space 5 pretzels on each half sheet.
7. Sprinkle the tops with coarse salt and bake for 15 to 20 minutes or until a deep golden brown.
8. Remove from the oven and place on a baking rack to cool completely.

*add the baking soda to a sheet pan lined with parchment paper and spread in a thin layer. Bake at 350°F (170°C) for 90 minutes. Be careful when handling.

STEAMED BUNS

Mixing Method: Full Knead

Yield: 16 buns
Prep Time: 30 minutes
Inactive Time: 2 hours
Steam Time: 25 minutes

Special Equipment

Saucepan
Steamer basket

Ingredients

1½ cups (341g) water

1 tablespoon instant yeast

3¾ cups (525g) bread flour

⅓ cup plus 2 tablespoons (70g) potato starch

½ cup (100g) granulated sugar

2 tablespoons (28g) vegetable oil

2 teaspoons table salt

Method

1. Follow the Full Knead Method outlined on page 48. In step 4 of the Full Knead Method, the dough should be divided into 16 equal pieces (approximately 65g each) and shaped into rounds. Place each round in the center of a small circle of parchment paper so that there is a ¾ inch (2cm) ring of parchment all the way around.
2. While the dough balls rise to one and a half to two times their size in step 5 of the Full Knead method, bring a saucepan of water to a boil. Once the water is at a boil, turn down the heat to medium to medium-low.
3. Add the risen buns to a steamer basket so that they have approximately 2 inches (5cm) between them.
4. Steam for 25 minutes. When time is up, turn off the heat, and leave the steamer on top of the saucepan. Wait an additional 5 minutes before opening the lid.

LEARNING WITH

NOT JUST BAKED BREADS

THE EFFECT OF BOILING

One of the most important steps in traditional bagel making is boiling the dough in a solution of water and just a little barley malt syrup right before baking. This boiling helps pre-gelatinize the starches in the crust and coats the exterior in a thin layer of this sugar. Once baked, this leads to a glossy exterior even without egg wash. More importantly, boiling a bagel before baking prevents the dough from expanding when baked. The result is a characteristically dense and chewy bagel that differentiates itself from a lighter and fluffier bread roll.

THE EFFECT OF AN ALKALINE BATH (SEE PHOTO)

Traditional pretzels are made by dipping each pretzel in a lye solution right before baking. This extremely alkaline solution coats the exterior of the pretzel and encourages deep browning when baking. But the very property that makes lye such a good browner of pretzels makes it dangerous to deal with at home. Alkaline burns can result from improperly handling lye, and they are painful. As a home replacement, I suggest boiling the pretzels in a baked baking soda solution. Baking the baking soda beforehand raises its pH and gets it closer to the use of lye in commercial kitchens. Be sure to follow the proper precautions when working with the baked baking soda, even though it's not as dangerous as lye.

LAMINATED BREADS

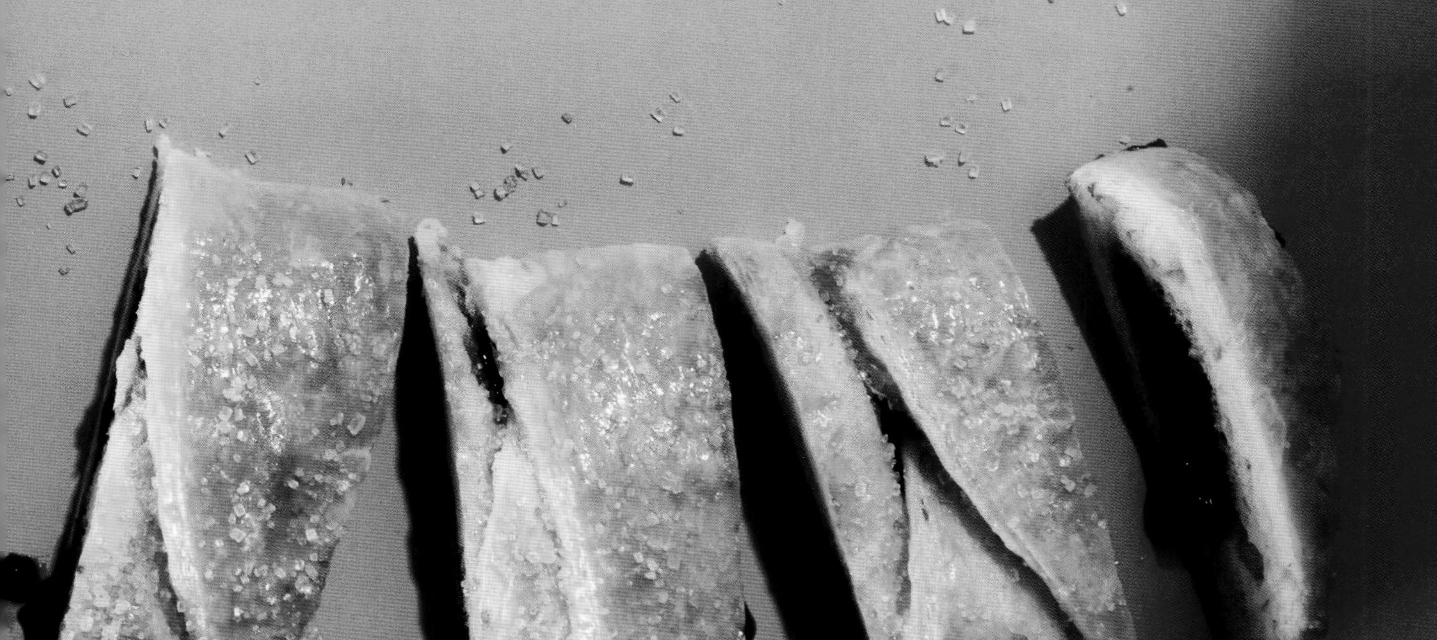

A CLOSER LOOK AT LAMINATED BREADS

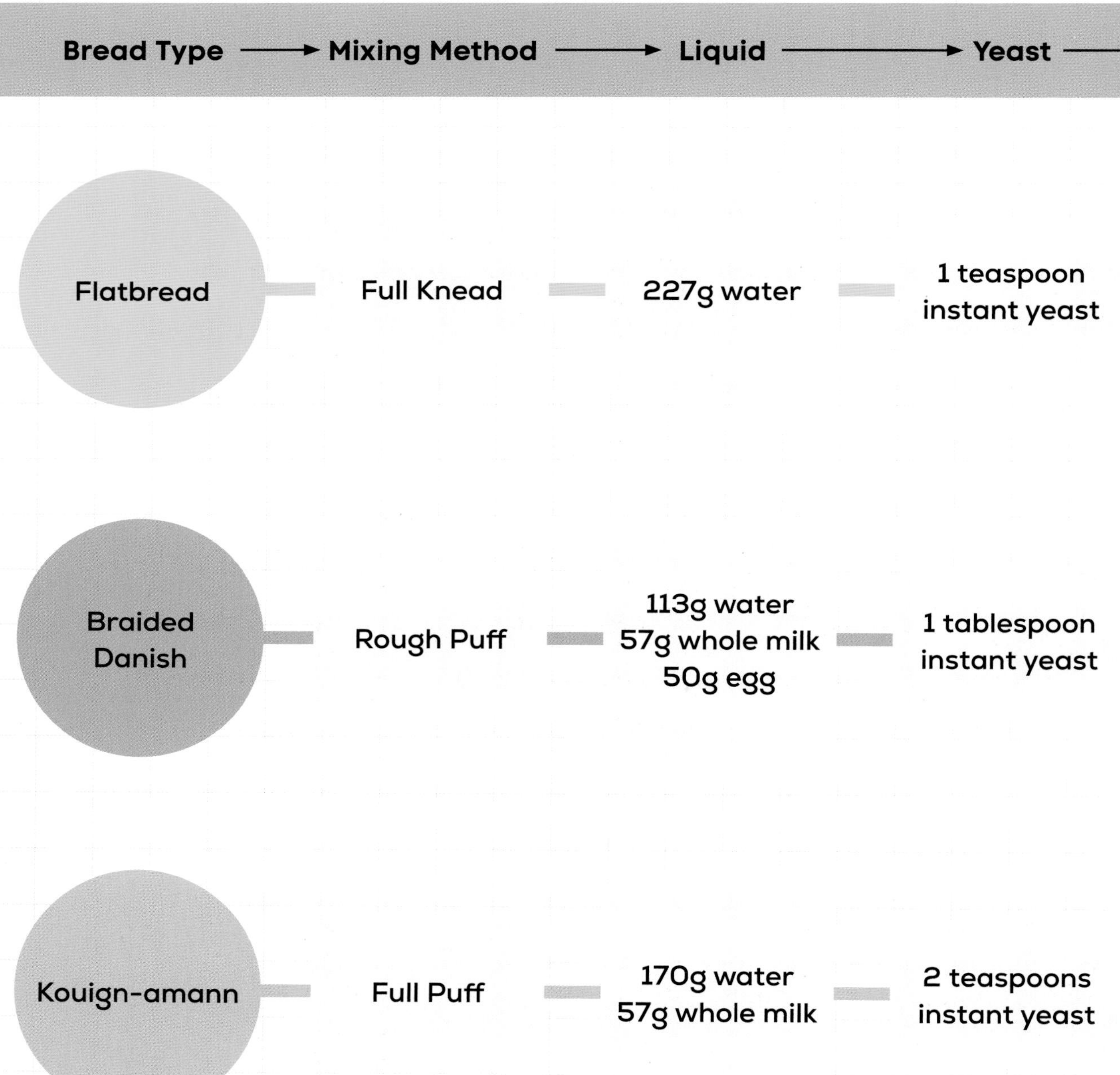

Bread Type	Mixing Method	Liquid	Yeast
Flatbread	Full Knead	227g water	1 teaspoon instant yeast
Braided Danish	Rough Puff	113g water 57g whole milk 50g egg	1 tablespoon instant yeast
Kouign-amann	Full Puff	170g water 57g whole milk	2 teaspoons instant yeast

Flour + Salt	Sugar	Butter
350g bread flour 1 teaspoon table salt	25g granulated sugar	113g unsalted European-style butter, softened for lamination
350g all-purpose flour 1 teaspoon table salt	50g granulated sugar	227g unsalted European-style butter, cold and cut into ½ inch (1cm) cubes for lamination
70g all-purpose flour 280g bread flour 1 teaspoon table salt	200g sugar	43g unsalted European-style butter for the dough, plus 184g cold and rolled into a block for lamination

LAMINATED FLATBREAD

Mixing Method: Full Knead

Yield: 4 flatbreads
Prep Time: 1 hour
Inactive Time: 1 hour
Cook Time: 10 minutes

Special Equipment

Stand mixer with the hook attachment, optional

10-inch (25cm) cast-iron skillet

Ruler

Ingredients

1 cup (227g) water

1 teaspoon instant yeast

2½ cups (350g) bread flour

2 tablespoons (25g) granulated sugar

1 teaspoon table salt

1 stick (113g) unsalted European-style butter, softened

Method

1 Make the dough following the Full Knead Method outlined on page 48, reserving the butter for lamination later on. Stop after step 3 in the Full Knead Method and continue below.

2 After the dough has risen, divide into 4 equal portions (approximately 150g each).

3 Beginning with one piece of dough, roll out on an oiled work surface until the dough is as thin as possible without tearing (don't worry about the shape of the dough yet).

4 Spread 2 tablespoons (28g) of the softened butter all over the surface of the dough and then roll it up like a cinnamon bun. Working along the length of the tube you just created, roll up one more time to create a snail shape, tucking the tail of the dough underneath the dough ball created. Set aside. Repeat with the remaining dough portions.

5 Go back to the first portion of dough, flatten the round, and, on an oiled work surface, roll into a circle with a diameter of 10 inches (20cm). Cover and repeat with the remaining rounds.

6 Preheat a skillet over medium heat. Once the pan is hot, add one flatbread and cook for 8 to 10 minutes, flipping halfway through. The final flatbread should have golden brown spots across its surface.

7 Remove to a baking rack to cool completely and continue with the remaining flatbreads.

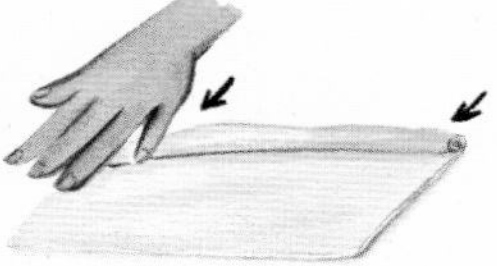

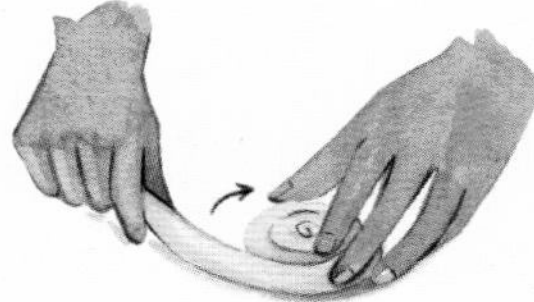

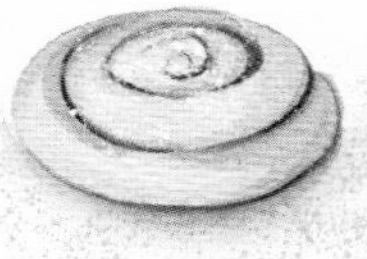

BRAIDED DANISH

Mixing Method: Rough Puff

Yield: Two Danish braids
Prep Time: 2 hours
Inactive Time: 12 hours
Bake Time: 20 to 25 minutes

Special Equipment

Rolling Pin
Ruler
Half sheet pans

Ingredients

½ cup plus 1 tablespoon (120g) water

¼ cup (57g) whole milk

1 egg

1 tablespoon instant yeast

2½ cups (350g) all-purpose flour

¼ cup (50g) granulated sugar

1 teaspoon table salt

8 ounces (227g) unsalted European-style butter, cold and cut into ½-inch (1cm) cubes

1 batch Banana Cream Pie filling (minus the bananas) (page 146)

1 cup (340g) fruit jam

1 large egg, beaten for egg wash

1 batch Honey Syrup (page 292)

Coarse sugar for sprinkling on top, optional

Method

1. Make the dough following the Rough Puff Method on page 54, extending step 4 to a full 12 hours in the fridge.
2. Complete 4 total rolls and folds, refrigerating the dough for 30 minutes after each pair of folds.
3. After completing all 4 folds and a 30 minute rest in the fridge, divide the dough in two, moving half to a lightly floured work surface and leaving the other half in the fridge.
4. Roll the dough out into a rectangle with dimensions approximately 10×14 inches (25×36cm). Move the dough to a half sheet pan that has been lined with a sheet of parchment paper.
5. Repeat with the other half of the dough.
6. Looking at the dough perpendicular to the long edge and imagining that the dough is in thirds, use a knife or pastry wheel to cut strips in the left third and right third of the dough every 2 inches (5cm).
7. Line the center third of the dough first with ½ cup of the vanilla cream pie filling, and then with ½ cup of fruit jam on top of the cream.
8. Braid the danish by bringing the strips on the right and left into the center, alternating from right to left to create an almost zipper-like pattern.
9. Loosely cover each Danish with greased plastic wrap and preheat the oven to 375°F (190°C).
10. Let the danishes sit at room temperature for 45 minutes or until just puffy (they will not double in size).
11. Brush with egg wash and bake for 20 to 25 minutes or until golden brown.
12. Remove from the oven and immediately brush with honey syrup and optionally sprinkle with coarse sugar.
13. Let cool on the pan for 10 minutes before moving to a baking rack to cool completely.

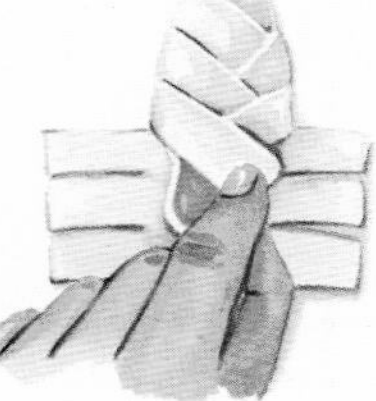

KOUIGN-AMANN

Mixing Method: Full Puff

Yield: 12 Kouign-amann
Prep Time: 1 hour
Inactive Time: 12 hours
Bake Time: 30 to 40 minutes

Special Equipment

Rolling pin

Ruler

12-cup muffin tin

Ingredients

¾ cup (170g) water

¼ cup (57g) whole milk

2 teaspoons instant yeast

½ cup plus 1 tablespoon (70g) all-purpose flour

2 cups (280g) bread flour

3 tablespoons (43g) unsalted European-style butter, softened

1 teaspoon table salt

13 tablespoons (184g) unsalted European-style butter, cold for lamination

1 cup (200g) granulated sugar, for lamination

4 tablespoons (57g) unsalted butter, softened for the pan

½ cup (100g) granulated sugar, for the pan

Method

1. Make the dough following the Full Puff Method on page 55 with the following adjustments: In step 1, knead the dough until the dough passes the windowpane test (see page 50) (approximately 7 to 10 minutes by machine or 12 to 15 minutes by hand). In between steps 1 and 2, let the dough sit out at room temperature until doubled in size (approximately 1 to 1½ hours). In step 9, complete a total of 4 folds, refrigerating the dough after the first two folds and again after the third fold. During the last fold, sprinkle half of the sugar on the work surface instead of using flour and sprinkle the remaining sugar over the top of the dough before folding up. Skip step 10.
2. Preheat the oven to 375°F (190°C) and prepare a muffin pan with softened butter and a coating of sugar.
3. Immediately after the last fold, roll the dough out one more time in the remaining sugar that didn't find its way into the dough during the last fold. Roll out into a rectangle that is ¼ inch (6mm) thick. Roll the rectangle up like a cinnamon roll and cut into 12 equal pieces.
4. Distribute the pieces into the muffin cups and cover loosely with greased plastic wrap.
5. Let rise at room temperature for 20 to 30 minutes or until puffy (they will not double in size).
6. Bake for 30 to 40 minutes or until golden brown.
7. Remove from the oven and let cool for 5 minutes before moving to a baking rack to cool completely.

LEARNING WITH

LAMINATED BREADS

HOW THE BUTTER IS INCORPORATED (SEE PHOTO)

Layers of fat and dough create flakiness as the dough is not able to completely bind to itself. The degree to which there is full or partial separation between the layers of dough depends on the state of the butter during lamination. A solid block of butter creates the most separation between each layer of dough, while using softened butter creates the least. Some of this softened butter is absorbed into the dough and as a result the difference between layers is not as apparent. Using solid butter also allows the liquid in the butter to evaporate, creating steam that further helps the puff and separation between the sheets of dough.

THE IMPACT OF THE NUMBER OF FOLDS

As the number of folds increases, so too does the number of layers. Depending on the type of fold (single or double/letter or book) and the number of folds, the separation between the layers will be more or less dramatic. With just a few folds, there are thick sheets of butter separating the layers of dough. This can cause some of the butter to leak out when baking and result in a final product with a modest rise. On the other hand, folding the dough too many times creates layers of butter so thin that they become almost indistinguishable from the dough. At this point you have created an almost brioche-like dough with an extremely tender texture that lacks flakiness.

GANACHE

A CLOSER LOOK AT GANACHE

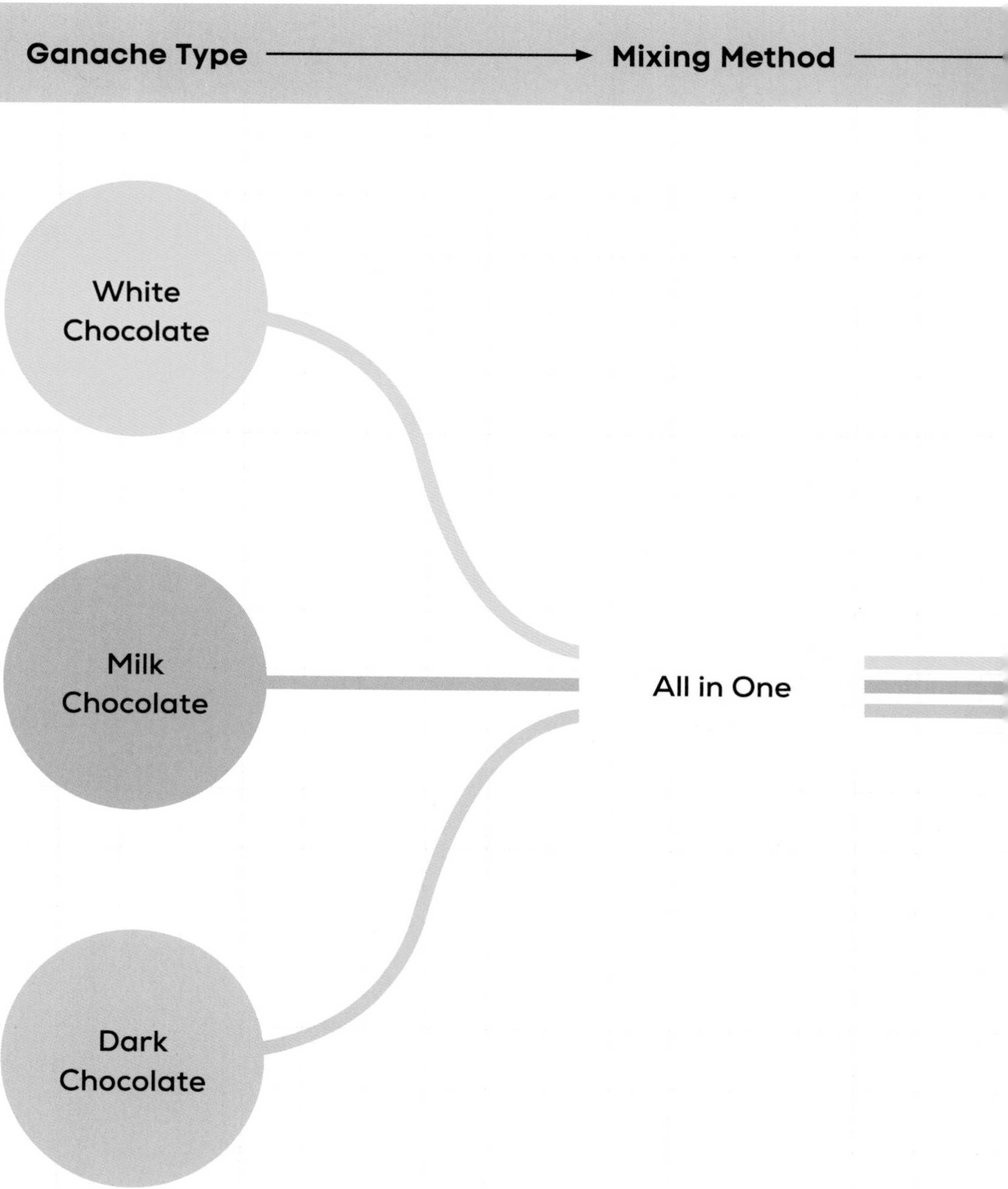

Ganache Type ⟶ Mixing Method ⟶

White Chocolate

Milk Chocolate

Dark Chocolate

All in One

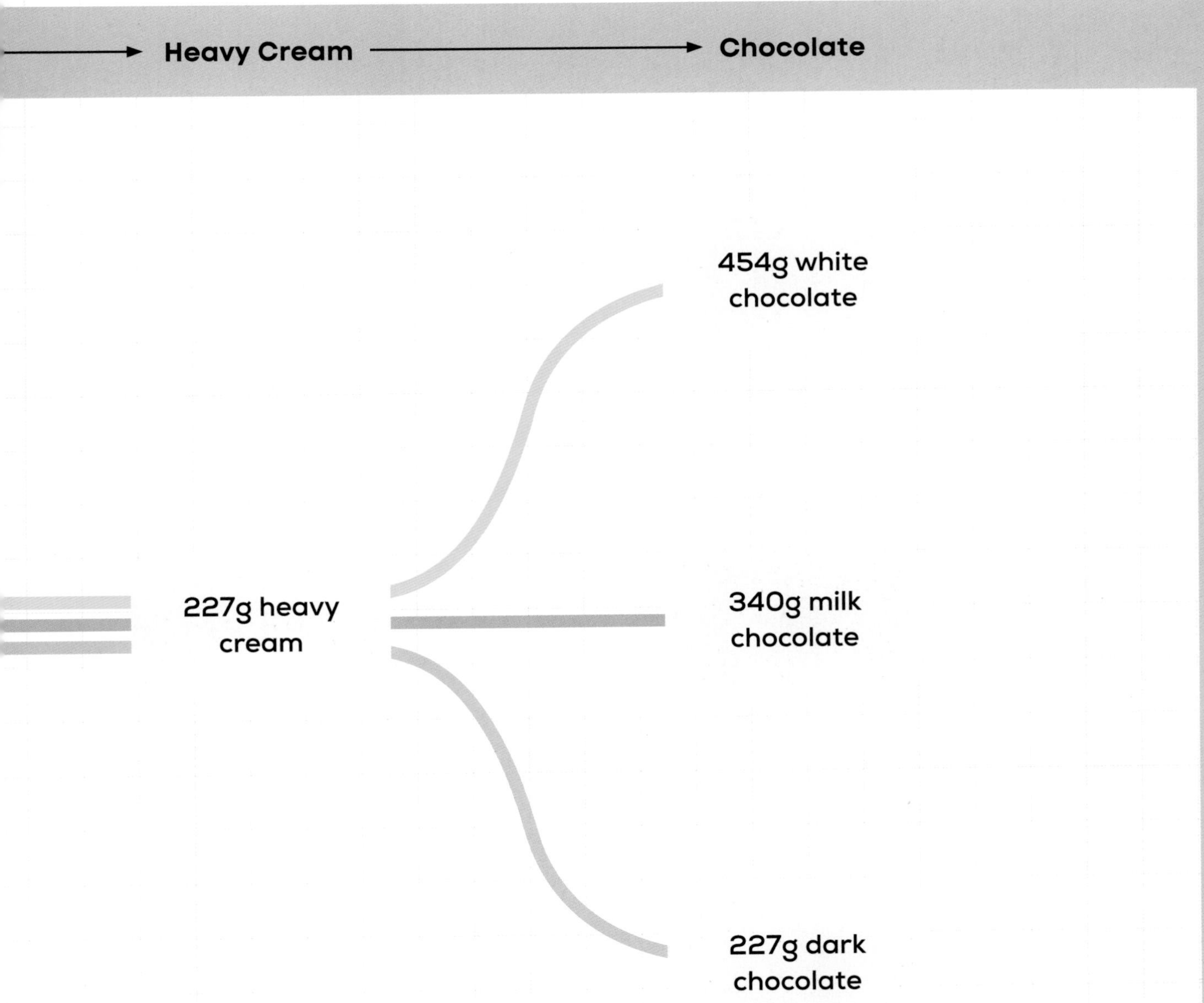

Heavy Cream → Chocolate

227g heavy cream

454g white chocolate

340g milk chocolate

227g dark chocolate

WHITE CHOCOLATE GANACHE

Mixing Method: All in One

Yield: 2½ cups
Prep Time: 15 minutes

Special Equipment

Saucepan

Ingredients

1 cup (227g) heavy cream

16 ounces (454g) white chocolate, chopped fine

Method

1. Heat the heavy cream until it just comes to a simmer.
2. Remove the saucepan from the heat and add the chocolate to the pot. Let sit for 2 minutes.
3. Using a spatula, begin in the center and stir in tight circles until the ganache starts to come together. As it comes together, widen your circles and continue stirring until the ganache is an even texture.

MILK CHOCOLATE GANACHE

Mixing Method: All in One

Yield: 2¼ cups
Prep Time: 15 minutes

Special Equipment

Saucepan

Ingredients

1 cup (227g) heavy cream

12 ounces (340g) milk chocolate, finely chopped

Method

1 Heat the heavy cream until it just comes to a simmer.

2 Add the chocolate to a heatproof bowl and pour the cream over top. Let sit for 2 minutes.

3 Using a spatula, begin in the center and stir in tight circles until the ganache starts to come together. As it comes together, widen your circles and continue stirring until the ganache is an even texture.

DARK CHOCOLATE GANACHE

Mixing Method: All in One

Yield: 2 cups
Prep Time: 15 minutes

Special Equipment

Saucepan

Ingredients

1 cup (227g) heavy cream

8 ounces (227g) dark chocolate, finely chopped

Method

1. Heat the heavy cream until it just comes to a simmer.
2. Add the chocolate to a heatproof bowl and pour the cream over top. Let the chocolate sit for 2 minutes.
3. Using a spatula, begin in the center and stir in tight circles until the ganache starts to come together. As it comes together, widen your circles and continue stirring until the ganache is an even texture.

LEARNING WITH
GANACHE

THE RATIO OF CHOCOLATE TO CREAM (SEE PHOTO)

Depending on the amount of cocoa mass and sugar in a bar of chocolate, you will have to adjust the amount of cream added to the ganache to get a similar consistency. With the most cocoa mass and least amount of added sugar, dark chocolate needs the least amount of chocolate to cream for a ganache sauce that has just enough viscosity to settle on top of your dessert. Adjust any of these ratios to create a whipped ganache filling. Double the amount of cream in each ganache and once the mixture has come together, refrigerate overnight. The next day, whip the ganache in a stand mixer with the whisk attachment until soft peaks form. On the other hand, increase the amount of chocolate relative to cream and you will end up with a thicker ganache that is suitable for piping on desserts.

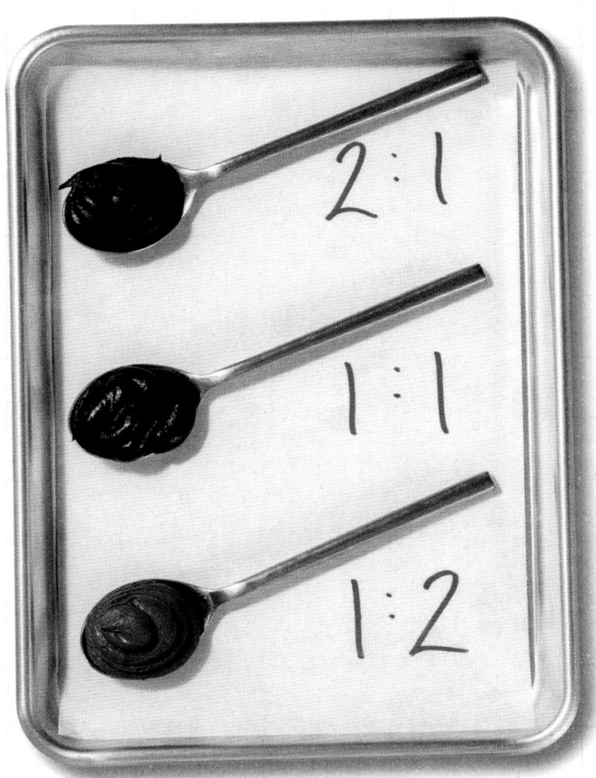

SAVING A BROKEN GANACHE

Ganache is a delicate emulsion of fat and water. Depending on temperature and the amount of each ingredient, this emulsion can break and the ganache can become grainy. In many of these instances, the ganache can be saved by gently warming it over a hot water bath while whisking continuously. If that does not work, the ganache may need more liquid (without much added fat) in order to come together. Add a tablespoon or two of warmed milk at a time and whisk continuously in order for the ganache to come together.

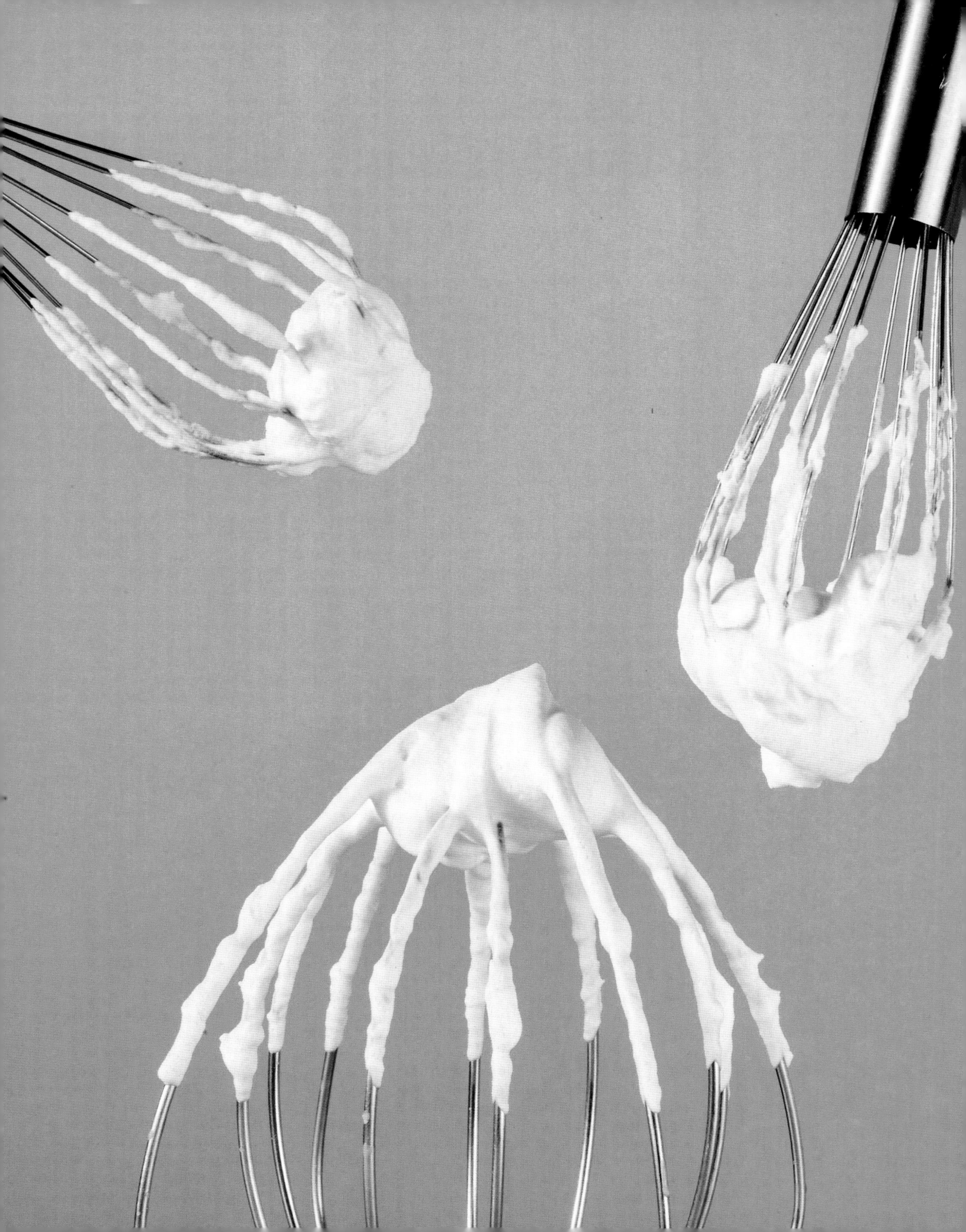

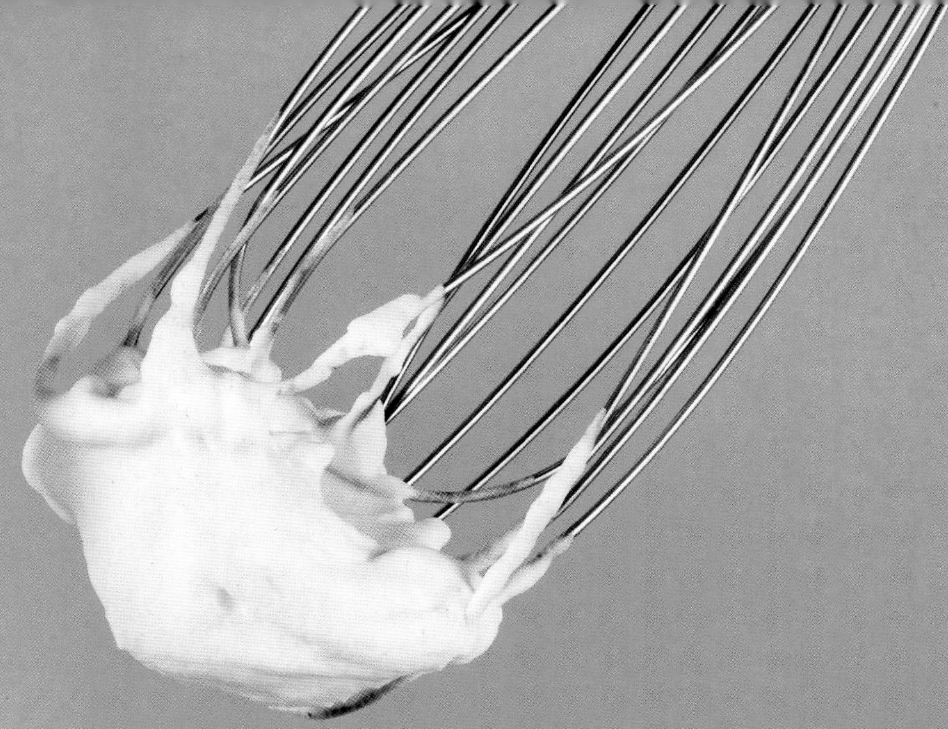

WHIPPED CREAMS

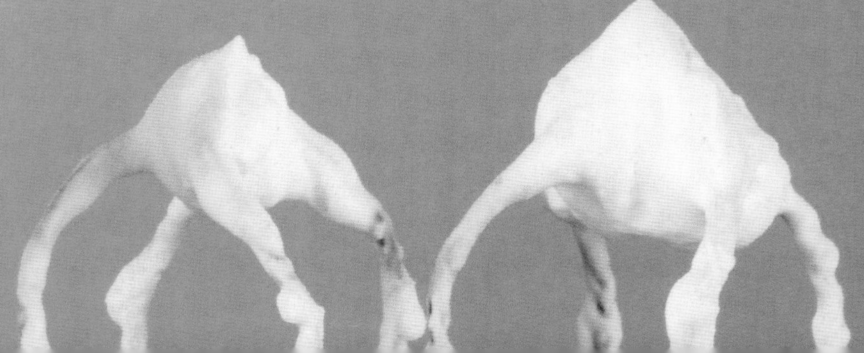

A CLOSER LOOK AT WHIPPED CREAMS

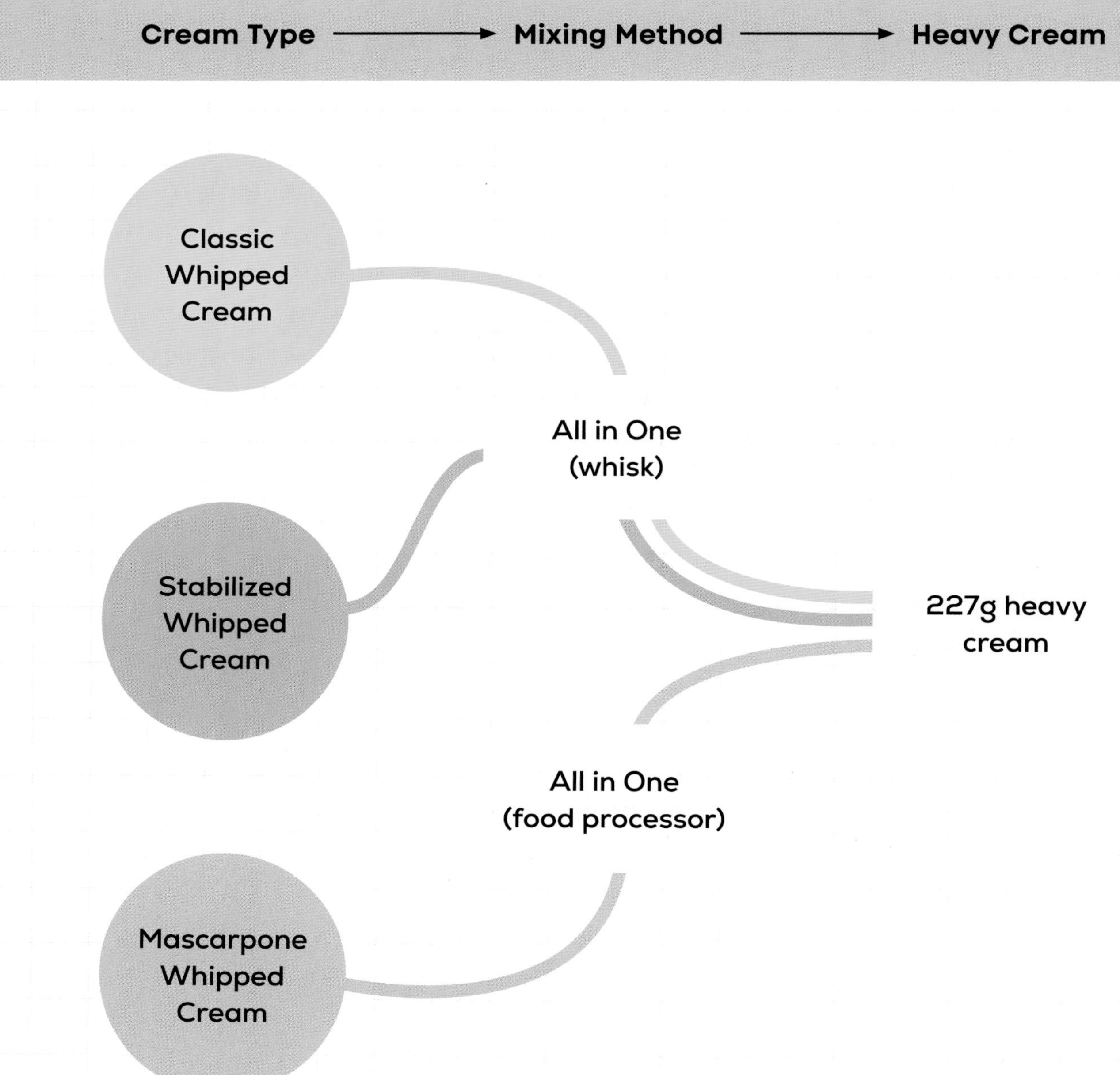

28g powdered sugar

¾ teaspoon powdered gelatin

227g mascarpone cheese

1 teaspoon vanilla extract
Pinch of table salt

CLASSIC WHIPPED CREAM

Mixing Method: All in One

Yield: 2 cups
Prep Time: 10 minutes

Special Equipment

Stand mixer with the whisk attachment

Ingredients

1 cup (227g) heavy cream

¼ cup (28g) powdered sugar, sifted

1 teaspoon vanilla extract

Pinch of table salt

Method

1. Add all the ingredients to the bowl of a stand mixer and whisk on medium-low speed until foamy (approximately 1 to 2 minutes).
2. Increase the speed of the mixer to medium and continue whisking until medium to stiff peaks form (approximately 2 to 4 more minutes).

STABILIZED WHIPPED CREAM

Mixing Method: All in One

Yield: 2 cups

Prep Time: 15 minutes

Special Equipment

Stand mixer with the whisk attachment

Ingredients

¾ teaspoon powdered gelatin

1 tablespoon water

1 cup (227g) heavy cream

¼ cup (28g) powdered sugar, sifted

1 teaspoon vanilla extract

Pinch of table salt

Method

1 Mix the gelatin and water together and set aside for 5 minutes. After 5 minutes, melt the gelatin mixture over a hot water bath. Once completely melted, stir 2 tablespoons of the cream into the gelatin mixture.

2 Add the leftover cream and all the remaining ingredients to the bowl of a stand mixer.

3 Whisk on medium-low speed until foamy (approximately 1 to 2 minutes). Increase the speed of the mixer to medium and continue whisking until soft peaks form (approximately 2 to 4 more minutes). With the mixer running, pour the gelatin mixture in and continue whipping until medium peaks form (approximately 1 to 3 more minutes).

MASCARPONE WHIPPED CREAM

Mixing Method: All in One

Yield: 2½ cups

Prep Time: 10 minutes

Special Equipment

Food processor

Ingredients

1 cup (227g) heavy cream

¼ cup (28g) powdered sugar, sifted

8 ounces (227g) mascarpone cheese

1 teaspoon vanilla extract

Pinch of table salt

Method

1 Add all the ingredients to a food processor and pulse until thickened and medium to stiff peaks form (approximately 3 to 5 minutes).

LEARNING WITH
WHIPPED CREAM

THE IMPORTANCE OF A CHILLED BOWL (SEE PHOTO)

Whipped cream whips because the high amount of fat in the heavy cream clumps together and holds onto the air. Crucial in this procedure is the temperature of the fat: it must be cold enough to hold on to this air. As the cream warms up to room temperature and beyond, the fat softens and resists its former air-catching properties.

WHISK VS. FOOD PROCESSOR (SEE PHOTO)

For a fluffy whipped cream with the greatest possible aeration, use a whisk. The tines of a whisk disrupt the fat globules in the cream and form large bubbles. Add the cream to a food processor, though, and the amount of air incorporated is not the same. The blade of a food processor can't create the same amount of aeration and large bubbles. Instead, there are multiple small bubbles that give a denser and more stable foam.

SAUCES

A CLOSER LOOK AT SAUCES

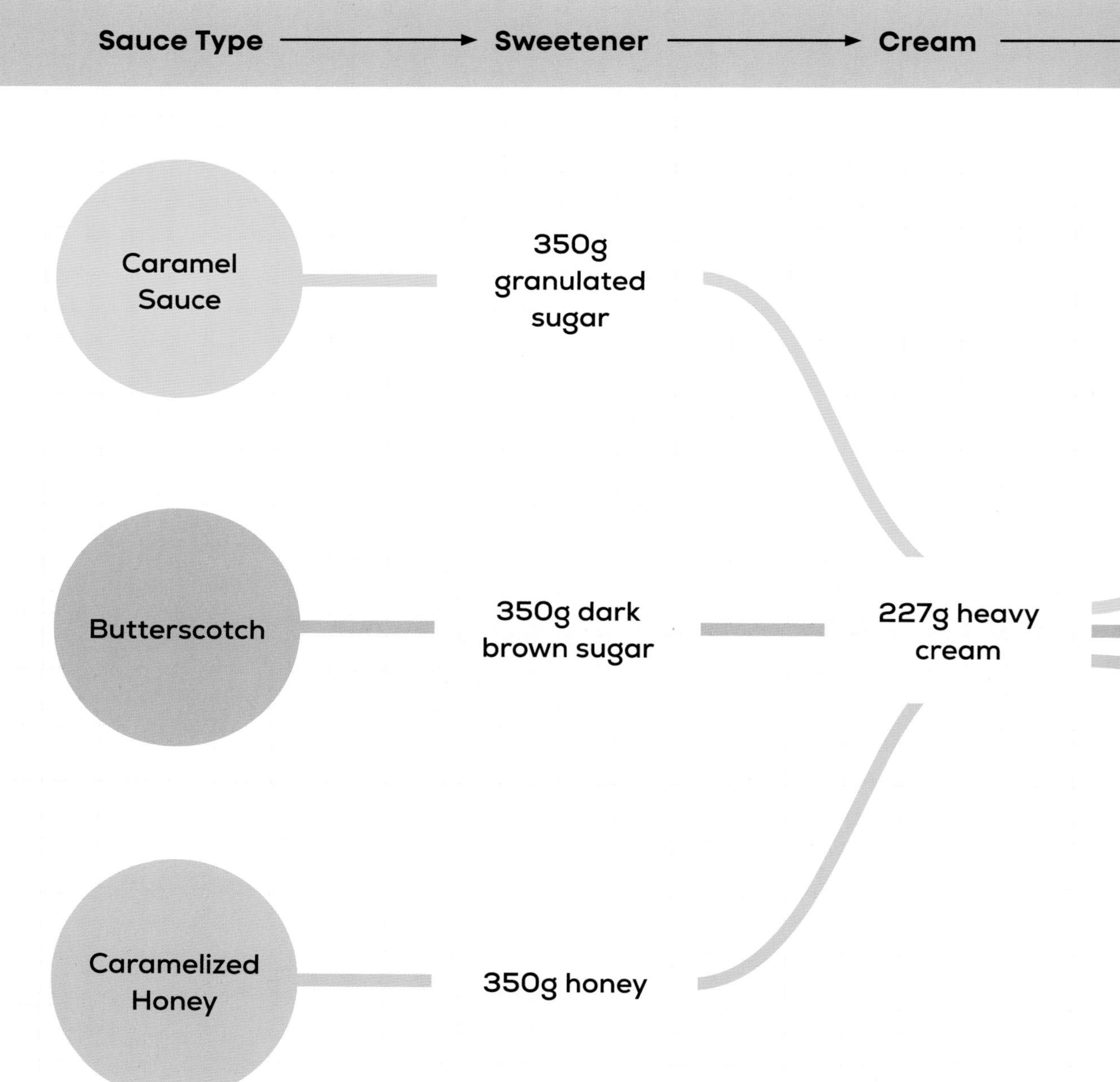

28g unsalted butter

57g unsalted butter

1 teaspoon table salt
1 teaspoon vanilla extract

CARAMEL SAUCE

Mixing Method: All in One

Yield: 2½ cups
Prep Time: 20 minutes

Special Equipment

Saucepan

Ingredients

1¾ cups (350g) granulated sugar

¼ cup (57g) water

1 cup (227g) heavy cream, warmed

2 tablespoons (28g) unsalted butter

½ teaspoon table salt

1 teaspoon vanilla extract

Method

1. Add the granulated sugar and water to a saucepan and set over medium heat. Leave undisturbed to cook until the sugar caramelizes and begins to turn a light amber color (approximately 5 to 10 minutes).
2. Lift the saucepan and swirl to evenly distribute the caramel in the pan. Continue cooking the caramel until it turns a deep amber color (approximately 1 to 3 more minutes)
3. Remove from the heat and slowly and carefully whisk in the cream. Add just a few tablespoons at a time at first. The mixture will bubble up, so make sure you're using a saucepan with plenty of space above the surface of the caramel.
4. Finish by whisking in the butter, salt, and vanilla. Serve warm.

BUTTERSCOTCH SAUCE

Mixing Method: All in One

Yield: 2½ cups
Prep Time: 20 minutes

Special Equipment

Saucepan

Ingredients

1¾ cups (350g) dark brown sugar

4 tablespoons (57g) unsalted butter

1 cup (227g) heavy cream, warmed

½ teaspoon table salt

1 teaspoon vanilla extract

Method

1. Add the sugar and butter to a saucepan and set over medium heat. Cook until the butter melts and the mixture comes to a boil (approximately 3 to 5 minutes). While whisking continuously, boil for a full 2 minutes.
2. Remove from the heat and slowly and carefully whisk in the cream. Add just a few tablespoons at a time at first. The mixture will bubble up, so make sure you're using a saucepan with plenty of space above the surface of the butterscotch.
3. Finish by whisking in the salt and vanilla. Serve warm.

CARAMELIZED HONEY SAUCE

Mixing Method: All in One

Yield: 2½ cups
Prep Time: 20 minutes

Special Equipment

Saucepan

Ingredients

1 cup (350g) honey

¼ cup (57g) water

1 cup (227g) heavy cream, warmed

½ teaspoon table salt

1 teaspoon vanilla extract

Method

1. Add the honey and water to a saucepan and set over medium heat. Leave undisturbed to cook until the honey caramelizes and turns a deep amber color (approximately 5 to 10 minutes).
2. Remove from the heat and slowly and carefully whisk the cream into the honey. Add just a few tablespoons at a time at first. The mixture will bubble up, so make sure you're using a saucepan with plenty of space above the surface of the honey.
3. Finish by whisking in the salt and vanilla. Serve warm.

LEARNING WITH SAUCES

THE FINAL TEMPERATURE OF YOUR CARAMEL (SEE PHOTO)

The final texture of your caramel is determined by its final temperature. After adding the warmed cream, the temperature of the caramel should be right around 225°F (107°C). This will give a caramel that, when cooled, will be smooth and will easily flow off of a spoon. For a thicker caramel, continue to cook until it reaches 240°F (115°C). The final texture this time will be thicker and fall off the spoon in ribbons. For an even thinner caramel, add more cream so that the final temperature is below 225°F (107°C). For an even thicker caramel that holds its shape, cook beyond 240°F (115°C). When at your desired temperature, finish with butter, salt, and vanilla for a classic flavor.

PREVENTING CRYSTALLIZATION

Once a syrup of sugar and water comes to a boil, leave the sugar to cook until it starts to caramelize. The reason you don't want to mix it is to prevent crystallization. Crystallization will happen if the syrup is agitated or dry crystals find their way into the pot. This can happen when the syrup splashes onto the sides of the pot, dries, and then this dry sugar finds its way into the rest of the syrup. When it does, it encourages large sugar crystals to form. If this does happen, though, you can still save the caramel. Add more water and heat to dissolve all the sugar crystals before continuing on.

SYRUPS

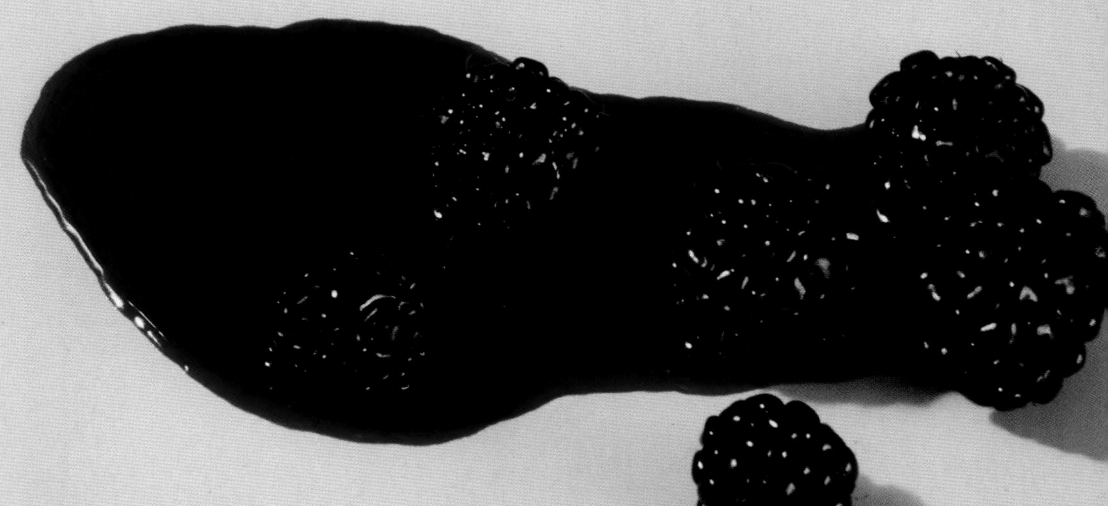

A CLOSER LOOK AT SYRUPS

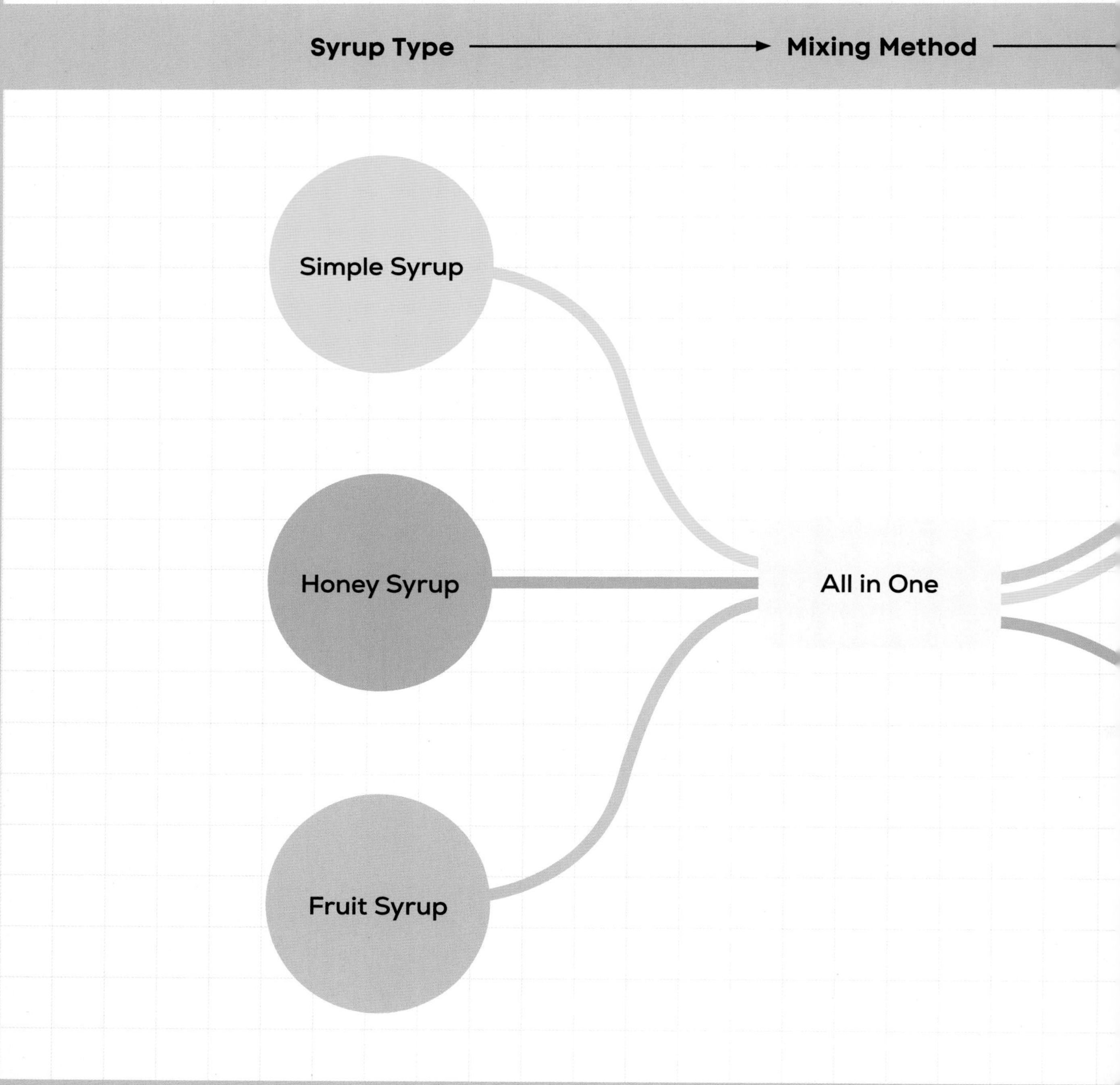

Syrup Type → Mixing Method →

Simple Syrup

Honey Syrup

Fruit Syrup

All in One

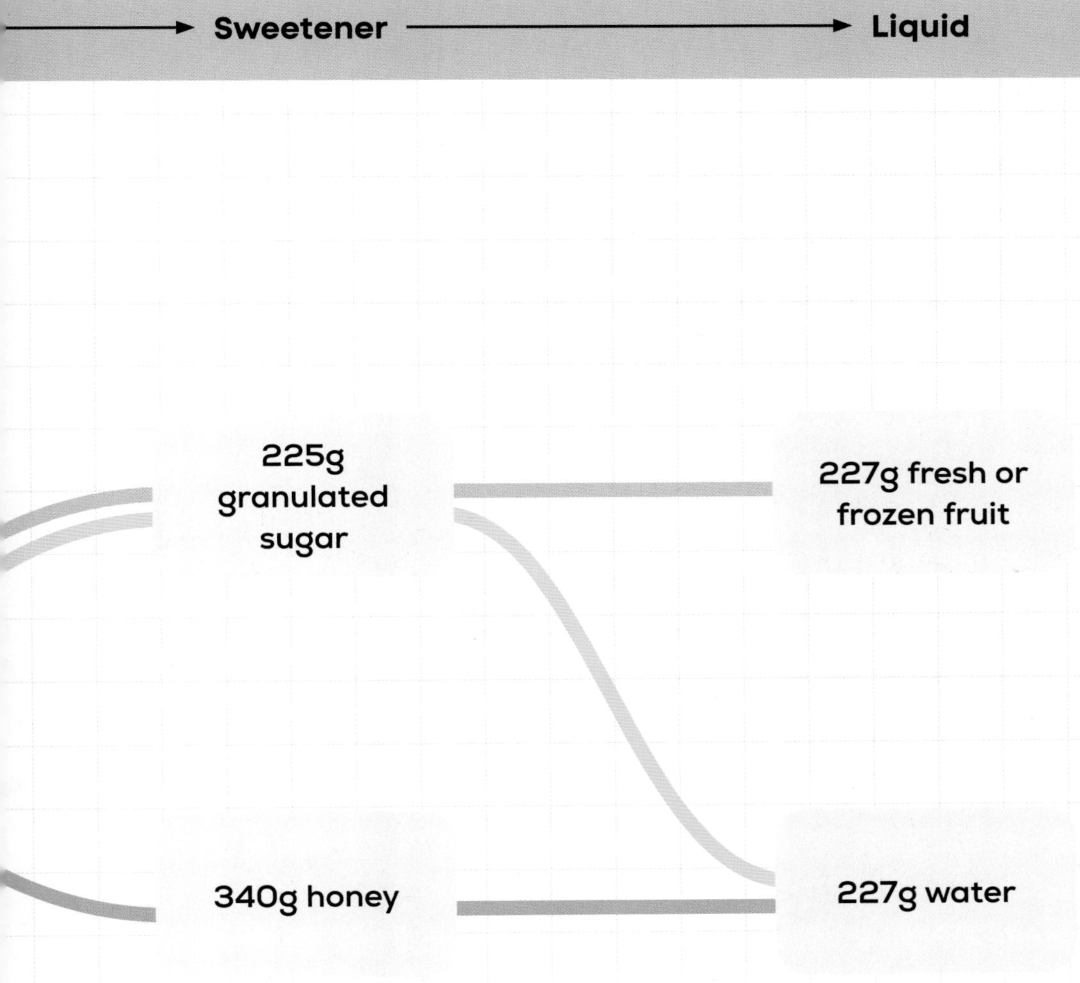

Sweetener → Liquid

225g granulated sugar

227g fresh or frozen fruit

340g honey

227g water

SIMPLE SYRUP

Mixing Method: All in One

Yield: 2 cups
Prep Time: 10 minutes

Special Equipment

Saucepan

Ingredients

1 cup plus 2 tablespoons (225g) granulated sugar

1 cup (227g) water

Method

1 Add all the ingredients to the saucepan and set over medium heat. Cook until the sugar dissolves (approximately 3 to 5 minutes).

HONEY SYRUP

Mixing Method: All in One

Yield: 2 cups
Prep Time: 10 minutes

Special Equipment

Saucepan

Ingredients

1 cup (340g) honey

1 cup (227g) water

Method

1 Add all the ingredients to the saucepan and set over medium heat. Cook until the honey dissolves (approximately 3 to 5 minutes).

FRUIT SYRUP

Mixing Method: All in One

Yield: 2 cups
Prep Time: 30 to 60 minutes

Ingredients

1 cup plus 2 tablespoons (225g) granulated sugar

8 ounces (227g) frozen fruit

Method

1. Stir all the ingredients together in the saucepan and set over low heat on the smallest burner. Cook until the fruit has given up most of its liquid and a syrup has formed (approximately 30 to 60 minutes).
2. Store in the fridge with the fruit and strain before use.

LEARNING WITH SYRUPS

THE RATIO OF SUGAR TO WATER (SEE PHOTO)

A simple syrup, named for its simplicity in ingredients and ratio, is made with an equal weight of sugar and water. It is the most versatile syrup for soaking sponge cakes or brushing pastries, but it is not the only option. Increase the amount of sugar to twice the weight of water to create a heavy syrup. This heavy syrup is a great option for candied citrus peel or ginger. Reverse the ratios and include twice the weight of water compared to sugar for a light syrup that is perfect for poaching whole pieces of fruit. The fruit will become plump and juicy.

FRESH VS. FROZEN FRUIT SYRUP

Most fruits have enough water content to create their own syrup when mixed with sugar alone. I suggest frozen fruit for this syrup for two reasons. Both rely on the changes that happen to the cells in a piece of fruit when frozen. The sharp ice crystals break down the fruit cells and soften the fruit. This means that the fruit is already primed to release its water and mix with the sugar to create a syrup. This also means that a defrosted piece of frozen fruit does not have the same tender texture that a fresh piece of fruit does. For this reason, I like fresh fruit for its texture and frozen for its willingness to give up water.

REFERENCES

Books

Amendola, Joseph, and Nicole Rees. *The Baker's Manual: 150 Master Formulas for Baking.* Wiley, 2003.

Amendola, Joseph, and Nicole Rees *Understanding Baking: The Art and Science of Baking.* Wiley, 2003.

Beranbaum, Rose Levy. *Cake Bible*. William Morrow, 1988.

Brown, Alton. *I'm Just Here for More Food: Food x Mixing + Heat = Baking*. Stewart, Tabori & Chang, 2012.

Corriher, Shirley O. *Bakewise: The Hows and Whys of Successful Baking with over 200 Magnificent Recipes.* Scribner, 2008.

The Culinary Institute of America. *Baking and Pastry: Mastering the Art and Craft.* Wiley, 2016.

El-Waylly, Sohla. *Start Here: Instructions for Becoming a Better Cook.* Alfred A. Knopf, 2023.

Figoni, Paula. How Baking Works: *Exploring the Fundamentals of Baking Science.* Wiley, 2013

Friberg, Bo. *Professional Pastry Chef: Fundamentals of Baking and Pastry.* Wiley, 2013.

Gisslen, Wayne. *Professional Baking*. Wiley, 2022.

Labensky, Sarah R., et al. *On Baking: A Textbook of Baking and Pastry Fundamentals*. Pearson, 2020.

Mcgee, Harold. *On Food and Cooking: The Science and Lore of the Kitchen.* Scribner, 2004.

Myhrvold, Nathan, and Francisco J. Migoya. *Modernist Bread*. The Cooking Lab, 2017.

Ruhlman, Michael. *The Simple Codes behind the Craft of Everyday Cooking.* Simon Spotlight Entertainment, 2010.

Wing, Frank, and Michel Suas. *Advanced Bread and Pastry a Professional Approach.* Delmar Cengage Learning, 2009.

Internet Resources

americastestkitchen.com

cooking.nytimes.com

kingarthurbaking.com

seriouseats.com

INDEX

A

B

C

D

E

F

G

H

I

J

K

L

M

N

O

P

Q

R

S

T

THANK YOU

To Steph, whose appreciation for the beauty of writing inspires me beyond measure. Though there is plenty of math and science in this book, the words on the page might've sounded like they were written by the Cookie Monster if not for your care in editing. Despite your preference for light blue bags of potato chips over emerald green packages of cookies, you never hesitate to taste and analyze each new recipe with me. Quite too many shared cupcake quarters, traded photos of fancy schmancy and turkey cupcakes, and never-ending searches for the perfect cellophane-wrapped supermarket cookie fill a box of my fondest memories. I can't wait for our future trips to bakeries and bookstores with Graham, who will be experiencing the places we love most with brand new eyes. I love you.

To my family. The hours spent at the kitchen table together will always be my favorite memories from growing up. Meatballs and sausages one night, and chicken thighs with bell peppers and onions another. I'm sorry for waking up early to sneak a few Oreos from any of your lunch bags, but I know that we all appreciate the value of dessert...and have done the same. Once we were old enough, our high standards for each other's baked goods always inspired me to keep learning so that no dessert of mine disgracefully made it to the next day. Sharing food and conversation with all of you has shaped me indelibly. Each of you is in this book, in your own way.

To my teachers in bakeries around the country, who always encouraged and indulged my endless baking questions and observations. All those who shared with me everything they know. Jess, Ned, Dylan, TTB, and everyone in Baltimore. What started as carefully cutting at the right notch with a ruler meant only for brownies has become a lifelong love of baking and learning. Karen, Richard, Suzie, Becca, John, Marsha, and everyone in Boston. Away from home, you were and will always be my family. Whether I was making danishes, decorating cakes, or learning how to drive, I am so thankful for your no-questions-asked love and support. Brianna, Megan, Mayra, and everyone in Los Angeles. Adapting to a new coast and new place was tough, but it was your acceptance into the small, corner-separated kitchen that eased my transition and brought me joy.

To the incredible artists that helped make this book come alive. Ryan and Haley, I so appreciate the creative and culinary vision that you brought to each photo. Whether performing a high-wire act of steamed buns and pretzels or capturing an egg yolk mid-flight, you made sure each image was perfect before moving on to the next. Enya. Your illustrations and artistry served as the inspiration for this book years before any conversation with a publisher. To have those same drawings adorn the pages of my book is a dream. Michelle. You tessellated the words and images together in a way that only a geometry teacher could truly appreciate. Thank you for your keen eye.

To my team who helped me realize this incredible opportunity of writing a book. Molly, your belief in me and my concept gave me the extra motivation to elevate my teachings and put them on the page. Your vision and perspective have been invaluable throughout this process, and I am grateful for your patient and measured feedback. Josh, you have stuck with me since the early days when I could only dream of my baking experiments reaching a much larger audience. You have always encouraged me to see the value in what I am doing, and you fight for me so that others see the same. Your support has been instrumental to my success.

To my followers. Your engagement and support for what I do has kept me going. It is never lost on me that my videos could help someone think about baking in a new way or inspire someone to come home from the market with a bag full of ingredients. The comments and feedback you give me push me to approach baking in ways that I had not previously considered, and I am a better baker and teacher because of it.

ABOUT THE AUTHOR

Ben Delwiche is a math teacher and a baking content creator based in Los Angeles. Known for his informative baking experiments and engaging instructional videos on social media (@benjaminthebaker), Ben is especially interested in how science and math inform key principles of baking. He aims to use his background in education to equip bakers of all levels with the knowledge and techniques that underpin all kinds of sweet treats. He lives with wife, his son, and his cat, Cookie.

Equipmen
RATIO MICHAEL RUHLMAN
UNDERSTANDING BAKING THE ART AND SCIENCE OF BAKING
THE BAKER'S MANUAL 150 MASTER FORMULAS FOR BAKING